# NATIONALISM
## and
# Violence

# NATIONALISM
## and
# Violence

## CHRISTOPHER DANDEKER
### editor

## TRANSACTION PUBLISHERS
### New Brunswick (U.S.A.) and London (U.K.)

This book is printed on acid-free paper that meets the American National standard for Permanence of Paper for Printed Library Materials.

Library of Congress Catalog Number: 97–30500
ISBN: 1–56000–339–1
Printed in the United States of America

**Library of Congress Cataloging-in-Publication Data**

Nationalism and violence / edited by Christopher Dandeker.
    p.  cm.
   Included bibliographical references and index.
   ISBN 1-56000-339-1 (cloth : alk. paper)
   1. Nationalism. 2. Ethnic relations. 3. Political violence. 4. World Politics—1989– I. Dandeker, Christopher.
JC311.N2954 1997
320.54—dc21
                                         97-30500
                                           CIP

# Contents

# Preface

The Harry Frank Guggenheim Foundation is a private foundation which makes grants to individual scientists and scholars for research which promises a better understanding of violence, aggression, and dominance. When Harry Guggenheim proposed this mission for the foundation in 1959, he argued that traditional responses to the problem of human aggression were simply not working and that the only hope for new and productive ideas would be to support smart and creative people to study these problems and think about how insights about the nature of violence, aggression, and dominance might suggest solutions. When James M. Hester was elected president of the foundation in 1989, he suggested that the time had come to take stock of what we know and to integrate that knowledge in books which would survey specific problems of violence across the many perspectives by which individual grantees were coming to a clearer understanding of them.

*Nationalism and Violence* is the product of a series of meetings organized by the foundation in 1991 and 1992, during which a group of scholars from diverse disciplines and nations discussed the problem of nationalist violence comparatively and prepared and criticized papers. These explicated particular cases or explained the views of particular disciplines, some not usually involved in a subject which is seen as mainly the domain of political science. The foundation had funded individual projects related to religious, ethnic, and nationalist violence over the years, and nationalism itself was a hot theoretical topic in the social sciences—although the discovery that communities are "imagined" and that tradition is "invented" was beginning to wear thin as innovative thinking by that time. However, the concern that fueled much scholarly interest in nationalism was oddly absent from the academic discussion: Nationalism, however fictive, recent and imaginary, leads to real bloodshed. We asked participants in our project to explore the inevitability of that connection and to think creatively about the future of a world in which old-fashioned loyalties to kin and tribe coexisted with transnational movements of people, commodities, and funds which made nations as political entities less salient. As nation-states lose their role as the principle actors on the global stage, their citizens have retained and demonstrated a willingness to kill and die in their service.

We know that cynical politicians have manipulated nationalist feelings to consolidate their own power. We know that social scientists have also contributed to such nationalistic projects by the recovery and invention of ethnic distinctiveness with little trace in contemporary memories. But we also know that people are quick to feel the advantages of their own group and the deficiencies of another, that perceptible variations in language, customs, and beliefs can make group differences more salient, and that when there is competition over resources, power, and interests, people often believe that to insure justice for their group they must fight others.

What we "know" is not invariably a direct guide to what to expect. When tested against the conditions of the real world, theories of conflict tend to overpredict situations of conflict. And people who have lived peacefully together for generations can surprise observers by engaging in battles over identity which seem to heat up overnight and have little practical payoff. The essays in this book provide a survey of current thinking about ethnic and national group loyalty and suggest some ways to use these understandings to think productively about nationalist conflict and war, in particular in relation to the current dilemmas of the post-war Balkans and identity politics in the United States.

Many people participated in the discussions which helped to produce this book. Assaad Azzi, Christopher Dandeker, Orfeo Fioretos, Harold James, Bruce Kapferer, David Laitin, Bruce Lawrence, Emmanuel Sivan, Reed Ueda, and Arthur Waldron participated in one or more of the foundation's meetings about nationalism and violence. Glenn Bowman, Richard Goldstone, James Gow, E.L. Jones, Janet Kentridge, and Klaus-Peter Koepping contributed papers for discussion, and members of a foundation advisory board from disciplines usually far removed from considerations of political violence—psychologists Leonard Eron and Clark McCauley, family sociologist Richard Gelles, and biologists Menno Kruk and Michael McGuire, along with my foundation colleagues James Hester and Joel Wallman—

reviewed parts of this manuscript. The discussions produced this book (and will produce further publications) and served as guides for the foundation's grantmaking in this area, which increased substantially during these years as our attention—and the world's—was drawn to the connection between nationalism and violence and towards the problem of devising better predictors, responses, and guardians against political and personal processes which justify and maintain the destructiveness of nationalist war.

Karen Colvard, Senior Program Officer
*The Harry Frank Guggenheim Foundation*

# Introduction

*Christopher Dandeker*

Both scholarly and public interest in the study of nationalism has increased dramatically in recent years. This is reflected in the sheer number of works on the subject, the range of topics and regions investigated, and the fact that academic contributors have been drawn from across the spectrum of disciplines in the humanities and the social sciences, including history, political science, international relations, economics, sociology, anthropology and social psychology.

Studies of nationalism have examined a wide variety of themes such as the nature and types of national identity and nationalist movements. Others have focused on the origins of the national idea, reflecting, for example, on its deep roots in religion and warfare or its more recent links with democratic citizenship and other elements of "modernity." There have also been studies on the spread of the national idea from Europe throughout the rest of the globe and the historical relationships between the national idea and the political organization of the nation-state including the implications of nationalism for international relations. Finally, taking up the earlier reference to warfare, some writers have been concerned to analyze the relationships between nationalism and violence—whether to do with national and ethnic groups within the same state or between groups of different states.[1] This last subject provides the main theme for the chapters in this book.

Nationalism has the potential of attracting the interest of those working in the humanities and social sciences—including the contributors here—because it poses fundamental questions about the nature of human societies. Not the least of these are the extent to which group identities are generated by biological or sociohistorical factors; the

1

mechanisms whereby such identities are transmitted from one generation to the other; the extent to which collective identities can be reconstructed—sometimes forcibly—through such processes as assimilation
and nation-building; the impact of historical memories on how different groups relate to each other and their perception of the "other" as
hostile—and, indeed, their willingness to change those perceptions.[2]

How these issues are resolved depends a good deal on the first of
these questions: whether national identities—and thus humanity itself—are social constructs or the historical realization of pre-social
group differentiations. Different answers to it have been termed
"primordialist" and "modernist."[3] Primordialists view nationalism as
predating "modernity"—specifically the democratization of politics and
industrialization in western Europe between 1780 and 1850. Far from
being created by modernity, national identities are built into the human species because they are rooted in language, and long collective
memories of affinities with territory and landscape. While it might be
recognized that the full force of nationalist feelings were released
under conditions of modernity, nationalism itself can be found centuries earlier.

In contrast, for "modernist" writers such as Gellner, Deutsch,
Hobsbawm, and Benedict Anderson, the national idea is a recent development dating from the French Revolution and the doctrine of popular
sovereignty whereby the state became the property of the people rather
than that of the dynastic monarchy.[4] This position can be reinforced by
arguments stressing that national identity is a modern phenomenon
because it presupposes conditions found only in industrial society: the
spread of literacy and compulsory education, including the compulsory
use of a national language, allowing for the possibility of "imagined
communities" beyond narrow circles of intellectual classes; the technical infrastructure of industrialism that unifies national populations
through improved transport and communications; the impact of universal conscription on national identity; and the creation of the nation-
state as a "bordered power container" with sharp boundaries between
external and internal relations, giving rise to the idea of the nation as an
entity with purpose and presence. Thus the "societies" studied by sociologists are actually quite new: they are extrapolations from the recent
development of the nation-state system.[5]

It is possible to synthesise these competing traditions of social theory
and, as I argue in chapter 1, this is one of the reasons why A. D.

Smith's work commands attention. As a result of the developments of modernity indicated above, Europe in the nineteenth century became a plurality of nation-states rather than just a state-system which had been created by the Treaty of Westphalia in 1648. During the twentieth century, the national idea became the dominant form of legitimizing the state and played a critical part in the disintegration of empires (including the Soviet one) and the legitimacy of the imperial *idea*. During the twentieth century nationalism provided the legitimacy of both established nation-states and the newer, more fragile, "state-nations" despite the fact that, in the latter, beneath their sovereign equality, lay marked differences in their social unity, and internal or external capacities to exert power.[6]

This book brings together authors from number of different disciplines in order to focus on the relationships between nationalism and violence. As Nairn argued twenty years ago, nationalism is "Janus-faced" (as we shall see, a point that underpins the economic and historical analysis in Harold James's contribution to this volume and my own sociological chapter).[7]

That is to say, nationalism can provide the basis of peaceful coexistence amongst peoples who are lifted out of the limitations of local allegiances and horizons into a common public life; one that extends to an exchange with other peoples on the basis of mutual respect and tolerance of different national identities.[8] Both liberal and Marxist writers have hoped that, under conditions of modernity, nationalism, having served its historical purpose will "wither away." Thus for liberals, a world of free-trading democracies will render national identities increasingly irrelevant because of the complex linkages binding the individuals of different countries in the international division of labor: nation gives way to humanity as the object of people's affection and loyalty. As a mirror image of liberalism, Marxism has regarded nationalism as, at worst, an authoritarian ideology of capitalism, masking the true interests of the international working class and as, at best, a way-station whereby class consciousness can be built up on a national and then international basis: in the short term, nationalism can be a most progressive force, especially in traditional societies where localism and religious superstition are dominant.[9] Revealingly, Marx referred to the proletariat as the "universal class."[10] For both, at heart rationalist and utilitarian schools of social thought, the survival of nationalism in the modern world is an anachronism, as can be seen most clearly perhaps in Hobsbawm's recent reflections on the subject.[11]

The alternative face of nationalism is that it can provide the basis of a regimented life in which the individual is a vehicle of the collective will in hostility towards the hated "other." This image is associated with nationalist authoritarianism of the late nineteenth and early twentieth centuries, as the idea of nation became transformed by Social Darwinism, culminating in the fascisms of Germany, Italy, and—too often forgotten—Central and Eastern Europe.[12] Showing this face, it would seem that national differences and struggle between nations are built into the human species. In sharp contrast with the liberal and Marxist understandings, the real author of history is not the rational individual or class, but the collective nation. It is interesting to note that this image of nationalism appealed to some of those Marxists who witnessed the power of national loyalty compared with that of class in the crisis and subsequent war of 1914—chief amongst these was Mussolini.[13]

The contributors to this volume draw on different disciplines—sociology, economics, history, social psychology, politics, and international relations. Using material drawn from old and new world nations, each is concerned with understanding the circumstances in which nationalism reveals one or other of its peaceful and violent faces. Although the book is concerned with the theme of nationalism and violence, there are important links between it and a number of other issues within the literature. Some consideration of these will provide a useful background to the chapters which follow.

Although, as I argued above, nationalism has the potential to attract the interest of those working in the humanities and social sciences, in fact, this interest has waxed and waned. While the renewed concern for the study of nationalism is at least two decades old, the recent upsurge of analysis and debate in scholarly and public debate has been encouraged by a number of overlapping developments. Three of these can be identified: first, the impact of "globalization" on national identities and nation-states—both established and more recent creations; second, the problems of ensuring that nation-states composed of different national and ethnic groups can continue to live together without violent conflict or, when such arrangements have failed, of reconstructing societies in ways that facilitate such relations of peaceful coexistence; and finally, effects of the end of the cold war on the revival of nationalism and nation-states in Central and Eastern Europe and the former Soviet Union.    Turning first to the impact of global economic integration on nationalism and the nation-state, this theme underpins my own chapter and the contribution from Harold James (chapter 2). My chapter applies a sociological approach to the task of explaining the links between nationalism, the nation-state, and violence, and in particular focuses on the impact of "globalization."

With the removal of the bipolar military confrontation between the superpowers it became easier to focus on the effects of "globalization" on social life in general and national identity in particular. Here there are complex links between the global and the local. "Globalization" refers to a process of international economic integration promoted by technological improvements in and reduced costs of transportation of goods, and in the processing, storage, and transmission of information. Both developments have made possible the organization of economic production and distribution on a transnational basis by companies able, indeed compelled, to think globally but operate locally—a process that has accelerated since the 1970s.[14]

These changes have posed the question of the extent to which transnational economic processes, and in particular the power of global corporations, have reduced the autonomy of the nation-state. For example, recent developments in the European Union (EU) and the formation of other trading blocs of nations such as the North American Free Trade Agreement (NAFTA), illustrate how nation-states have sought collective, more supranational forms of political organization as a means of exercising more effective control over the economic, environmental and other transnational processes that are increasingly beyond their capacities when operating independently.

However successful these political strategies might be, there is some evidence to suggest that they encourage the development of subnational (and other types) of communal identities within even the more established nation-states. Such communities—the Catalan or Scottish examples come to mind—seek to establish direct political relations with and the resulting benefits from such emergent supranational political authorities. It would be a mistake to perceive such subnational developments as being confined to the least economically advantaged members of a national community. They can flourish in regions that are economically dynamic and feel that they could do even better if they were to operate with less control exercised by the central state which, as in the case of Italy, might be perceived as inefficient—even corrupt—and organized to divert resources to less dynamic regions.[15]

In addition, such subnational movements provide their supporters with some sense of identity and relative stability at a time when changes in their life chances are the result of transnational processes which the governments of their own nation-states seem less able than before of controlling. Even when participating in supranational organizations in order to *increase* their capacity to exercise control such processes, these benefits, such as they are, can be quite opaque to those subnational groups whose lives are so distant from such political and administrative structures. All of this has led some commentators to conclude that, from a cultural point of view, globalization at one and the same time can break down barriers between national identities *and* reinforce them.

It can be argued that the impact of globalization and its recency have been overstated. For example, globalization of economic life is hardly new: there have been movements toward global economic integration since the sixteenth century with, as it were, mercantilist reversals. Thus a substantial process of economic integration occurred during the nineteenth century only to be reversed by the process of economic and military nationalism associated with the rise of fascism. Indeed 1913 levels of economic integration were not achieved until about 1970.[16] Even if the extent of global integration *is* qualitatively greater than before—largely because of modern information technologies—has the reduction in the autonomy of the nation-state proceeded far enough to justify talking of its decline? It might be suggested that the global social order requires the continuation of the nation-state as a central mechanism in the maintenance of international society built on a combination of old and new principles. As Horsman and Marshal have argued,"What may now be developing is a system where states, regions, international companies and transnational companies vie *more equally* for power."[17]

One of the reasons for the continuing importance of the nation-state concerns the issue of legitimation. Even if it is possible and desirable that the nation-state become involved in supranational organizations, a significant limitation on this process is the extent to which public attachments and loyalties to them can be generated: such organizations do not have the potential of legitimacy that nation-states have. In any case, nation-states are reluctant both to give up core elements of their sovereignty, particularly in matters of defense and security policy, and commit themselves to continued and deeper involvement in such organizations if their strategic economic and other goals are not being met.

The examples of France and Germany's roles in the development of the EU come to mind. Here a significant consideration is that any subordination of such goals to supranational interests can create subnational discontents.

"Subnational" developments can be found in mature and less well-established nation-states. In both cases, issues of legitimation are involved. As Mayall has argued, today all nation-states have to contend with the fact that the rights—civic, political, and social[18]—of minorities provide obstacles to the supremacy of sovereign state. This limit on state sovereignty derives in large part from the impact of liberal ideology on international society; and indeed has grown in importance now that the UN (United Nations) is less stymied by ideological confrontation between the superpowers and the global media are able to dramatize the plight of those minorities whose rights are threatened by their state. One resulting problem is an increase in the tension between the sovereign state's internal authority and the ways in which rights based ethics can fuel not simply opposition to legitimate government by disaffected ethnic or national minority groups, but the withdrawal of that legitimacy by some sections of the population to such an extent that secessionist movements are created.[19] There are overlaps between this question and the earlier discussion of globalization and the "new medievalism." It is possible to argue that because *all* nation-states face such potentially violent fissiparous tendencies the "new world order" will comprise less a network of nation-states and more a sort of Hobbesian drama of "small wars" of all against all.[20] As I argue in chapter 1, in the light of the available evidence, this seems to me to be too extreme a view.

Harold James analyzes the links between nationalism, economic development, and violence, arguing that explanations fall into two camps. The pessimistic view sees economic modernization as leading to the breakdown of traditional social structures and acts of violence against those groups perceived as gaining—illegitimately—from the new economic order. Such violence may well be projected externally, as foreign enemies can serve as a mechanism of domestic social integration. Alternatively, militaristic aggression and conquest can provide economic compensation for the troubles created by modernization at the expense of other peoples. This view was a riposte to the liberal idea that economic modernization, based on rational economic conduct and the division of labor—both nationally and internationally—

would lead to peace and prosperity under the rule of law. For those of this persuasion, the coincidence of global economic integration and the apparent revival of nationalism is a puzzling anachronism.

James shows that whether, in fact, nationalism does create tensions in international society or promotes stability depends on the links between nationalism and economics. Too close a connection has indeed led to such tensions; however, these are not inevitable but depend upon *beliefs* about what the nation should be and how economic affairs should operate. There is no historical logic leading to one or other of the scenarios sketched above. For example, in the mid-nineteenth century, the concept of national community was seen by countries such as Germany and Italy as an economically desirable means of responding to the already established colonial powers of Western Europe: national existence would underpin economic development and this in turn would provide for the military wherewithal of defending national integrity.

However, with the continuing revolution of transport and communications and the awakening of continental economies, especially the dynamic United States, the idea of the nation-state as the basic for economic decision making was put into question by those who claimed that far larger economic spaces were more appropriate: thus the new found enthusiasm for concepts of *empire*, *lebensraum*, and *mitteleuropa*. At the same time, in many industrial nations in the late nineteenth century, distributional problems between rich and poor within nations led to a critique of the idea that the national market alone could provide the basis of peace and prosperity. A welfare state was seen as a critical mechanism to meet the needs of social cohesion that could not be met by the market alone. These distributional problems spread into the international arena with a parallel social market debate on protection and managed trade creating the prospect of international tensions and war.

The critical problem was, and remains, how to prevent these international tensions drifting to violence. After the First and Second World Wars policymakers faced the same basic problem: how to reconcile national sovereignty with transnational economic processes. As in the interwar period and more successful efforts after 1945, one method was to rely on international organizations to maintain economic cooperation and smooth tensions amongst nations. Another method has been to shift to supranational mechanisms such as the EU. However, as we are witnessing today in the EU, as it debates the arguments for and against European Monetary Union (EMU) this creates problems of its own in connection with distribution and legitimacy. If such a supranational system adopts technocratic performance criteria distanced from politics this will promote demands for accountability. If accountability is produced then the politics of national interest and redistribution will loom, creating legitimacy problems for supranational institutions as some nations perceive them as operating for narrow interests rather than for the wider community.

In the context of global economic integration, how will the relations between nationalism and economics play out? One possibility is that nationalism will be associated with xenophobia and protectionism based on the belief that a nation and its leaders can mould economics to meet national objectives. On the other hand, nationalism can underpin continued participation in the global economic system and its shifting cycles of good and bad times. The question posed by James's chapter is: is this easier to do if a country is equipped with a strong national identity and a widely held belief that the nation-state cannot solve all economic problems or bend transnational economic processes to its will?

However, whether nationalism becomes connected with peace and stability or violence cannot be answered by social structural and institutional analysis alone. Psychological factors are also important as Assaad Azzi suggests in chapter 3 which is concerned largely with the problem of ethnic nationalism and conflict within nation-states and the consequences for international society. Indeed, the significance of the psychological perspective is indicated by its shedding further light on the question of the nature of national identity and thus the debate between modernists and primordialists discussed earlier.

Azzi (chapter 3) questions those who suggest that national identities are "imagined communities." He accepts that such categorizations are social constructions rooted in psychological mechanisms of differentiation and homogenization involving an accentuation of individual and group differences and similarities. However, this social construction process works on *preexisting* differences between social categories, whether physical, linguistic, or territorial. These processes are not without paradoxes: nations celebrating their independence are not immune from seeking to homogenize their own internal differentiations while emphasizing their differences from other nations—a process also present in ethnic nationalist movements seeking to secede from an existing nation-state.

What are the psychological mechanisms that facilitate intergroup conflict and ethnic conflict in particular and what are the circumstances in which that conflict will be expressed in violent forms? Azzi shows that the existence of incompatible goals is a necessary condition of conflict between groups. However, contrary to common stereotypes and myths of group behaviour (whether based on class, ethnicity or gender), the "working class," "women," "blacks," or Bosnian Serbs do not behave in the same way: that is to say, not all members of a group will be willing to engage in collective action in pursuit of group goals. Their willingness to do so will depend upon a number of factors: for example, whether the social structure of power and distribution of rewards that orders intergroup relations is perceived to be just. Here Azzi is analyzing the distributional and legitimation issues that are raised in other chapters, especially that of Harold James. The propensity of individuals to engage in collective action on behalf of the group in confrontation with others will also depend upon whether individuals perceive a congruence between their own concrete interests and those of the group. In addition, such action will be affected by the multiple allegiances that characterise all groups in complex national communities: that is to say, in some circumstances, individuals will identify more with their own ethnic group or the wider community of the nation-state of which they are a part.

This argument highlights the problem of whether there is an inherent tension between ethnic identity and the identity of the nation-state and, therefore, whether successful nation-building necessarily involves the attenuation of these subnational identities—as in the "peasants into Frenchmen" modernist thesis of Eugen Weber discussed by Harold James. Azzi questions this way of looking at the problem, suggesting that the two identities are on separate rather than the same scales or dimensions. While one condition for an individual's participation in collective action and ethnic nationalism would be a stronger identification with the ethnic group than the broader national category, it is possible for an individual to have strong allegiances to *both* identities. At the same time, it is too simplistic to assume that group identification is driven exclusively by material interests: symbolic needs are also important drivers of the process. It appears that rather than there being an inherent clash between these two levels of identification, arising from, say, basic cognitive processes of social categorisation, this is most likely to be the consequence of "particular political ideologies and structures which pit the two against each other".[21] This process works differently depending upon the historical context: while a civic nation-state requires a separation of ethnic and national identity, this separation can occur in two quite different ways—through fusion or merger of constituent national groups into one national culture or assimilation into one group's culture by another more or less against their will.

The question of the relationship between national and ethnic identity is a major issue faced by all multiethnic nation-states operating in an international climate that underpins the legitimacy of minority rights. It is most evident in new world societies and of these the United States provides a striking example. Today all nation-states—whether well-established or more recent creations—experience the problem of sometimes violent, fissiparous tendencies which can develop, as we have witnessed in Canada and Spain and the United Kingdom, into "separatism." This point leads on to the second of the developments I identified earlier as promoting interest in nationalism in general and, here, in the study of the relations between nationalism and violence. This concerns the conditions under which peaceful relations of co-existence amongst the national and ethnic groups of which nation-states are composed can be maintained or reconstructed if they have broken down. While we must be aware of the—somewhat blurred—line dividing internal and external affairs of nation-states, at this point we are concerned with the problem of nationalism and violence within their boundaries.

This is the context for Reed Ueda's chapter (chapter 4). It is now generally accepted by scholars—if not concerned political activists committed to a particular interpretation of nation-building—that *all* nation-states, even the most established, are composed of a variety of different ethnic and national groups. Of course, the extent to which this is so varies considerably: some nation-states are explicitly multinational like Switzerland; others are more clearly structured on the basis of a successful strategy of nation-building by what Smith has called a dominant *ethnie*. The history of, say, France and Britain come to mind, although in the latter case, the English construction of Britain has always been limited by the fact that it is a United Kingdom of different nations—and one whose continued framework of unity is open to debate.[22] The rights-based ethic of the liberal tradition will ensure that the past record of nation-builders will be held up for question by those who seek to remember the identities apparently erased by such strategies. By the same token, it provides a difficult environment for those in new "state-nations" who are in the process of nation-building and seeking to use a "dominant ethnic" strategy, even if, as some analysts such as Smith suggest, this is, perhaps, the strategy most likely to be successful.

An alternative model of nation-building is to identify a set of principles or values, such as multiculturalism, as a basis on which a nation-state of—different but equal—national and ethnic groups can live together. This approach, it can be argued, is critical to the future of new world countries, such as the United States—designed explicitly to depart from the ways of old Europe—and Australia and New Zealand. In these cases, the possibility of a white European ethnie strategy of nation-building is no longer possible not least because of changes in the ethnic and national composition of their populations due to the impact of globalization on the size and distribution of populations amongst nation-states.[23] Indeed, as no part of the world is or can be isolated from these processes of change, the strategy of multiculturalism might well be the most appropriate mechanism for reconstructing nations under the conditions at the end of the twentieth century.

Yet this is hardly an uncontroversial view and can be opposed by those who would suggest that the only way in which such different populations can coexist in the same political community is for one set of principles, held by the core national ethnic group(s)—in terms of proportion of the population, social power, and longevity of national membership to provide the basis of national coherence. Multi-nationalism—rather than multiculturalism—is only possible when a small number of national groups come together to form a political state as the result of a political settlement which commands legitimacy amongst the participants as in Switzerland. It will be interesting to observe how Switzerland will manage the ethnic tensions likely to arise as its traditional multinational social structure becomes more multicultural as a result of population shifts due to the globalization of economic relations.

Ueda analyses ethnic nationalism in the context of the historical development of the U.S. nation-state. He focuses on the problems associated with implementing a civic national identity in a rapidly expanding, multiethnic community produced by successive waves of immigration from different parts of the world. Ueda shows how the United States evolved a pattern of "differentiated status that reinforced a ranked ethnic order."[24]

The Northern pattern of ethnic relations was based on the liberal, civic concept of nationhood in which ethnic identity was subordinated to the equal opportunity to participate in a superordinate national community. In contrast, the South was based on segregation of blacks and whites while the Western and territorial patterns were based on a multiracial but hierarchically organized system of status groups. Government played a key role in sponsoring the differentiated ethnic status system during the first half of the twentieth century through the control of migration and definition of rights of different groups. While this social order could produce stability, as in the social distance created by segregation or the acceptance of the system by some groups who perceived social mobility as a beneficial consequence of such acceptance, xenophobia and violence were, nonetheless, integral to it.

Ueda shows how progressivism sought to universalize the Northern, civic pattern of ethnic relations during the period between the New Deal and the Great Society of the 1960s. He explores the part played by this model in promoting the socioeconomic and cultural integration of European immigrant groups without internecine violence—a significant achievement given the historical context of European violence from which such groups had been drawn. Yet this process was not preordained but dependent upon key social structural features of the modernizing city.

Ueda shows how developments in ethnic corporatism have undermined the civic model of multiethnic national identity in the United States since the 1960s. Such corporatism increases the risk of ethnic subgroupism flourishing away from a shared public life in which the agenda is dominated by increasingly fractious distributional disputes. He suggests that a revitalization of the Northern pattern is critical for the reinvigoration of national identity in the United States. He argues that this must be based on "a constructive equilibrium between cultural unity and diversity."[25] While the value of ethnic diversity should be respected, government should not underwrite ethnic separatism but encourage the development of those values that can provide the basis of a superordinate national identity and shared public life. However, this argument leaves us with a problem: such values—an American creed for the twenty-first century—can only generate sufficient cohesion if citizens regard them as absolute, sacred values and do not perceive them as attempts to universalise the values and standards of particular privileged status groups within the polity: a national identity based on a contract of convenience between ethnic groups will be fragile. If such a scenario emerges as a realistic possibility, it will then surely encourage more restrictive immigration policies and assimilationist strategies to counter nascent ethnic separatism. Such nativist strategies could be conjoined with the forms of trade protection discussed earlier in connection with the links between nationalism and economics. Just such links were made in the 1890s in the United States and there are some suggestions of a repeat of this at the end of the 1990s.[26]

I turn now to the third of the broad themes underpinning the chapters in this volume. This concerns the impact of the end of the cold war on the national question: specifically, the disintegration of the Soviet Union, and the formation or reinvention of independent nation-states in the old Soviet republics together with the recreation of new nation-states in Central and Eastern Europe. Conflict and tensions mark the relationships between Russia and some members of the former Soviet Union with, it seems, Russia being destined to remain troubled by anticolonial style, independence struggles on its borders however the Chechnya crisis resolves itself. Meanwhile, in Central and Eastern Europe, the break-up of, and subsequent war amongst, the components of the former Republic of Yugoslavia has stimulated interest in nationalism not least because of fears concerning the spread of nationalist based violent conflict in the region and the ways in which these developments resonate earlier patterns of violence and war in twentieth-century Europe. This provides the setting for James Gow's chapter (chapter 5) although his arguments touch on many of the issues raised in the other chapters.

The war, and current moves towards a tentative peace, have posed the question, in an acute fashion, of the circumstances in which different nations can reconcile their differences peacefully and the political arrangements that provide the most favourable conditions for peaceful coexistence. Here the question of how to order the boundaries of national identity and the state loom large. This, in turn, suggests a number of other problems. For example, recent events in Central and Eastern Europe and the former Soviet Union have forced analysts to ask whether the survival of national identity beneath the four or seven decades of Soviet domination suggests that the roots of these identities might go back far further than those writers—convinced that nationalism is a modern phenomenon, created by the idea of citizenship and popular sovereignty at the end of the eighteenth century—would care to admit. In addition, however this issue is resolved, analysts have also had to consider the extent to which the longevity of national identity also applies to the conflicts that mark the relations between some nations. Do such conflicts and the violence to which they can lead flow from the nature of group life and memory or are such phenomena in part created and manipulated by political leaders as part of their strategies to gain or maintain power, particularly when their communist basis of legitimacy has been undermined? If so what are the techniques underpinning such strategies and on which social and psychological factors do they depend for their success? Here there are fruitful lines of enquiry thrown up by Gow and Azzi's chapters that require further research and analysis.

Gow's chapter shows how the wars in the former Yugoslavia raise far wider questions about the links connecting a family of concepts—nationalism, sovereignty, statehood, self-determination—and the potential these have to create violent instability in international society. At the same time he shows how developments in the post-cold war security context provide an opportunity to develop a more effective response to these problems and this is created in large part by rethinking the key concept of sovereignty.

The wars in the former Yugoslavia are placed in the context of three waves of nation-state formation in the twentieth century. Each wave has been generated by a linkage between nationalism, sovereignty and statehood. The first occurred after the dissolution of the German, Russian, Austro-Hungarian, and Ottoman Empires and led to the revisionist nationalisms of the interwar period culminating in Nazism. After World War II, a second wave was created by Western decolonization in Africa and Asia. The third wave is a phenomenon of the post-cold war period when nation-states have been created by the disintegration of communist federations. In each wave, "nationalist" pressures for self-determination have played a key part in promoting the formation of new states.[27]

During the post-World War II period, the principle of national self-determination was restricted to "anticolonial self-determination." Thus, with the exception of the successful secession of Bangladesh, no ethnic group was allowed to continue the process of "self-determination" beyond the phase where anticolonialism had succeeded in detaching the colonial state from empire and constituting it as a sovereign entity.

However, in the post-cold war context the problem is rather different as the sovereign state system is confronted not by the challenge of anticolonial nationalism but by components of states motivated by ethnic or what I have called subnationalism.

This point leads Gow to consider the implications of two meanings of nation: on the one hand the population "living within the territorial boundaries of a given political community" and, on the other, a politically mobilized ethnic community within a state no longer willing to accept the political and territorial status quo.[28] Both senses are intertwined in the Yugoslav wars.

The key problem in international affairs is that there are very few cases where these two senses of nation politically coincide. Thus, in the many cases where significant numbers of the same ethnonational group are found in more than one state—especially where these are contiguous and connected with economic and strategic conflicts—the potential for problems of sovereignty and self-determination disputes is substantial. Indeed, if it becomes easier for ethnonational secession to occur than was the case during the second phase of twentieth-century European nation-state formation, there could be very serious consequences for international security.

The Yugoslavia case poses the problem, in an acute form, of how to manage the tensions created when the international legal sovereignty of the state clashes with the claims of an ethnic nationalism embarked on a strategy of political sovereignty. Gow suggests that one part of a solution to the problem is to question the indivisibility of the concept of sovereignty. This involves creating a division of sovereign powers not only within states in the international community but also between them and international bodies. Today, the internal affairs of states are a legitimate concern for international bodies such as the UN, for example, when the human rights of its citizens have been threatened, on matters connected with the rights of national minorities, or where fragile states have collapsed.

This concern of international bodies, and the questioning of the sovereignty of states in their internal affairs, can be exercised on a more or less consensual basis. Under certain circumstances, it can involve the legitimate intervention in the internal affairs of states. In extreme cases, this can involve the use of armed force where the intervention is just but a state is unwilling to permit it. Gow shows how various UN Security Council resolutions in connection with Bosnia and Herzegovina, Libya, and Somalia involved radical departures from traditional concepts of sovereignty in international relations and how these emerged from the way in which the international community responded to the Gulf crisis in 1990–91. As a result, states can no longer view the sovereign rights in their internal affairs under Article 2 (7) of the UN Charter as inviolable in face of UN judgments about "threats to international peace and security" stemming from the final clause of that Article in the UN Charter. Their sovereignty is part of an international division of labour with the UN.

All this creates an outline of a working solution to some of the problems of nationalism and violence. Ethnic nationalism can lead to the violent disintegration of states and to create international disorder. This can be limited by international bodies having a role to play in ensuring that much—not all?—of the autonomy many ethnonational groups desire (and, as Ueda argues in this volume), have a legitimate right to expect, can be achieved within the existing boundaries of a state. With sovereignty divisible rather than indivisible, the very importance of these boundaries in causing ethnic and national violence, with all the pain for those involved, can be lessened significantly.

To conclude, as I suggested earlier, as with all aspects of the study of nationalism, scholarly investigations are never very far away from political controversy—particularly when these do not coincide with the strongly held ideologies of particular nation-states or ethnonational groups. In an acute way, we are reminded of the importance of our commitment to the core academic values of dispassionate analysis and respect for the rules of logic, evidence and clarity in the formation and use of concepts. This is the spirit in which the chapters in this volume were written and it is a pleasure to acknowledge the support of the Harry Frank Guggenheim Foundation which supported our endeavours by providing the means for the authors to meet and discuss their contributions in a congenial environment. I should like to thank Karen Colvard, senior program officer of the Foundation for her encouragement and support during the preparation of this volume.

Christopher Dandeker
*Department of War Studies,*
*King's College, London.*

# Notes

1. Recent reviews include: A.D. Smith, *Theories of Nationalism*, Duckworth 1971; *The Ethnic Origin of Nations*, Blackwell 1986; *National Identity*; A.D. Smith and J. Hutchinson, *Nationalism*, Oxford 1995; M. Guibernau, *Nationalisms: The Nation-State and Nationalism in the Twentieth Century*, Polity Press 1996; J. Hutchinson's *Modern Nationalism* Fontana, 1994, includes a brief, well-balanced, and excellent discussion of the key intellectual debates in the field; E. Hobsbawn, *Nations and Nationalism* Clarendon 1990; J. Mayall, *Nationalism and International Society*, Cambridge 1990; P. Alter, *Nations and Nationalism* Edward Arnold 1989; B. Anderson, *Imagined Communities*, Verso 1991. Mayall divides the literature on nationalism into three: sociology, with the works of A.D. Smith being the most important; history, with A. Cobban's *Nationalism and National Self-Determination*, Oxford University Press 1969, remaining one of the best studies of the efects of the national idea on international relations and political science. He cites Breuilly's *Nationalism and the State*, Manchester University Press 1982, and E. Gellner, *Nations and Nationalism*, Blackwell 1983 and B. Anderson, *Imagined Communities*, London Verso 1983, but does not indicate to which of the disciplines these can be considered contributions. See Mayall 153, note 2. Breuilly's work straddles history and politics while Gellner draws on three of the disciplines in addition to that of anthropology.
2. Scholarly debates on nationalism, by raising such fundamental issues about collective identity, can become connected with heated political and policy debates. This is illustrated by the recent decision of a university press not to publish a controversial book on Macedonia and the process of nation-building or "Hellenization" by Greece. See the report and discussion on Cambridge University Press's decision not to publish Dr. A. Karakasidou's manuscript because of fears of terrorist attacks on its representatives, in *The Times Higher Education Supplement*, 9 February 1996, 1, 15.
3. See J. Hutchinson, *Modern Nationalism*, Fontana 1994, 3–7 for a brief and lucid discussion of this theme.
4. See Hutchinson, 1994, p, 3.
5. This idea is developed by A. Giddens in *The Nation State and Violence*, Polity Blackwell 1985; C. Dandeker, *Surveillance Power and Modernity*, Polity Blackwell 1990.
6. On this theme see the brilliant discussion in J. Mayall, *Nationalism and International Society*, Cambridge University Press 1990, 35–49;111–144.
7. T. Nairn, *The Break-up of Britain*, New Left Books 1977.
8. Durkheim's liberal conservatism provides a good example of this view. See É. Durkheim, *The Division of Labour in Society*, Free Press Glencoe 1971. On the liberal view of nationalism and violence see M. Howard, *War and the Liberal Conscience*, Oxford, 1981.
9. On Marx's view of India see the discussion in S. Aviweri, The Social and Political Thought of Karl Marx. Cambridge University Press. 1968, 168–71. On the general question of Marx and Engels on Nationalism see W. Connor, *The National Question in Marxist-Leninist Theory and Strategy*, Princeton University Press, 1984. See also M. Shaw (ed.) *War State and Society*, Macmillan 1984, and B. Semmel, *Marxism and the Science of War* Oxford 1981.
10. On this point see the discussion in S. Avineri, *The Social and Political Thought of Karl Marx*, Cambridge University Press 1971.

11. E. Hobsbawm, *Nations and Nationalism Since 1780*, Clarendon, 1990.
12. The literature on fascism is now immense. Useful guides to the literature include W. Lacqueur, *Fascism, A Reader's Guide* Penguin, Hamondsworth 1979; A. J. Gregor, *The Ideology of Fascism*: the ideology of Totalitarianism NY. 1969; P. Hayes, *Fascism*, M. Kitchen, *Fascism*; R. Eatwell, *Fascism: A History*, Chatto and Windus 1996; A. J. De Grand, *Fascist Italy and Nazi Germany: The Fascist Style of Rule*, Routledge 1996.
13. This is one of the themes in A. J. Gregor, *The Ideology of Fascism*.
14. See V. Cable, "The Diminished Nation-State," in *Daedalus*, Spring 1995 23–51; in the same issue see also, S. Strange, "The Defective State," 55–74 and V. A. Schmidt, *The New World Order, Incorporated: The Rise of Business and the Decline of the Nation-State*, 75–106; S. Strange, *States and Markets*, Pinter 1988; M. Horsman and A. Marshall, *After the Nation-State*, Harper-Collins 1994; J. Hutchinson, *Modern Nationalism*, Fontana 1994, 134–163.
15. M. Horsman and A. Marshal, *After the Nation-State*, Harper Collins, 1994, 87;131.
16. See V. Cable, "The Diminished Nation-State: A Study in the Loss of Economic Power," *Daedalus*, Spring 1995, for a discussion of this issue.
17. M. Horsman and A. Marshall, *After the Nation-State*, Harper Collins, 1994, 166, emphasis added. A key problem with this work is that its central argument veers between the problematic claim that the nation-state is in decline and the more defensible thesis that nation-states continue to play a central, albeit different role in international life in the lives of those who live in them. In this argument, they are drawing on the "new medievalism" thesis: the idea that the new world order, in some respects, comprises elements of the pre-1648 era, when the supremacy of the sovereign state was not accepted. See A. Roberts, "A New Age in International Relations," *International Affairs*, vol. 67, no. 3 July 1991.
18. On citizenship rights see the classic sociological discussion in T. H. Marshall Class, Citizenship and Social Development, Greenwood Press, 1973. Other useful discussions include, J. M. Barbalet, *Citizenship* Open University Press, 1988, A. Giddens, *Nation-State and Violence*, Polity 1985.
19. On these points see J. Mayall, *Nationalism and International Society*, Cambridge University Press 1990.
20. This is the main theme of M. Van Creveld, *On Future War*, Brassey's 1991.
21. Asaad Azzi, ch. 4, p. 129.
22. On the historical background to this point see L. Colley, *Britons Forging the Nation 1707–1837* Yale University Press 1992.
23. See J. Hutchinson, *Modern Nationalism*, 165–197.
24. Ueda, ch. 5, 139.
25. Ueda, ch. 5, 158.
26. I refer here to the Buchanan campaign in the 1996 Republican primaries the success of which surprised some commentators.
27. Gow ch. 6, 1.
28. Gow, ch. 6, 14.

# 1

# Nationalism, Nation-States, and Violence at the End of the Twentieth Century: A Sociological View

*Christopher Dandeker*

The decline of war and the waning of national identity are both central themes in the history of modern sociological thought. Today there are thinkers, such as Hobsbawm, who argue that the process of globalization will push nations and nation-states to the margins of contemporary history.[1] As for violence, writers like Fukuyama claim that nationalism in Europe—particularly Central and Eastern Europe— will entail violence only in the short term, and that, unlike the situation earlier in this century, such violence will not embroil other na- tion-states in major wars. To such thinkers, the twenty-first century promises the realization of the liberal vision of a peaceful concert of nation states.[2]

Yet up to now, nationalism has been closely connected with vio- lence and, as we shall see, some have argued that the twenty-first century is unlikely to be different, at least on that score. I shall argue that there are two reasons for this connection between nationalism and violence: the first is conceptual and has to do with the essential con- nection between nationalism and political autonomy. The second con- cerns the formation of national communities and the ways in which these have been—and will continue to be—forged in the political framework provided by the modern state and its monopolization of legitimate violence within a given territory. Have these relationships changed? This essay examines this fundamental question from the point of view of sociology.

In doing so, these connections between nationalism[3] and violence will be explored by focusing on two themes. The first is the part played by violence in the creation of nation-states, and the circumstances in which their internal relations and external conduct can be peaceful. The second is the significance of the seeming renewal of nationalism at the end of the twentieth century. Does this process indicate that nationalism will continue to be an important factor, or does it, in fact, signal the emerging dominance of other forces, thus rendering any interest in nationalism and violence of little contemporary relevance? Here the link between globalization and national identity figures strongly. Before proceeding further, some conceptual clarification is in order.

### Nations, Nation-States, and Modernity

National identity and nationalist ideology have been key features of modern history, in large part through their close connection with the creation of the nation-state system. This system was first forged in the pluralistic civilization of Europe and then spread to the rest of the globe over the last two hundred years with the result that, at the beginning of the twenty-first century, global society will be subdivided into nearly two hundred nation-states. Nationalism not only underpins the nation-state but also encourages those who wish to rectify what they perceive to be disparities between established political-territorial and cultural-ethnic boundaries. This shows little sign of waning at the end of the twentieth century. Yet such arguments presuppose a definition of nationalism, hardly an uncontroversial matter.

The approach to nationalism adopted here is influenced by the ideas of A. D. Smith, whose work synthesizes the insights of what have been termed the "primordialist" and "modernist" strands of thinking on the matter.[4] Central to his argument is the distinction between "ethnie" and nation. Smith emphasizes continuity and change in history: ethnicity is socially constructed and manipulated in intergroup struggles for power; but it is also an identity having deep historical roots that are more than simply politically convenient mythical constructions. Ethnic communities—that is, self-aware collectivities as opposed to objective, observer-created ethnic categories—are characterized by six features:

> (1) a collective proper name (2) a myth of common ancestry (3) shared historical memories (4) one or more differentiating elements of common culture (5) an *association* with a specific homeland (6) a sense of solidarity for significant sectors of the population.[5]

Smith argues that ethnic communities have played a significant role in the creation of modern nations and nation-states. The generic features of *national* identity are encompassed in the following definition:

> a nation . . . is a named human population sharing an historic territory, common myths and historical memories; a mass public culture, a common economy and legal rights and duties for all members.[6]

The critical differences between ethnies or ethnic communities and nations are as follows. First, whereas in the case of ethnies the link with territory may only be one of historical association or myth (or put another way a dimension of "imagined community"[7]) in the case of nations "it is physical and actual: nations *possess* territories."[8] Thus, ethnic communities need not be "resident" in their territorial homeland; indeed, rectifying a mismatch between symbolic boundaries and the actual territorial state of affairs may well be a key political objective of an ethnic community. Secondly, national culture may not be common to all members perhaps being confined to an intellectual or religious elite. Thirdly, an ethnie may not have a common division of labor and economic unity nor, fourthly, legal codes with common rights and duties for all.[9]

Under conditions of modernity it has been possible for ethnic communities to become transformed into nations. Such an argument allows us to recognize the ways in which modernity changes national identity. For example, Fukuyama has made the modernist claim that

> Nationalism did not exist in pre-industrial societies. It was born out of the process of industrialization, because economic modernization requires a common linguistic culture and vastly higher levels of mass education based on common language.[10]

There *is* a good deal of truth in this view. The formation of modern national communities took place once institutional structures for the organization of political authority had developed. As Giddens has suggested, if by society one means a clearly demarcated and internally well-articulated social entity, it is only relatively recently that large human populations have lived under such arrangements; and these have been the administrative achievements of modern nation-states.[11] Yet it is important to recognize that while modernity transformed national identity, it is not necessary to make the modernist error of assuming that it created it.[12]

Against this background, the distinctive features of nation-states become clearer: first, the greater mobilization of mass involvement in the political process and the significance of public opinion as a factor that state elites have to consider in their decision making; second, the greater collective awareness or self-consciousness of modern nationhood because of the conditions of modernity such as literacy and education; third, the clear boundaries of the modern nation-state as a power container and the sovereign authority exercised within its borders in contrast with the parcelled sovereignty of pre-modern polities and their more ragged and contested borders.[13]

Nationalism continues to flourish today for two main reasons. First, the end of the cold war and the disintegration of the Soviet Union have resulted in the formation, or reconstitution, of new nation-states and the spread of more or less violent national, ethnic, and separatist struggles in Central and Eastern Europe. Second, the dramatic impact of the globalization of world society on established political economic and cultural institutions means that these struggles are destined to become generic features of all modern nation-states, even long established ones. There is, I shall suggest, no reason to believe that nationalist conflicts within and between different nation-states (and their potential to become violent) will be confined to the less developed parts of global society. Let us turn first to the problem of the part played by violence in the creation of nation-states, and the circumstances in which their internal relations and external conduct can be peaceful before addressing the impact of globalization on nationalism and violence.

## Violence and the Two Faces of Nationalism

That the creation of the modern nation-state system has, so far, been intimately connected with violence is attested by many examples: the creation of the Netherlands in the seventeenth century from the

Habsburg Empire; the emergence of the United States in the eighteenth century through the defeat of the British Empire; the foundation in the nineteenth century of Latin American nation-states in the wake of the withdrawal of Spain; the disintegration of the Austrian, Turkish, and Russian Empires in Europe and the Middle East at the conclusion of the First World War in 1918; and the creation of new states from the colonies of the West European empires of Britain, France, and Belgium after the Second World War. This process has culminated in a remarkable recognition of the nation-state under international law. As Mayall has observed, "With the passage of UN General Assembly Resolution 1514 in 1960, the international community ruled that empires were no longer acceptable political entities." [14]

A key feature of twentieth-century history, however, was the seventy-year attempt by Soviet communism to resist this trend: to create what was in effect a socialist empire that the international community would accept. Democratic class ideology was invoked, while the social currents of national autonomy and secession were actively repressed, as in the case of the forced incorporation of the Baltic republics into the Soviet Union (they had been part of the old Russian empire) in 1940. The Soviet attempt to create a legitimate, non-national polity ultimately failed, however, and its end—the collapse of the Soviet Union and the delegitimation of communist ideology—is perhaps best viewed as the failure and dissolution of the last global empire. [15]

With this collapse has come a new wave of democracy, which underpins nationalist movements and the establishment or recreation of new nation-states in Eastern Europe, such as Croatia, Slovenia, and the Baltic states. One must ask, however, whether this latest process of nationalist renewal and nation-state formation will be as violent as earlier examples, as the Soviet empire is broken up, and new states struggle to formulate a framework for security. The wars in the former republic of Yugoslavia and the continuing violence in Russia's dealings with Chechnya suggest that it will not be easy for this process to be free of violence. [16] To answer this question will require considering a further problem: whether, and under what conditions, internal relations and external conduct of nation-states, once formally recognized by the international community, can be freed from violence. Our response will depend on how we see the connection between democracy and nationalism. Is liberal democracy really the best antidote to the internal and external violence of nations and, if it is, how can it be encouraged?

Looking back at the European experience of the formation of national communities, how then, might we account for the link between that process and violence? Nationalism has been connected with violence in two ways. The first is conceptual, having to do with the essential link between nationalism and political autonomy. A. D. Smith draws a distinction between the concepts of state and nation, while admitting certain overlaps between them.[17] Following Max Weber, he argues that the state refers to "public institutions, differentiated from, and autonomous of other social institutions and exercising a monopoly of coercion within a given territory."[18] In contrast nation, "signifies a cultural and political bond, uniting in a single community all who share an historic culture and homeland."[19]

This distinction helps use to recognize the implications of ethnic and national diversity for nation-states. Smith argues that the distinction between an ethnie and a nation rests on *possession* of rather than *association* with territory. There is a crucial difference between, on the one hand, an ethnic group which, despite its historical association with a territory, is actually content to live in a given nation-state and, on the other, an ethnic group which is not and thus seeks to separate the territory it is associated with from the state in possession and the group or groups that control it. Accordingly, an ethnic group may become an aspiring nation, or, if it is related to a nation already in existence in another territory, seek to join it through territorial reorganization. This could involve secession from a state or being engaged in strategies of irredentism emanating from outside its borders.[20]

It is precisely because national identity is bound up with territory and political autonomy that national conflicts are fundamentally associated with the risk of violence: control of the instruments of coercion and regulation over territory and thus the framework within which other activities are decided upon are at issue. Some writers, such as Hutchinson, have questioned the idea that nationalism presupposes a political strategy to construct its own state.[21] They draw a distinction between political and cultural nationalism, arguing that the latter focuses on educational, literary and related activities in order to encourage the formation of culturally distinct identities. Indeed, it is often associated with a suspicion of political organizations and the state. However, in order to achieve the goals of nationalism—some form of autonomy for the nation, if not independence—cultural nationalism has to become conjoined with, or become transformed into, political nationalism. Such are the territorial realities of nationalism.

The second link between nationalism and violence concerns warfare and the historical development of the nation-state. That is to say, warfare helped to create national communities *before* as well as during the development of the modern nation-state. A key feature of European civilization has been its national and ethnic diversity. This "patchwork quality" is in part owed to patterns of conquest and invasion in the period 700–1200.[22] These helped to forge feudal structures which provided the political basis for pluralism. They also helped to create relations of non-kin personal bonding and loyalty of significance for the later expansion of contractual market relationships. In addition, the heterogeneous nature of the invading groups of conquest added to the ethnic and national diversity of European civilization. This pluralism in Europe provided a barrier against the development of a continent-wide despotism.

By sustaining geopolitical pluralism, national/ethnic divisions helped to promote continuous and intense warfare in Europe. War had great costs, but it also promoted economic development, by making kings, nobility, and church dependent upon money lenders, bankers, and armament manufacturers, all of whom grew independently wealthy as result. This pattern of development strengthened the formation of independent capitalist classes based in autonomous cities and city states; they were able to play one state off against another, freely moving between them, depending upon which provided the most favorable financial environment. Warfare in Europe also stimulated technological and tactical innovations in military organization and the modernization of other administrative structures of the state including its financial system. These in turn meant that when the West eventually expanded overseas in the sixteenth century, it was able to defeat the armies and navies of societies that had stagnated militarily—even if they were more advanced in non-military matters. Thus, the West's world leadership in arms manufacture and military organization was a capacity later translated into global, economic, and political supremacy and the spread of the nation-state system as the basis of international society. The upshot of all this was that war created nations, nations created states, and states created further wars. In turn, these stimulated the modernization of the state as a power container in which national communities could be consolidated.[23]

Such arguments and the long-term perspective they encourage, provide a sobering perspective from which to view the relationships between violence and the newer nation-states—for example, those created in Europe after the collapse of the Soviet Union and those formed in the aftermath of earlier phases of decolonization by the Western european powers, Britain, France, Belgium, and Portugal.

In European history, there have been two faces of nationalism. First, it has been linked with the emancipatory, democratic liberation of peoples—as in the creation of citizenship states from absolutist polities in nineteenth-century Europe and the associated liberal ideal of a network of peaceful republican democracies. However there is a second face of nationalism; one associated with the repressive and violent side of human conduct through the xenophobic and authoritarian organization of citizenries in militarized confrontations with and subordination of other peoples. The prime examples are the development of authoritarian nationalism and imperialism in Europe between 1880 and 1918 and the rise of fascism between 1918 and 1945. A key component of current debates on the future of European security is which side of the "Janus-face" of nationalism will be revealed in Eastern Europe and Russia over the next decade and whether and how the emancipatory potential of nationalism can be fostered.[24]

Under conditions of modernity, whether nationalism takes an emancipatory or repressive course will be determined, in part, by the form of democratic politics in the countries concerned. Although it is right to suggest, as Smith does, that national identity is a deep-rooted social phenomenon, it receives particular forms and intensity under the conditions of modernity. The impact of the capitalist market and division of labor, the industrialization of transport and communication, and the surveillance capacities of the modern bureaucratic state all give modern nationalism particular features lacking in pre-modern contexts. In particular, the emancipatory potential will be favored if economic, cultural, and political conditions are favorable for the development of liberal democracy. Societies organized on such basis are rather less likely than other types of political systems to resort to war to resolve conflicts amongst *their own kind* and to experience violence as the prime mechanism of ordering the relations amongst the subgroups of the national community.

A well-developed literature discusses the relationships between liberal democracy, industrial society, and peace. Three mechanisms appear to be at work.[25] First, such a system makes its participants prosperous, and thus less likely to turn to war to resolve their economic difficulties; indeed their very prosperity gives them more to lose by turning to war. They have a vested material interest in peace, which promotes international cooperation, further prosperity, and more cooperation in a self-reinforcing feedback cycle. Second, economic interdependence promotes mutual vulnerability and this means that states acquire interests in cooperation and in devising trust and confidence building measures. Third, economic and social interdependence amongst nation-states promotes conditions under which forms of global governance, based on the values of democracy, individual rights, and the rule of law, can flourish. Such mechanisms can provide diplomatic resolutions of residual conflicts and the means of managing the more violent disputes likely to emerge in those parts of the world still undergoing modernization.

A further implication of all of this is that the best chances for peace *within* a nation hinge on the development of a political framework of liberal democracy which is able to command widespread legitimacy and a market economy. That is to say, conflicts between interest groups take place within sets of rules and understandings which are themselves not at issue, and a politically managed socioeconomic system that generates prosperity or the *hope* of an acceptable standard of living for the major elements of the population.[26] By contrast, when these conditions are absent, conflict is much more likely. When social and economic disadvantages (real or perceived) are linked closely with regional and ethnic divisions and sources of identity, then violent conflict can ensue, as recent riots and unrest in the United Kingdom and United States testify.

In the European context, the disintegration of the Soviet Union and the consequent "final wave" of the long process of decolonization, poses, in acute form, the question of how difficult will be the process of converting communist states into liberal-democratic members of a prosperous and peaceful Europe. Yet it is best to view this problem as a regional component of a far broader *global* question: how can relations amongst the core capitalist countries, and the less developed nations be configured to reduce the chances of war and violence.

We might expect a continuing upsurge of assertive, even xenophobic, nationalism in the aftermath of the cold war. In Eastern Europe and elsewhere, the "unfreezing" of deep-seated regional and ethnic bases of conflict has been reinforced by the gulf between the prosperous (and, as with the EU, increasingly defensive) core countries and the developing world. However, from a liberal-capitalist perspective, there are stronger grounds for optimism and for questioning the supposed power of ancient conflicts to resist changes in social conditions. It can be argued that the intensity and assertiveness of nationalism reflects different stages of industrialization. For example, Fukuyama has suggested that, national feelings "become most intense just at or after the initial phase of industrialization, though they can be suppressed by political forces."[27]

This judgment allows him to explain why

> Third World nationalism has been much more zealous than European nationalism in the second half of the twentieth century, and why within Western Europe, the two countries that industrialized and unified the latest, Italy and Germany, were the initiators of fascist ultra-nationalism. It also explains why nationalism is so intense in the southern half of Eastern Europe and in the Soviet Union today, for these regions industrialised later than Western Europe, and are only now being permitted a degree of democratic self expression.[28]

Fukuyama goes on to suggest that while "[y]oung nationalisms are frequently chauvinistic and imperialist, demanding dominion over other people" [29] they also mature as national identities gain wider recognition and ultimately become more secure. Thus in Eastern europe, the process of dismantling a failed empire and the establishment of a number of new nations may be violent in the short term but, in the longer term, a peaceful and more stable outcome can be anticipated. With successful industrial development and commitment to the values of the market, technology and political pluralism, new nations can be at peace with themselves and with their neighbors.

The key question raised by arguments such as these is how easy will it be for post-colonial societies and other new nations facing external barriers to development and internal ethnic divisions, to advance successfully to a liberal industrial society. Fukuyama argues, that the short-term violence associated with the creation of new nations today simply does not have implications for global peace and security comparable to that associated with the Balkan disputes of the late nineteenth and early twentieth centuries. The reason is that the broader context of conflict has changed. Great powers are no longer competing for control of these areas via alliance structures and other military means; their competition is now focused on economic means. The question remains: is this too optimistic a view?

Whatever the difficulties faced by the new nation-states in contemporary Europe in constructing peaceful internal and external relations, these are far worse in some of the new "state-nations" created by earlier processes of decolonization. Such entities have fragile infra-structures of territorial control and weak national identities.[30] In many parts of Africa, for example, disputes have arisen that were based on the inherent structure of post-colonial society. Not the least of these were the incorporation of conflicting ethnic groups into one state and, indeed as the case of Rwanda illustrates, the encouragement of such conflicts as a component in an imperial strategy of divide and rule. The momentum of such conflicts has, indeed, often been maintained, at least until the cold war ended, by structures of clientship that linked such regional conflicts to superpower global rivalry. In addition to these problems, strategies of nation-building are also inhibited by the economic and political power disparities between developed and de-veloping countries. As we shall see later, these will be exacerbated by any increase in protectionist tendencies on the part of the dominant centers of global economic power. The obstacles to successful nation-state building are, therefore, profound.

A. D. Smith suggests that it might be possible for these societies to create Western style nation-states, based on shared values rather than presumed common descent. This could be achieved either through a strategy of constructing national identity on the basis of the values of a hegemonic ethnic core or through reliance on a supra-ethnic political culture. This latter approach might be especially appropriate in a soci-ety of such ethnic complexity that a candidate for hegemon cannot be clearly identified, as in Nigeria. More disturbingly, Smith argues that there is another possibility—what he calls ethnonationalism. This en-tails a recurrence of the populist ethnic nationalism, based on myths of shared descent in the form of separatist movements similar to those of late-nineteenth-century Eastern Europe. Today for many ethnic groups, "the new states into which colonialism incorporated them are viewed with sentiments that range from reserve, to outright hostility, which may spill over into protracted wars of ethnic liberation, threatening the stability of whole regions."[31]

The evidence suggests, moreover, that potentially violent separatist ethnic nationalism will *not* be confined to developing or new nations, but will be a significant feature of the developed world as well. In recent years there has been a third wave of ethnic nationalism much closer to the core of industrial societies such as France, Italy, Canada, and the United Kingdom. Why? As I suggested earlier, part of the answer lies in the drive towards democracy—or at least the celebration of self-determination—despite the difficulties associated with that concept. This has been given added momentum by the end of the cold war and the delegitimation of communism. However, another part of the answer lies in fundamental social transformations connected with global interdependence and the restructuring of the links between local, regional, national, and international relationships—issues to which I now turn. It is in this context that we can answer the question posed above: is the liberal democratic perspective on nationalism and violence overly optimistic?

## Globalization and New Times— ## The Future of Nationalism and Violence

The end of the cold war has thrown into prominence once again the abiding sociological themes of the decline of war and the waning of national identity. But important as the end of the cold war was, it is best seen as one aspect, albeit a very important one, of an even broader and far-reaching social transformation.

What I have termed the "new times" of late modernity are characterized by a number of related social processes.[32] The first and most obvious feature of these new times is the end of the cold war itself and a shift from the certainties of the bipolar standoff between the two superpowers to a more uncertain, fragmented world of competing centers of economic, political, and military power. In this new era of risk uncertainty it is now difficult for any of the advanced societies to establish the circumstances in which a bewildering array of risks (defined as capabilities not matched to intent) might become identifiable threats. For example, the proliferation of nuclear and other weapons of mass destruction increases the risk of their use, but specific identifiable threats cannot be charted without an analysis of the intentions of the users of those weapons. Consequently, in this uncertain and turbulent world it is more difficult than ever before to identify where one's international interests lie and thus what appropriate mix of military and non-military (economic, diplomatic) instruments of security should be developed.

Now that the four-decade military confrontation between the superpowers has concluded, it is easier to observe a second process. This is "globalization": the growth of an interdependent world economic system coordinated through transnational corporations and other international and transnational organizations, the operations of which are facilitated by the electronic revolution in communications.[33] World-economic integration is being accelerated by a growth in trade; for example, there was a thirteen-fold increase in the trading of goods and services between 1950 and 1990.[34] In addition, integration is promoted by the increase in the volume of financial flows and the migration of people, companies, and other organizations from one country to another. Modern means of transport and communication—especially electronic information storage, processing, and transfer—facilitate the rapid spread of cultural and other products from one society to another, including the movement of populations. A good example of this is the impact of television images of the West on the revolt against communism in the 1980s in Eastern Europe and on migratory movements today in the east and south of the EU.[35]

Globalization has spread the Western systems of economic capitalism, political democracy, technology, and military power to other parts of the globe. It has at the same time brought about a relative shift in the distribution of global power, as between the old West and Pacific rim, although the extent of this is a matter of heated debate. However this may be, globalization entails an "intensification of worldwide social relations which link distant localities in such a way that local happenings are shaped by events occurring many miles away and vice versa."[36]

The third process to which I want to draw attention concerns the interplay between regionalization and transregionalization. Globalization has not only integrated the world economy to a greater degree than before; it has also made different regions of societies susceptible to the consequences of shifts of capital, raw materials, and population from one part of the world to another, as for instance in the global sourcing of modern manufacturing products such as automobiles and computers.[37] The cycle of good and bad times is increasingly dependent upon transnational processes that interconnect regions in different nation-states in different parts of the world, rendering autarchic, national economic strategies more and more difficult. Populations of all states—including their leaders and advisors—have to come to terms with the paradox that global unification and regional fragmentation of national communities are two sides of the same coin.

The fourth feature of these new times is an increase in the number and types of international actors. To be sure, there is nothing especially peculiar about a multipolar international state system—regional and world politics have experienced cycles moving from uni-, multi-, and bipolar systems in different historical periods. What is new about the post-cold war world is the coincidence of the structural principles of multipolarity and multicentric orders. By multicentric, I mean centers of power and global action that are not sovereign states.[38] A plethora of such "sovereignty-free" state actors—nongovernmental organizations (NGOs), corporations, parties, and media organizations, and so on—now play a role in international politics. They complicate the environment in which nation-states operate, both in regard to their external and their internal affairs. These organizations can achieve a global presence and ensure that the space of international politics is no longer the exclusive preserve of the state. States now have the difficult task of designing a legal and normative basis for a multipolar and multicentric order; and in doing so they have to weigh the relative value of military and non-military instruments in securing it.

In this multipolar and multicentric world, sovereign states are also joined by emergent politico-economic blocs, e.g., those of NAFTA, the EU, and similar entities in the Pacific region. The full significance of this trend is difficult to assess. On the one hand, with the end of the cold war the world has become multipolar, producing a geopolitical system that is more unpredictable and less stable at least in terms of threat assessment as opportunities for independent action by nation-states increase.[39] On the other hand, global economic pressures force many states to become attached to one or another of the emerging economic blocs or to create other blocs. This is in order that states can exercise some control over global economic and other processes (such as ecological risks) by participating in supranational agencies because their capacities when operating alone are so limited. For example, for most new European nation-states, one of the first steps after national independence is to consider how best to take advantage of some type of association with nearby blocs such as the EU.[40]

The crucial and paradoxical issue here is that bloc formation, which arises from attempts to take economic and political advantage of globalization, can lead to mercantilist-like processes of "deglobalization" such as protectionism and unilateral approaches to security problems. This is one of the key debates in the EU in connection with its views on opening membership to Central and Eastern European nations;in maintaining relatively free trade with other blocs such as NAFTA; and of course in connection with policy on Bosnia-Herzegovina.

The fifth feature of the new times of later modernity concerns the impact of international law on the conduct of states. An example of this is the role of the European Community and Court of Human Rights on member states. However, the broader trend has direct relevance to the response of the international community to nationalism and violence. There is a much greater questioning of the legitimacy of unilateral use of military force as a means of resolving international disputes. Furthermore, as the issue of Iraq's treatment of the Kurds illustrates, there is also greater doubt about the absolute sovereignty of states over even their internal affairs. While Rosenau has noted a "world wide trend towards valuing human rights,"[41] this poses the question of how might the conflicting imperatives of state sovereignty on the one hand and the rights of the individual and minority groups within state borders be managed?

How this issue is resolved in any given case such as Rwanda or Bosnia-Herzegovina, is affected by a sixth element of new times: the impact of global electronic media, especially television. The media can use and be used by public opinion to pressure governments into intervening in order to ameliorate the suffering associated with ethnic conflicts within states.[42] We are witnessing the increased capacity of public opinion to exercise its political influence in ways that transcend the boundaries of states. The increased focus on human—individual and minority—rights and toleration can be viewed as a recent addition to the concept of security. To return to the implications of the case of the Kurds in the aftermath of the Gulf conflict: earlier definitions—for instance, in Article 2(7) of the UN charter—were emphatic that there should be no interference in the "internal affairs of states . . . Events in the last few years have changed all that. Under a Security Council resolution, outside powers [were] intervening in Iraq in an attempt to protect the Kurdish minority in the North and the Shi'ites in the South."[43]

Consequently, the democratic core of industrial states have considered mounting more robust interventions in favor of democracy and human rights around the world.[44] At the same time this has stimulated debate over the criteria for deciding when and where to intervene— not least how far to question the internal affairs of sovereign states— as well as the costs of such actions. Since the Gulf war a growing number of such interventions can be identified such as the Kurdish case and Yugoslavia. Such interventions and peacekeeping necessarily entail consideration of a wider agenda of legitimacy and organizational issues than that of managing the conflicting imperatives of state sovereignty on the one hand and, on the other, the rights of the individual and minority groups within state borders. For example, should state intervention be subcontracted to UN authorized regional groups of states or should there be strong UN control of such activities? How might the military-political interface, made more complicated by the multinational nature of these operations and media scrutiny of their initiation and conduct, be managed more effectively?[45]

These problems will remain of critical concern because current trends are likely to produce a continuing series of violent national and ethnic conflicts posing risks at the regional and global level. This point is connected with a seventh feature of late modernity and is something of a counterreaction to globalization. It concerns the development of subnationalist regional and separatist movements within nation-states.

Most "nation-states" are multiethnic or multinational. Even the most established nation-states in Western Europe, which have experienced long-term political and administrative rationalization and the consolidation of different groups into the nation still retain significant subnational elements—Basques, Catalans, and Scots, for example.[46] With the shifts in population associated with the globalization of economic relations, the national and ethnic complexity of all nation-states will continue to grow—whether this be in Western Europe or in the Pacific region as in Australia. In addition, national minorities are increasingly likely to express their rights to be recognized as distinct elements in the nation-state; or, in the extreme case, even to form their own state by appealing to the liberal principle of autonomy that underpins international society.[47]

These movements within nation-states can be viewed as nationalisms of frustration, directed against the transnational cycles of good and bad times I referred to earlier. Together with processes of supranational political organization, their development has led some to argue that the nation-state is being eroded from both above and below.[48] Giddens has argued, convincingly in my view, that globalization and localism, or regionalist and subnational trends are dialectically related.[49] Such developments as Quebec separatism in Canada, schisms within India, the disintegration of the Soviet Union and Yugoslavia, and separatism in Italy, Spain, and the United Kingdom are occurring not in spite of, but because of, the larger processes already mentioned. European integration means that politics becomes more distant in terms of the location of centers of power. The result is that issues of locality become more important. These points connect with my earlier arguments on regionalization and transregionalization. Globalization is uneven in its effects: economic integration can exacerbate regional inequalities, and thus provide a basis for nationalist attempts to seek better terms from the cores of dominant power centers. In the European context, shifts in a federal direction in the EU have "given many small nations such as the Scots, Basques, and the Catalans the impression that they could trade in their former minority status and become full members of a multinational European state—a new Europe of all nations."[50]

The dialectical character of nationalism in the age of globalization is further revealed in nationalist perceptions that economic integration provides *risks* as well as opportunities. One example is concern about core (i.e., U.S.) cultural hegemony over regional and local values and lifestyles. For this reason, a key element of the many contemporary nationalist agendas is to obtain more resources and recognition from transnational political and economic entities than was traditionally provided by the nation-state—but not to fall into new forms of subordination.

In all of this, a critical question for the EU and similar political entities is how to ensure that core-periphery inequalities do not create nationalisms of resentment from the periphery and counter-nationalisms from core areas. If this is a difficulty for the EU, then how much more difficult will it be for the other regions of newer nation-states such as post-communist Eastern Europe?[51]

An answer to this question can be generated by considering the implications of my analysis of "new times" for nationalism and the nation-state and for the relationships between nationalism and violence. There are, I suggest, four related effects. First, nation-states at the core and periphery of global society are tending to decompose into smaller units. Second, relations of economic, political, and cultural interdependence are undermining both the sovereignty and the autonomy of nation-states. Third, as liberal social structures spread, war and military power will decline as mechanisms of resolving disputes between established nation-states organized on those principles. Fourth, and paradoxically, while the advanced industrial states experience peaceful ways of resolving disputes with one another, they will have to respond to national and ethnic violence within the nation-states of the developing world and within *their own*, increasingly multiethnic countries.

The process of gradual breakdown of nation-states has been called "sub-groupism"[52]; "regionalism"[53] and, by the present author, "sub-nationalism." However, it should not be thought of as the end of the nation-state. Rather, it is best seen as a reconfiguration of linkages of local, regional, and global social relationships, in the management of which the nation-state remains a key player.[54] For example, given the fragility of many third world state-nations I referred to earlier, it will be difficult for them to avoid the more extreme forms of subnational disintegration. However, that said, for these state-nations—*and* secessionist groups—maintaining or gaining status as independent nation-states provides a principal means of extracting favorable treatment from privileged societies, and from international and transnational organizations such as the International Monetary Fund (IMF).

The second effect of new times concerns national sovereignty. David Held has argued that relations of economic, political, and cultural interdependence across the globe undermine the sovereignty (the legal-constitutional independence to make decisions) as well as the autonomy (the effective power to implement decisions) of nation-states. For nation-states, including new ones, operation in an

> ever more complex international system both limits their autonomy and infringes ever more upon their sovereignty. Any conception of sovereignty which interprets it as an illimitable form of public power is undermined. Sovereignty itself has to be conceived today as already divided among a number of agencies national, international and transnational and limited by the very nature of this plurality.[55]

Yet, this loss of sovereignty, however, is a complex and double-edged process. The shift from a bipolar to a multipolar world can, in fact, lead to greater autonomy for some states, such as regional powers (Nigeria in west Africa for example), while core nation-states attempt to use their power to influence the conduct of the UN Security Council and other agencies such as the IMF in order to respond to the instabilities created by globalization.

The third effect of new times is that, as globalization is strongly associated with the spread of liberal capitalism, war, and military power will decline as mechanisms of resolving disputes among liberal capitalist societies. They will increasingly be confined to the interface between the capitalist and noncapitalist world. Moreover, this interface will no longer be structured by a bipolar superpower conflict; it will develop in a context where the communist road to modernity has lost legitimacy. Although this opens up the prospect for the further advance of liberal democracy it would be foolish to deny that non-democratic regional powers will continue to pose threats to the values of a liberal international society. Threats from this quarter might increase the possibility of the formation of stronger collective security arrangements focused on the UN and backed by the military might of the remaining superpower.[56]

Although war might well become limited to the interface between the capitalist and noncapitalist world, it may be wondered how successfully the developing world will tread the road to liberal democracy, particularly those parts which control scarce resources crucial for the survival of industrial societies. The advanced societies will probably seek to maintain their advantages by military means if necessary. This raises the whole question of how the nation-state system grapples with problems of conflicts between and within nations created by such core-periphery tensions.

So far this chapter's argument has paralleled some of the ideas of liberal social theory.[57] It has suggested that under current conditions of globalization (and so long as mercantilism or deglobalization does not become influential), interstate war among core industrial nation-states is most unlikely. The most likely focus of collective violence will be regional conflicts among developing countries or subnational conflicts within one or more of these societies. Furthermore, it has maintained that such violence will be extruded from the core countries to focus on the interface between core and periphery, with the core drawn in willingly or unwillingly in peacekeeping-type roles in regional security operations legitimated through the UN. However, the argument need not end there. Two rather different directions can be taken. One is to develop Rosenau's ideas on the implications of globalization for violence; the second is to follow the argument of Van Creveld.[58]

Rosenau focuses on four dynamics that are leading to a global decline in the likelihood of interstate war. The first is complexity: complexity of loyalties and centrifugal tendencies within nation-states make it more difficult than before for a state to mobilize its population for the sustained effort of war. Meanwhile, the external complexity of an opponent's social structure makes it difficult to control even if one has the motive and means of conquest.[59] Second, "weariness": populations are tired of wars for distant and abstract goals (although, as will be seen presently, interest in more local goals might well be *increasing*). Third, "paralysis": precisely because of the difficulties faced by the world's governments in managing economic, ecological, and other planetary problems, the time and motive for war has declined. Fourth, "the worldwide trend toward valuing human rights serves as a vital constraint on war-proneness of states."[60] As I suggested earlier, this trend is reinforced by the impact of global media. However, it should be stressed that the same trend can encourage public opinion to press for military action in pursuit of just interventions—when, for example, humanitarian or other rights are threatened by ethnic strife within a nation-state. How robust the will of the public remains when casualties of their *own* soldiers and citizens mount is a question that, naturally, vexes their governments.

Rosenau, in an argument similar to that defended by Moskos, warns that the decline of war may, in fact, be connected with the *growth* of violence. He suggests that " . . . other forms of war may well mar the global landscape as the complexity and paralysis of states encourages subgroups to contest each other and resort to coercive action on behalf of subgroup aspirations."[61]

This point is taken to its logical conclusion by Van Creveld who makes what Rosenau calls "sub-groupism" a central theme in his thesis. Low-intensity conflicts fought by subnational groups have been the prevalent form of war since 1945. These conflicts are "irregular" in that at least one of the parties to the conflict is not an army—that is, not a conventional, legitimate state organization—while the protagonists do not rely on the high- technology weapons systems so beloved of modern armed forces. Such conflicts have been characteristic of the less developed parts of the world, although in recent decades the forms of terrorist violence associated with them have spread to established industrial nation-states including France, Great Britain, Italy ,and Spain. Indeed, he suggests that this process will continue: thus Israel's deep-seated problems with Palestinian autonomy and the implications for the Israeli state can be expected to have parallels in all multiethnic nation-states.

Despite the significance of low-intensity conflicts and their future importance, the record of modern armed forces in dealing with them has been a dismal failure. Van Creveld argues that if states are less and less effective in deterring or fighting one another in order to defend the interests of their populations, then other groups will take up the challenge. As the modern state loses its monopoly on the means of legitimate violence, "war will not be waged by armies but by groups whom today we call terrorists, guerrillas, bandits and robbers."[62]

Van Creveld is probably right to draw our attention to the fact that the post-cold war world *is* a break with the past and that the armed forces of the advanced states will have to adjust accordingly. But whether their destiny is to wither away and die along with the authority of their own states may be doubted. This is because of the continuing capacity of the nation-state to provide services and a focus of loyalty for its populations by linking their local concerns with supranational questions and institutions under conditions of globalization. This is not to underestimate the problems nation-states will face in playing this role; it *is* to suggest that arguing that the established nation-states are already failing is too premature. Indeed, Van Creveld severely underestimates the continuing military capacity of the industrial nation-state to contain if not defeat the violent strategies of subnational groups. Van Creveld's image of a world of violent medievalism—a "back to the future" of the Thirty Years War, or an extrapolation from the Israeli "Intifada" is overdrawn.

## Conclusion

This chapter began with two issues: the part played by violence in the creation of nation-states, and the circumstances in which their internal relations and external conduct can be peaceful; and whether nationalism and national identity are central or marginal social forces in late modern times. Our conclusions should now be clear.

With regard to the first issue, national identity and violence *are* closely related, as is shown by the close connections between nationalism, territory and political autonomy, and the historical record of nation-state building. The argument is usually made for Western Europe, but it can be applied as well to the centerpiece of the modern West: no War of Independence and Civil War, no modern democratic United States.[63]

Furthermore, there is a strong association between industrial capitalism and liberal democracy, and the decline of war as a means of resolving disputes among states of that type. However the risks of deglobalization or protectionism for war between one state and another and xenophobia and intolerance between one group and another *within* nation-states are profound. In addition, societies in the difficult process of making a transition to democracy, might be expected to experience internal conflicts and external outlets for them in the form of war with regional neighbors.[64] This point does not apply necessarily in regard to conflicts between liberal democracies and other—especially nondemocratic types of society.

On the second issue—the significance of nationalism today—contrary to the claims of the dominant traditions of classical social theory, nationalism and national identity remain key features of group identity and intergroup relations. Conditions today are, of course, very different from those of the nineteenth century. With globalization, integrative and transnational social processes are dialectically linked with localist and regional trends, thus undercutting the modern nation-state from above and below. Hence a certain "subgroupism" is common to societies on either side of the core-periphery division in the post-cold war world.

Clearly, these arguments do not necessarily add up to a conflict-free future. The risks of violence associated with forging new national identities as separate states are high not least because of particular difficulties associated with the idea of self-determination in a world defined largely by the rules of the nation-state system. In these new times, statehood remains a critical part of the answer to the questions of how to promote prosperity and autonomy for a people. Thus, insofar as the trend of nationalist separatism and the associated risks of violence are deeply rooted, the challenge to the global community is immense.

So we are left with questions. Will the consequences of recognizing new states like Croatia, Slovenia, Bosnia-Herzegovina encourage an acceleration in secessionist movements, and what criteria will be used in awarding or withholding state status? As Marc Weller has argued

the dissolution of Yugoslavia poses inconvenient and possibly dangerous problems for Europe and other regions. Once it is established that self-determination is not only a pretty principle but a substantive right that may include the right to secede, then nationalist fervour will be fuelled the world over, it is feared. However, separatist violence is already much in evidence, in Europe and elsewhere, precisely because there are *no* peaceful procedures available to negotiate about the implementation of the right to self determination.[65]

One must ask whether following the Organization of African Unity (OAU) principle that post-colonial state boundaries, however illegitimate on some grounds, nonetheless has provided at least some aspects of a basis for collective security. Disposing of this or similar rules in any region is fraught with danger. As the relations between nationalism and violence continue to evolve, much will depend on how the international society of nation-states deals with the issue of ethnonational minority rights.[66] Few would accept that every social entity asking for state status should be offered it. In order to maintain global political order and satisfy the demands of peoples for self-determination, minority rights buttressed by international guarantees may well become more significant than hitherto. The challenge is to establish effective political and military mechanisms to implement these guarantees. These will necessarily be international in character, involving the UN, and will pose difficult questions for participating governments who will need to justify their participation to their own peoples. This will not be easy as they might be inclined to view the legitimacy of such activities as weak and ephemeral. Significant progress in closing the gap between what is institutionally appropriate and what commands legitimacy or public acceptance would constitute an appropriate response to the problems of nationalism and violence in the twenty-first century.[67]

## Notes

1. E. Hobsbawm, *Nations and Nationalism Since 1870*, Canto Press 1991.
2. F. Fukuyama, "The End of History?" *National Interest*, Summer 1989, 3–18, and subsequent discussion, 18–35; F Fukuyama, "Democratization and International Security," in *New Dimensions in International Security*, part 2, Adelphi Paper 266, 14–24, 1991–92. For the background to this tradition of thinking see M. Howard, *War and the Liberal Conscience*, Oxford 1976. Although Marxism and the liberal theory of industrial society both predict the decline of violence and nationalism with modernization, there is a third tradition of sociological realism premised on the idea that these phenomena are chronic and recurrent features of human societies. Max Weber is a representative of this tradition. See the discussion in C. E. Ashworth and C. Dandeker, "Warfare Social Theory and West European Development," *Sociological Review* 35, 1, 1987, 1–18.
3. In this analysis, national identity and nation refer to a type of social group. Nationalism is an ideology and/or movement committed to the idea of creating and defending an existing or anticipated national identity by political cultural or other means. A nationalist is a person motivated, at least in part by such ideals.

4. A. D. Smith, *The Ethnic Origin of Nations*, Oxford Blackwell 1986, *National Identity*, Penguin, Harmondsworth, 1991. The terms "primordialist" and "modernist" are used by J. Hutchinson in *Modern Nationalism*, Fontana 1994, 3.

5. A. D. Smith, *National Identity*, Penguin, Harmondsworth, 1991:21, emphasis added.

6. A. D. Smith, *National Identity*, 40, emphasis added.

7. See Benedict Anderson, *Imagined Communities*, Verso 1983.

8. A. D. Smith, *National Identity*, 40, emphasis added.

9. Ibid.

10. F. Fukuyama, *Democratization and International Security*, 20.

11. A. Giddens, *Nation-State and Violence*, Polity, Blackwell 1985;172; C. Dandeker, *Surveillance Power and Modernity*, Polity, 1990, Blackwell.

12. On this see the excellent discussion in Hutchinson, particularly his critique of Connor's ultra-modernist position. J. Hutchinson, *Modern Nationalism*, 11–12, 14,16,17.

13. A. Giddens, *The Consequences of Modernity*, Polity Press, 1991, 303.

14. J. Mayall, "Nationalism and International Security after the Cold War," *Survival*, Spring 1992; 19–35, 22.

15. On this theme see S. P. Huntington, *The Third Wave: Democratization in the Late Twentieth Century*, University of Oklahoma Press, 1991.

16. See James Gow's chapter 5.

17. A. D. Smith, *National Identity*, 14–15. See also J. Breuilly, "The Nation-State and Violence: A Critique of Giddens," in J. Clark, C. Modgil, and S. Modgil, Anthony Giddens: *Consensus and Controversy*, Falmer Press 1990; 271–288; 291–293.

18. A. D. Smith, *National Identity*, 14.

19. Ibid; 14–15.

20. On secessionism and irredentism see J. Mayall, *Nationalism and International Society*, 57–63; 80–81.

21. J. Hutchinson, *Modern Nationalism*, 39–63.

22. The following analysis draws on, W. McNeill, *The Pursuit of Power*, Blackwell 1983; M. Howard, *War in European History*, Oxford 1976; C. Cipolla, *Guns, Sails and Empire: Technological Innovation and the Early Phases of European Expansion, 1400–1700*, Collins 1965; P. Contamine, *War in the Middle Ages*, Blackwell 1984; J. A. Hall, *Powers and Liberties: The Causes and Consequences of the Rise of the West*, Blackwell 1985; C. E. Ashworth and C. Dandeker, "Capstones and Organisms: Political Forms and the Triumph of Capitalism: A Critical Note," *Sociology* 20, 1, 1986, 82–87; C. E. Ashworth and C. Dandeker, "Warfare, Social Theory and West European Development," *Sociological Review* 35, 1, 1987, 1–18.

23. This is not to deny important differences between trajectories of nation-state formation. Here one can point to the distinction between the largely Western, civic, or political concept in which national identity is derived from allegiance to common political values, and the cultural concept, in which national identity is rooted in a shared, presumed (i.e, often mythic) descent. The latter is a marked characteristic of the Eastern European tradition although, as Smith is careful to note both can be found in all parts of Europe. See A. D. Smith, *National Identity*, 43–70; also P. Alter, *Nationalism*, Edward Arnold 1989, 14–18.

24. See A. Smolar, "Democratization in Central-Eastern Europe and International Security," Adelphi Paper 266, part 2, 1991–2, 25–34; B. Kodmani-Darwish, "International Security and the Forces of Nationalism and Fundamentalism," Adelphi Paper 266, 1991–2, 43–52. The idea of the "Janus-face" of nationalism is taken from T. Nairn, *The Break Up of Britain*, New Left Books 1977.

25. See the useful, and critical, discussion in J. Mearsheimer, "Back to the Future, Instability in Europe after the Cold War," *International Security*, vol. 15, 1990, 5–56.

26. See R. Aron, *Main Currents of Sociological Thought*, Penguin, Harmondsworth 1968, 223–232.

27. F. Fukuyama, *Democratization and International Security*, 1991, 20.

28. Ibid: 20.

29. Ibid: 20.

30. Smith, *National Identity*, 106–108.

31. Smith, *National Identity*, 124.

32. See my essay, "A Farewell to Arms? The Military Profession and the Nation-State" in the collection edited by J. Burk, *The Military in New Times; Adjusting Armed Forces to a Turbulent World*, Westview, 1994, 117–40 as well as the editor's introduction; and C. Dandeker, "New Times for the Military Some Sociological Remarks on the Changing Role and Structure of the Armed Forces of the Advanced Societies," *British Journal of Sociology*, vol. 45, no. 4, 1994, 637–654.

33. For a brief review of this concept see M. Waters, *Globalization*, Routledge 1995.

34. *The Economist*: 22 December 1990, 74.

35. Mesny, A. (1993) "Globalisation, Communication et Guerre du Golfe," in M. Audet and Bouchikhi, Structuration du social et Modernite avancée, University of Laval Press, 223–30.

36. A. Giddens, *Consequences of Modernity*, 64.

37. P. Dicken, *Global Shift, Industrial Change in a Turbulent World*, Harper and Row 1986, 293–212.

38. On this theme see J. Rosenau, *Turbulence in World Politics*, Harvester 1992.

39. Although, in one sense the world is *uni-polar* in that the United States is the only power with capacity if not the intention to be a truly global military power.

40. M. Horsman and A. Marshall, *After the Nation-State*, 190–191.

41. J. Rosenau, "A Wherewithal for Revulsion, Notes on the Obsolescence of Inter-state War," paper delivered to the American Political Science Association 1991, 6.

42. I explore some of the issues in C. Dandeker, "Public Opinion and the Gulf War," *Armed Forces and Society*, vol. 22, no. 2, Winter, 1995/96, 297–302.

43. London European Security Working Group: 1992, 1.

44. For the United States at least, defense of human rights is part of the promotion of democracy and the capitalist markets that provide the economic underpinning of this institution. This argument forms one component of the current Clinton administration's foreign policy. See Remarks by the President in CNN Telecast of "A Global Forum with President Clinton—The Carter Center—Atlanta, Georgia, 3 May 1994. For this point, and the reference, I am indebted to Dr. Karin Von Hippel, MacArthur Post Doctoral Fellow in the Department of War Studies, King's College, London.

45. For a British perspective see M. Rifkind, "Peacekeeping or Peacemaking: Implications and Prospects," *The RUSI Journal*, (Royal United Services Institution for Defence Studies) April 1993, 1–7. J. Gow and C. Dandeker, "Peace Support Operations: the Problem of Legitimation," *The World Today*, August-September, 1995, vol. 51, nos. 8–9, 171–174.

46. See J. Mayall, *Nationalism and International Society*.

47. A theme explored in J. Mayall, *Nationalism and International Society*, Cambridge University Press 1990, 50–69. See also J. Hutchinson, *Modern Nationalism*, Fontana 1994, 164–197.

48. See the interesting discussion in P. Alter, *Nationalism*, 1985, 92–152.

49. A Giddens, *The Consequences of Modernity*, 72–78.

50. M. Keir, "The Strange Survival of Nationalism," *Geographical Magazine*, July 1992, 25–29, 27. Keir argues that enthusiasm for this strategy has been encouraged by the end of the cold war and the perception that the military security provided by the nation-state is less important and that any residual security requirements can be met at the federal level.

51. With regard to such regional tensions in the EU, the situation is complex. It can be argued that European monetary union, by freezing existing patterns of economic disadvantage between one region and another would promote violence insofar as these are connected with ethnic and national divisions. If political attempts were made to ameliorate such divisions by stronger transfers of resources from the rich to the poor regions, increased disaffection in the former may be the result. On other hand, a free trading union of nation-states which allowed competitive devaluations might promote tensions and even war between states seeking to use such strategies to gain advantages over their competitors. This is a position argued by the more enthusiastic supporters of a federal EU.

52. J Rosenau, *Turbulence in World Politics*, Harvester, 1992.

53. N. Ascherson, "Why the Future Waves a Flag," *Independent*, 8 September 1991, 21.

54. On this theme see P. Dicken, *Global Shift: Industrial Change in a Turbulent World*, 1988. Also see the recent discussion in M. Horsman and A. Marshall, *After the Nation-State*, Harper-Collins 1994.

55. D. Held, "Farewell the Nation-State?" *Marxism Today*, December 1988;16). This point is developed in a very interesting direction by James Gow in chapter 5. See his discussion of divisible and indivisible sovereignty: Gow chapter, 34–42.

56. But this is far from certain. The UN may be confined to providing a fount of legitimacy for coalitions of the willing to deal with threats to international peace and security.

57. See C. Moskos, "Armed Forces in a Warless Society," *Forum* 12, Sozialwissenschaftliches Institut der Bundeswehr; C. Moskos and C. Burk, "A Post Modern Military," in J. Burk, ed. *The Military in New Times: Adjusting Armed Forces to a Turbulent World*, Westview 1994.

58. M. Van Creveld, *On Future War*, Brassey's 1991, J. Rosenau, *Turbulence in World Politics*.

59. This is why industrial democracies like the United States are so concerned that wars be infrequent and, when they occur, are short with clear, achievable goals and well defined exit points.

60. J Rosenau, *A Wherewithal for Revulsion*, 1991, 6.

61. Ibid, 7.

62. M. Van Creveld, *On Future War*, 197.

63. This is a key theme in Barrington Moore, Jr. *The Social Origins of Dictatorship and Democracy*, Peregrine, 1968.

64. One of the consequences of the Falklands war was an improvement in the conditions for the development of democracy and market capitalism in Argentina. It will be interesting to see if economic interdependence and a shared commitment to democratic values will prevent any return to war in order to resolve the territorial dispute over the Falkland Islands/Malvinas.

65. M. Weller, "Breaking Up is Hard to Do," *New Statesman and Society*, 23 August 1991;19, emphasis in original.

66. This is a point developed in different, but I would suggest, complementary ways by Reed Ueda and James Gow in their contributions to this volume.
67. This is a major theme in chapter 5. See in particular p. 198 et seq.

# 2

# The Economics of Nationalism
# and Violence

*Harold James*

This chapter examines the connections between nationalism, economic development, and violence. Past explanations have been divided between pessimistic assessments of the violence involved in the process of development, and optimistic versions in which development provides a balm to atavistic violence.

The pessimistic argument runs as follows. Economic growth is always accompanied by profound, complex, and painful social changes. These may be sufficiently disruptive to lead to a breakdown of older structures of social integration. Such a collapse may itself lead to outbreaks of violence, directed particularly against those groups (defined in social terms, but in some societies also in terms of ethnicity) thought to be the illegitimate beneficiaries of the growth process.[1] The weakening of older cohesive institutions and attitudes may also produce violence between societies organized politically as states. The search for new integrative mechanisms to deal with the consequences of social disruption may lead to the search for an external enemy as an aid to a "negative integration."[2] Or alternately, the new search for economic gain in the developing society propels a quest for advantage at the expense of an external other.[3] Strong economies could be built easily on the basis of military triumph.

This pessimistic account is characteristic of many classic studies of

49

industrialization in Western societies, of marxist studies of the logic of imperialism, and of accounts which examine the disintegrative impact of imperialism and the world economy on societies that had previously been isolated.[4]

Such an interpretation arose primarily as a rejection of the optimistic picture (which could be described as the product of a complacent liberalism). That story dwelt on the rationality of economic activity and its implications for a world built on calculation, consensus, and contract. There is a consensus about the observation of contract; and contracts in turn reinforce consensus because the basis of a contract is the calculation of mutual advantage.[5] We will not agree to a business deal unless both sides see a potential benefit. In this way the calculation of what produces consensus leads to a rationalization and a displacement of conflict. This picture insists that the nineteenth-century-technical changes produced in the West a world that was more peaceful and harmonious than the ancien régime societies it replaced.

Applied to international society, this interpretation sees economic change as generating new codes of international agreement, a new international law and a system of preserving peace. On the basis of such an assessment, analysts from Norman Angell through Michael Doyle and Francis Fukuyama[6] have predicted the imminence of a new age of perpetual peace between peaceful democratic and liberal political societies.

Many contemporary political issues are argued in terms of the assertion of one or both of these very contrasting traditions of interpretation. Two of the most platitudinous of contemporary political verdicts are the direct outcrops of these rather venerable debates. When observers complain about the chaos that they say will result from the introduction of market processes into societies which had been previously believed to have been "planned," they are arguing a version of the first and pessimistic account. Sometimes it is exactly the same commentators who argue that the rise of nationalist and ethnic tension flies in the face of modern reality: when they make this claim, they are giving an airing to the liberal and optimistic picture of modernization.

The functions of the nation have proved problematical to modern commentators. Most analyses after 1945 presented the nation as a stage in a developmental modernizing process which had in the later twentieth century become nothing more than a defunct and obsolete relic of the nineteenth-century imagination. In this view, modern life was developing through integration across frontiers into the "one world" popularized by the vision of Wendel Wilkie.

In consequence, in the late 1980s many observers were surprised and profoundly shocked by the reassertion of nationalism. Not just in the area formerly dominated by Soviet imperialism, but also in highly developed industrial societies, in opposition to movements for supranational integration, defenders of the principle of the nation-state have reemerged. The major argument against their views is that modern nationalism flies in the face of the process of modernization, and defies an economic logic that points towards international integration.

Such a case assumes of course that there is an objectively ascertainable "economic logic" to which societies respond. It is an assumption which lies deeply embedded not only in the history of the nationalist phenomenon, but also in the history of its analysis. In order to understand why the economic dynamic should be felt to be such a powerful objection to national sentiment, it is necessary to examine the evolution of an identification of nation, state, and economy that lies at the heart of the modern experience.

The emergence of modern nationalism occurred in Europe at the same time as a profound economic and social transformation of life, at the end of the eighteenth and the beginning of the nineteenth centuries. Nationalism developed on the basis of a series of ideas and beliefs in Europe in the context both of a particular international order and an economic system that may be described as market capitalism.

In this chapter it is argued that the key to the question whether nationalism is harmful and internationally destabilizing, or whether it plays a stabilizing function by promoting a sense of identity and legitimacy, lies in the nature of the relationship between nationalism and economics. An excessively close association of national integration and economic forces has in the past led to tension and volatility in domestic and international politics. What creates that closeness, however, is by no means an inexorable process; but rather the intellectual association of beliefs about what the nation should represent and how the economy should function. There is no automatic path to smooth and peaceful modernization: the terrible examples of the twentieth century development of Germany, Japan, and Russia should warn us against that assumption.[7] But neither is there a necessary and inevitable process of disintegration and violence following from attempted economic change.

## Nationality and Economic Performance

The European state system in which the modern doctrine of nationalism originated had emerged rather earlier, in the sixteenth century in the era of the Reformation, after the defeat of universalist claims to imperial rule on the part of the Habsburg dynasty and the papacy. Europe's historical uniqueness lies in the resulting coincidence of a wide cultural community, with powerful intellectual links and substantial migration on the one hand, and a system of individual states with claims to sovereignty on the other.

The state system of the early modern period produced some proto-nation-states, with well developed central administrations which frequently possessed (as in the case of England or France) a strong sense of identity and patriotism.[8] Most scholars, however, see such states only as a foundation on which later nationalism might be constructed. It was in the eighteenth century that two intellectual currents made possible a broader, as well as potentially more contested, sense of nationality.

The first current had its source in 1772 when Johann Gottfried Herder in his *Essay on the Origins of Language* explored the notion that a social group might be defined primarily in terms of linguistic community. These communities ("nations") then developed a culture through the transfer of values across generations: "I came into the world and was subjected to instruction by my family: and so was my father, and so was the first son of the first father of the tribe."[9] Herder saw linguistic groups coexisting in a world marked by a recognition of difference. A nation only became fully aware of itself as a nation when it interacted with a different group. According to Herder, "otherness," but not necessarily conflict, would be the foundation on which a society built its identity. Such identity would emerge as a natural process. For Herder, this process was as simple and as unproblematic as the sentiment that grows in a family relationship.

The second eighteenth-century current ran in the direction of popular legitimation of the political process. Its theorists paid much more attention than did Herder to the problem of how a community would come to possess a particular belief system. They propounded a doctrine of self-determination and popular sovereignty associated with the French Revolution. According to Jean-Jacques Rousseau's conception, which provided a basis for the actions of the Jacobin revolutionaries of the 1790s, politicization and political education (or propaganda) were needed for the establishment of a general will of society that differed from and would override the chaotic mass of individual wills. These social theories coincided with an economic transformation of some European societies, often conventionally described as the "Industrial Revolution." The economic changes began in the seventeenth century with increases in agricultural productivity and a quick growth in export markets in England and the Netherlands, and a resulting rise in standards of living. In late-eighteenth-century England there followed the technological transformation of the cotton textile industry which acted as the motor for growth in the classical "Industrial Revolution."

Even though the original character of the processes might be quite separate, changes occurring simultaneously often have a profound effect on each other. Neither the theories of the Enlightenment nor Herder's linguistic definition of nationality can be directly linked to a new economic transformation. The French Revolution resulted from a fiscal crisis of the ancien régime caused by expensive dynastic wars rather than from any pressures for change from a new industrial class. Herder when he wrote his essay was a preacher in the remote and sleepy German town of Bückeburg, and was completely unaware that changes were taking place in the production of textiles in Lancashire in England. Rousseau wanted to live as far as possible away from cities, cultivated a romantic regard for natural man, and held up as ideal for self-determination and realization of a general will the democracies of antique Greece and the gatherings of peasant cantonal assemblies around the oak trees of Switzerland.[10] On the other hand, the innovators who made new machines, and the business men who sold new products scarcely cared about the apparently abstract world of continental European ideas.

Nevertheless, the new economics and the new technologies eventually facilitated the spread of the new doctrines: in the first instance because new technology provided a base for increased mobilization of resources in war, and thus put a greater strain on the inadequate fiscal structures of ancien régime states. Later, the transport revolution of the nineteenth century established larger communities by bringing more people into contact with others. Initially canals, and then railways, drew together people and goods from a wider area. A trading and industrial economy appeared to require larger political units.

The most simple and direct explanation of the connection between economics and ideas was given by the marxist tradition. Karl Kautsky, the most orthodox of late-nineteenth-century marxists, wrote: "In proportion as economic development has proceeded, there has grown the need for all who spoke the same language to be joined together in a common state."[11] This theory also became the prevailing interpretation of Russian bolsheviks. J.V. Stalin, for instance, applied the analysis to the peoples of the Russian Empire: "Georgia came on to the scene as a nation only in the latter half of the nineteenth century, when the fall of serfdom and the growth of the economic life of the country, the development of means of communication and the rise of capitalism, instituted a division of labor between the various districts of Georgia, completely shattered the economic self-sufficiency of the principalities and bound them together into a single whole. The same must be said of the other nations which have passed through the stage of feudalism and have developed capitalism."[12]

How did mental structures respond to the tremendous economic transformation of the nineteenth century? The sense of larger group identities followed, it is often argued (particularly influentially by Karl Deutsch and Ernest Gellner), from market integration and a communications revolution.[13] Nationalism, in its modern form, was said to be the child of the railway. Nineteenth-century writers such as Max Weber described the railway as the "great instrument of culture." For the modern historian Eugen Weber it is the railway (along with universal military service and compulsory primary education) that turned "peasants into Frenchmen."[14]

By the mid-nineteenth century, the railway had indeed completely changed the language in which nationalism was discussed. It was not just that a new economic order stimulated new ways of thinking about a wider social group that might happen to coincide with the boundaries of a real or desired nation-state. The nation also came to be advocated by many as a result of an economic reasoning, of the application to political and historical processes of a sort of economic determinism. Marx's reasoning about the economic laws of motion of modern society were widely accepted—not just by people who saw themselves as socialists or marxists.

Particularly in those areas where there existed no proto-nation-state with its established institutional structures to generate legitimacy and stability, the idea of economic development appeared as an answer to the question of how communities could be bound together. In England constitutional monarchy and a tradition of parliamentarism, in the United States a written constitution, and in France the principles of the French Revolution provided a focus and a guide for political life. On the other hand, in Central and Southern Europe there existed an institutional and political vacuum that cried out to be filled. A specific doctrine was required to create that national community which Herder's powerfully attractive theory had simply assumed to be natural. That new ideology was economics.

In early-nineteenth-century Italy, a group of liberal thinkers, publicists and economists, Giandomenico Romagnosi, Carlo Cattaneo, Carlo Ilarione Petitti, Cesare Balbo and Massimo d'Azeglio pointed out that new economic opportunities demanded a transformation of Italian life. D'Azeglio spoke of "these progressive improvements which are required by the necessity of the times." "To reduce things to a formula, I say that every social state has a political state which is its necessary consequence. This truth the princes have not seen for thirty years. We shall see how many years it will be before the people see it." [15]

On the political level, this new economic ideology was expressed most explicitly by Count Camillo di Cavour, who as minister-president of the Kingdom of Sardinia was the decisive architect of the diplomacy of national unification. Cavour justified the adoption of a liberal constitution simply on the grounds that "free institutions tend to make people richer."[16]

A very similar set of arguments gained widespread currency in Germany at the same time. As in Italy, they emerged out of the defeat of liberal dreams during the revolutions of 1848. Looking back, nationalist historians such as Heinrich von Treitschke, contrasted the operation of "real forces" with the liberal nationalist enthusiasm. According to him, the foundations of German unification were not so much liberal ideas as the military policy of the Hohenzollern dynasty in Prussia and the economic integration promoted by the German customs union of 1834. "The final result [German unification] was brought about by the very nature of things, and it produced a real Germany, united by economic interests, while Frankfurt [the liberal parliament of the 1848 revolution], like Regensburg in earlier days [the former Imperial Diet from the old Holy Roman Empire], was ruled by the mere phrases of politicians."[17] The insistence that nationalism was driven by material forces appeared also in the work of Georg Friedrich

List ("It is the duty of national economics to provide for the economic education of the nation"), and in the writings of the political journalist Ludwig August von Rochau. "For Germans," Rochau wrote in 1869, "unity is basically a pure business affair."[18] This materialism, that of course also characterized Karl Marx's almost contemporaneous analysis of the driving forces behind human history, also deeply influenced the German political elite. Otto von Bismarck, the minister president of Prussia and the primary architect of German unity, disliked what he termed the "swindle of nationalities," but applauded the new rule of realism and material interests. The latter alone could in his estimation provide a true foundation for a state.

The theory of the economic desirability of nationhood appeared first in Italy and Germany—in the two new nation-states of the mid-nineteenth century. But it rapidly spread to other would-be nations, who saw national existence as a prerequisite for satisfactory economic development, and economic growth as the only way of providing a basis for the military defense of national integrity. Intellectually, the most important influence came from the German writer Friedrich List's 1841 treatise *The National System of Political Economy*. Listian doctrines, which provided a neat statement of this case, were taken up with particular enthusiasm in Japan, as well as in Russia, where the reforming Finance Minister of the 1890s, Count Sergei Witte, had written extensively about List's work.[19]

Economic nationalism constituted the most important component in what W.W. Rostow has termed "reactive nationalism": the development of theories to challenge the apparently inexorable rise of the European colonial powers.[20]

It involved a double aspect: on the one hand, it linked economic development and military might. On the other, it treated growth as a way of dealing with the social problems arising out of increased demographic pressure in the nineteenth century.

The first aspect was in many ways quite conventional, and arose out of a long tradition of mercantilist thought. Money, according to this tradition, constituted the sinews of war. Policies of early modern states aimed at the accumulation of wealth chiefly in order to build up a powerful military position. Late into the nineteenth century mercantilist arguments were still set out by governments, and by business men trying to justify their activities in the eyes of their compatriots. The tsarist empire always justified its economic programs by saying that they would enhance Russia's military might. German bankers saw their role as central in forging the power politics of the imperial strategy of the Kaiser's government. Jakob Riesser, a director of the powerful Darmstädter Bank, wrote in his standard work on German banking in 1906 on the national responsibility of bankers: "They had to strengthen our financial, and with it our political influence abroad."[21]

Secondly, nationalism in its classical modern form also conjured up the ideal of a genuine social harmony that might be built on the basis of improved education available to all and also of enhanced prosperity. Economic intercourse would breed harmony. The theory was not so much that all men were equal because they were citizens of the nation—that would have been patently untrue—but rather that equal opportunities in the long run might generate the liberal utopia of greater equality and a national fraternity.

## The Challenge to Classical Nationalism

The classic doctrine of economic nationalism had been substantially undermined by the end of the nineteenth century. In the first place, it no longer appeared obvious that the nation was the most appropriate framework for economic development. A new transport revolution in the last quarter of the century opened much wider markets than those created by the nation-building railway of an earlier era. In the 1870s, the steamship cut oceanic freight rates by over a third (and the decline continued after this, with the results that rates in 1908 were a quarter of their 1873 levels)—and at the same time large agricultural areas in North and South America and in Russia were opened up to what was now a world market by the railway. If the railway and "classic" nationalism were inextricably connected, the steamship produced a postclassic nationalism, in which nations—if they wanted to continue to make the functional argument about the economic utility of the national form—needed to claim much bigger areas.

Reasoning of this sort produced appeals for empire, and no longer for the nation-state. According to many influential late nineteenth century writers, the world would be divided between three or four great imperial systems. Such a forecast was interpreted positively by historians and social scientists: Sir John Seeley in Britain, Paul Leroy-Beaulieu in France, Hans Delbrück, Erich Marcks, and Hermann Oncken in Germany. The economist Gustav Schmoller in 1891 wrote that "the history of the twentieth century will be shaped by the competition between the Russian, British, American, and perhaps also the Chinese world empires and by their aspirations to make all other smaller states dependent on them." He concluded that "the superior and ancient culture of Europe" could be defended against this attack only by a Central European customs union.[22]

Other writers (J.A. Hobson, Rudolf Hilferding, Rosa Luxemburg, V.I. Lenin) presented a critical analysis of imperialism as the "highest stage of capitalism," in which an economic imperative drove colonial powers to suppress and dominate other societies, but would eventually provoke a nationalist backlash as the oppressed peoples defended their independence and integrity.

At the same time, the marxist tradition also produced criticisms of the nationalism of small states as being culturally backward-looking and economically unproductive. Rosa Luxemburg's doctoral dissertation took as its theme how the development of capitalism in Poland had tied this territory to Russia and made Polish nationalism historically irrelevant. Later, she made the same point even more explicitly: "The restoration of Poland is already a mental illusion. . . . When industry developed in the Kingdom of Poland and a capitalist class emerged, it was from the beginning an enemy of national uprisings and the quest for independence."[23] Economics cut across the boundaries of small states.

By the early twentieth century, the functional argument about the superiority of the large market derived a great part of its attraction from the experience of the United States. The world's most dynamic economy grew at such a spectacular rate because of the availability of new land, and an ever open frontier. Some Central Europeans drew from this a doctrine of *Lebensraum:* that satisfactory economic development required large reserves of virgin territory. In its least aggressive form, such a vision produced demands of the kind laid out by Friedrich Naumann in *Mitteleuropa* (1915) for a Central European customs union stretching from the North Sea to the Danube. More extreme versions, such as that envisaged by Germany's military leadership during the First World War, saw an industrial heartland surrounded by food-supplying colonies. Adolf Hitler later took up this type of theory and elaborated vast imperial schemes.

As a result of the new economic experience, and the theories that it prompted, the old-style nation-state no longer seemed the most appropriate physical location for the economic legitimation of political systems. At the same time as new theory pushed at the state's geographic frontiers, domestic political demands about what the state should do became much more ambitious.

The original domestic version of economic nationalism had simply presented the nation as the most suitable setting for the generation of growth and hence prosperity. The simple size of the new national market would be enough to do the trick, if combined with political autonomy and freedom form foreign pressures. One way of presenting the argument in the new or would-be new nations of the nineteenth century had been to claim that there existed a simple choice: advanced development like England or France or Belgium, and increasing wealth, on the one hand, or on the other underdevelopment and mounting pauperization produced by political dependence or colonialism, such as that experienced by Ireland or India.

A few decades later this debate seemed outdated. Growth alone had not provided social cohesion: on the contrary, industrialization was accompanied by the emergence of new social problems and apparently very large disparities of wealth and income. A response to the social crisis appeared in the form of demands for reform programs: for sickness insurance, old-age pensions, and also unemployment insurance. The populist parties of the late-nineteenth century—Catholic and socialist movements—began to press for redistribution. As distributional rather than growth issues became the focus of debates about the economy, the capacity of economic reasoning to produce social consensus and harmony decreased. Politics split along class lines. In addition, by the end of the nineteenth century, every industrial country experienced deep divisions over tariff protection, which did not necessarily follow the lines of fissure between conventional political parties or social classes. The British conservative party was torn. Classical liberals who maintained free trade principles lost electoral support in Germany. In Anatole France's satire of Third Republic France, *Penguin Island,* politics were reduced to two major groupings: distillers of alcohol (graingrowers), and those who did not distill (winegrowers).

Distributional conflicts, when they become extreme, can destroy the stability on which the ideal of the nation depends. The nation implies a common framework in which problems can be resolved; but particular groupings interpreted their interests as those of the nation as a whole, and clashed with other groupings with alternative formulations. Factions within industry (most typically, exporters against those who produced for a domestic market), agricultural interests (also often split between livestock and cereal producers) contended for the control of economic policy-making. Most importantly the clash of labor and capital remained the central theme in the politics of advanced industrial countries for almost a century. Only after the middle of the twentieth century did the rise of a service economy make obsolete the old distinctions, and required a greater cooperation of previously conflictual sectional interests.

Some analysts (most notably Mancur Olson) have linked the new politicization of domestic economic debate to the rise of interest groups. According to Olson, this development reduces economic efficiency and thus eventually also the ability of the economy to satisfy social demands.

A small grouping may have a powerful gain (rent) that can be made at the expense of others in society by concerted lobbying action (for instance through tariff protection). The relative loss for the rest of the community is not necessarily immediately perceptible or sufficiently large for all the other individuals to have sufficient incentives to resist the demand of the interest groups. The unequal costs of social action in this way works to the benefit of organized pressure lobbies and imposes a net loss on the whole of society. Only a radical reordering of political forms, in which the distributional game can begin again from zero, could act as a corrective. Stable, well-established political systems in this view tend to breed special interests that impede economic efficiency.[24]

However, interest groups may also be constrained by a framework that imposes a regard for general national concerns ("national interest"). If that framework is sufficiently stable, the interest groups are less likely to be able to alter it in order to gain a distributional advantage (for instance, through new legislation or the introduction of new institutions). A well-established state structure can in consequence be a counterbalance to excessive interest group pressure. But interest groups may then have an incentive to work on the erosion of stability.

As distributional demands replaced the consensus on growth the intellectual climate changed against conventional liberalism. Some political liberals, in order to preserve voting support, took up the distributional demands. In France, one wing of the Radical party took this path, and tried to work with the socialist movement. In Britain, a similar stance (sometimes characterized as "Lib-Lab") was taken by the "new Liberals" around David Lloyd George. In domestic politics, the new approach involved the idea of correcting the workings of the market by securing improvements for the disadvantaged through political action at the expense of someone else.

The critique of economic liberalism inevitably spilled over into perceptions of international relations. If domestic politics involved altering the distributional game and benefiting at the expense of another group, then it appeared tempting to apply the same approach to interstate relations. Why not solve the internal distributional issue by gaining more resources from other states? In peacetime, this could be done through the application of trade policies (tariffs, quotas), or monetary policies designed to impose the cost of adjustments to changing technologies on to other states. During wartime, additional territory could be simply seized by force. In the course of the world wars of this century, the belligerents tried to define economic goals that could be achieved through combat. Both sides in the First World War claimed that the bill for the fighting would be met, after their victory, by the defeated powers. Germany in both world wars tried to create a Central European bloc under German control.

Wars thus became a continuation of conflictual economics by other means. Before 1914, many liberals had taken the stance, formulated in an extreme version by Norman Angell in *The Great Illusion* (1909–10), that modern economic forces made war impossible. (A milder version, that war had to be the result of atavistic aristocracies, and not of modern businessmen, was set out in Joseph Schumpeter's early work on imperialism.) But after 1914, a powerful military-industrial complex had shown that war had its own scheme of economic utility.

## Economics and International Peace

Once the nation and economic nationalism had become perceived as destabilizing influences on the world political setting, there arose a demand for greater international cooperation to preserve and guarantee peace. Two competing theories of how peace could be rescued appeared in the 1920s.

The first may be described as Wilsonian idealism: it was to work through international organizations (the League of Nations) established by a covenant of sovereign states. International institutions would put pressure on states to adjust policies that might be in the specific interest of individual countries but would undermine a broader international stability. The pre-war liberal confidence that rationality alone would restrain states was no longer sufficient: new international instruments had to be instituted in order to create adequate deterrents against aggression.

When this institutional vision collapsed (because of the rejection of the covenant in Congress), the United States tried to build a world stabilized by the actions of private businessmen. According to this vision (which was rather obviously little more than a recast version of older liberal politics), capital flows and universal prosperity would generate peaceful and harmonious relations between states. In this case, no international institutions were required to enforce the triumph of consensus.

The attempt to restore liberalism in this manner also failed dramatically: not least because of the intrusion of politics into international economic relations in the aftermath of the World War. Reparations and war debts poisoned the atmosphere and promoted redistributive rather than growth-oriented thinking. It was not just idealistic Americans who were deeply frustrated by the turn in events. The British Labour prime minister, Ramsay MacDonald, complained of the way in which continental politics interfered disruptively with a universal and peaceful economics. During the Lausanne Conference on reparations (1932) he noted in his diary: "Very much struck by the fact that both Germans and French think only of themselves in all of this and of politics more than economics and trade which are the deepest rock foundations of politics. Most tiring day." [25]

The lessons of failed reconstruction after the First World War appear to have been learnt and applied with conspicuous success after 1945. The fundamental problem was the same as that of the aftermath of the First World War: the reconciliation of national sovereignty with economic relations that crossed national frontiers. Irrational economic warfare had destroyed the chances of peace: "Economic warfare has in the past too frequently led to actual warfare. If we want to help keep world peace, we must also prevent the outbreak of international economic warfare."[26]

The new international system rested on two contrasting approaches: one explicitly intended to preserve national sovereignty, the second tending to limit or transcend sovereignty. The first approach produced the Bretton Woods conference in 1944, where a universal economic order was proclaimed as a way of beginning a liberalization of trade and financial relations. The international institutions of the Bretton Woods system, the World Bank and the International Monetary Fund, were explicitly designed to encompass any kind of national economic policy. The two architects of Bretton Woods, John Maynard Keynes and Harry Dexter White, had considerable differences during the course of their negotiations, and the United States had a very clear idea of the national policy it wanted to pursue in forcing the British imperial system to liberalize its trading practice. But both men agreed that the new institutions had to respect the principle of national sovereignty.

The British draft of April 1943 produced by Keynes stated: "There should be the least possible interference with internal national policies, and the plan should not wander from the international terrain. . . . The technique of the plan must be capable of application, irrespective of the type and principles of government and economic policy existing in the prospective member states." And White's version of April 1942 similarly claimed: "No restrictions as to membership should be imposed on the grounds of the peculiar economic structure adopted by any country." The eventual Bretton Woods agreements were specifically designed to encompass centrally planned economies. The original U.S. plan as drawn up by White actually stated that "a socialist economy like a capitalist economy engages in international trade and financial transactions which can be either beneficial or harmful to other countries."[27]

They reflected, however, not just an abstract commitment to the idea of sovereignty: the expectation was that postwar states would have as their highest priority the domestic objective of full employment. The Canadian negotiator at Bretton Woods, Louis Rasminsky, put the point most succinctly: "The International Monetary Fund is a new type of international monetary standard which seeks to reconcile the desire of all countries to carry out domestic economic policies which are aimed at high levels of income and employment, with the desire of countries to have orderly international economic and monetary arrangements so that trade can go forward and take place to the benefit of all."[28]

In other words, Bretton Woods allowed the pursuit of national interventionist policies, for which the participants recognized there was a pent-up demand, and sought to reconcile them with international stability. The agreements tried to make internationally harmless the cries for domestic economic regulation and management. As Keynes put it, they constituted "an attempt to reduce to practical steps certain general ideas belonging to the contemporary climate of economic opinion." [29]

The second pillar of the successful postwar stabilization tried to deal with the problem of national autonomy in a completely different way: by removing economics, and the politics of economics, to a higher, supranational frame, thus limiting the scope for traditional sovereignty. The European Recovery Program (ERP) of 1947 (or Marshall Plan) envisaged economic integration as a way of promoting stability. The ERP administrator Paul Hoffman saw it as his mission to attack the whole principle of national economic policies. He believed it necessary to unravel fifty years of European "indulgence in economic practices that are basically unsound. . . . It is, in our view, quite impossible for Europe to become enduringly self-supporting, with a reasonably high standard of living for its people, unless Western Europe's 270 million consumers are welded into a single great market."[30]

In Europe, parts of the most controversial areas of economic policy making (which had been the most destructive of the principle of national community) were transferred away from the nation-state towards multilateral institutions. In 1952 the European Coal and Steel Community (ECSC) solved a long-standing problem of the relationship of France (with large ore resources, but little coking coal) and Germany, which possessed Europe's most substantial coal-field. The six-member ECSC was a precursor of the European Economic Community (EEC) established in 1957 by the Treaty of Rome and functioning from January 1958. Its task was to desensitize the two economic issues which had plagued European politics for the previous century, the external tariff and the question of farm support, by transferring decisions to an international stage. Agricultural issues, and the politically desired subsidization of agriculture, could be handled less contentiously if it were to be managed through the Common Agricultural Policy from remote and politically insulated institutions in Brussels. Separating these controversial issues from the domain of national politics was part of the new anti-political prescription for the ills of Europe.

At the same time, the EEC existed in the world of nation-states: the cause of integration was vigorously promoted by the French President

General Charles de Gaulle not in order to create a European state, but to represent French national interest more effectively. "He talks of Europe, but he means France," was British Prime Minister Harold Macmillan's verdict—the product of bitter personal experience.[31]

From 1985, the drive to European integration acquired a new momentum, again for power political reasons. It seemed to some Europeans that the post-1945 dominance of the superpowers was coming to an end, and that a European economic and political challenge could be successful if accompanied by a further push for integration. As in the 1950s, the process was driven by a push for national power. France wanted to use German economic might as a compensation for France's weak international position, and at the same time to surround Germany with a cocoon of binding agreements. Germany, on the other hand, believed itself condemned by the postwar settlement to a future as a "political dwarf" (though it might at the same time be an "economic giant"). This meant that it needed international institutions (EEC, NATO, CSCE [Conference on Security and Cooperation in Europe], UN, etc.) to realize its policy goals without offending other states: a diplomatic strategy of using "alphabet organizations" which came to be known as "Genscherism" (after the foreign minister of the Federal Republic from 1974–1992, Hans-Dietrich Genscher).

There is a constant temptation to play power politics with international economic institutions, since their actions can be used to shift the distributional outcome in one direction or another. Economic relations do not of themselves intrinsically generate power or domination: because every transaction represents a process in which both sides see an advantage in participating. It is notoriously difficult to say in a trade relationship who is benefiting at whose expense; or whether a debtor or creditor has the greatest relative power. But institutions designed to regulate the international economic process are an altogether different matter, and can be manipulated in order to produce a gain in political power. This is the case both with regard to universal international regulation of the Bretton Woods type, and for supranational integration of the European Community variety.

Probably the most famous example of hegemonic manipulation in the post-war world concerns the gold-exchange provisions of the Bretton Woods system, in which other countries held claims on American assets as currency reserves. In the latter 1960s, this feature (de Gaulle called it America's "exorbitant privilege") was abused by U.S.

policymakers to make surplus countries, chiefly Japan and Germany, pay the costs of the deficits produced by the Great Society program and by the war in Vietnam. American leaders consciously manipulated an institutional arrangement. As Treasury Secretary John Connally put it rather picturesquely: "Foreigners are out to screw us. Our job is to screw them first."[32]

But the period of actual manipulation in the late 1960s was remarkably brief, and the collapse of the whole system in 1971 followed speedily. It may be concluded that the international order only worked while the manipulation was a potential and not a reality; and that an international order is not well suited to the exercise of effective hegemony.

Germany in the later 1970s tried to use the European Monetary System (EMS) in a similar way to the American political and hegemonic use of the Bretton Woods institutional apparatus, but with an opposite policy effect. The EMS was not designed to spread German inflation more evenly through the world (as the American had operated Bretton Woods in the 1960s) but to distribute throughout Europe the costs of the German domestic requirement for monetary destabilization and disinflation.

Here again there is a similar potential problem as with the U.S. use of Bretton Woods. Once the international arrangement is widely perceived as being used to further specific national advantages, it rapidly loses any widespread respect. Once this happens, the "rules of the game" are no longer credible and effective. In the German instance, the strain was not intolerable while other countries in the late 1970s also wanted to reduce their inflation rates. When however in the early 1990s, the difficulties of stabilization became particularly acute after the costly process of German unification, and coincided with high levels of unemployment in other EMS countries, the divergence in national goals became much clearer, and threatened the position of the Deutschemark. As in the case of the disintegration of the U.S.-based Bretton Woods system in 1971–3, the collapse of the German-centered EMS in the currency crisis of September 1992 was quite rapid, quite dramatic and quite foreseeable. The critical issue in the shaping of the proposed European Monetary Union will be the extent to which Germany modifies her institutions and traditions and accepts a greater share in the adjustment costs. One way of interpreting the easing of German interest rates in the 1996 is a step in this direction: a step to the self-abolition of monetary sovereignty.

## Dilemmas and their Solution

In the late twentieth century we find the economics of the nation-state troublesome. Its institutional framework is no longer the appropriate locus for economic decision making: indeed it had ceased to be that already before the end of the nineteenth century. Global economic problems appear to require management on a supranational level and cooperation between nations.

Such international cooperation faces a hard dilemma. If it is ostentatiously supranational and depoliticized, and concentrates on the solution of merely technical issues, as was the original vision underlying the growth of the European Community bureaucracy, it will produce demands for increased accountability. The European Union Commission and its relations with a parliament whose capacity to initiate legislation is zero and to amend drafts is severely limited is described as having a "democratic deficit." If, on the other hand, these supranational bodies are made accountable, they will suffer the temptation to practice the redistributive policies which clash with perceived national interests. And as this happens, other national interests will be excluded by a political process, and resentments and tensions will mount.

The greatest danger to the international system is when individual powerful states try to distort to their advantage the rules under which the system operates. Domestically strong states are least likely to attempt to transfer their national problems to an international arena. The disruptive examples of the post-1945 era are ones in which states which took on too much internationalized their difficulties. This sort of hegemonic manipulation was a symptom of political, economic, or psychic exhaustion. The United States in the 1960s simultaneously pursued too expensive a foreign and domestic strategy (whether either one on its own could have been managed more satisfactorily is an open question). It used its control of the international economic system in an attempt to make other states pay the costs of the war in Southeast Asia. At the beginning of the 1990s, Germany suffered from the temptation to impose her own problems on the rest of Europe because of a reduced ability to produce domestic consensus. The precariously evolved postwar foreign policy consensus, which reached a peak of sophistication in "Genscherism," wanted to tie Germany down by association in multilateral international organizations: the EEC, the CSCE, NATO, the UN, etc. Neither the 1960s United States nor 1980s

Germany were self-consciously "strong" states, and the attempt to dominate an international order coincided with intense domestic perceptions of weakness and strain. In the 1990s, German policymakers emphasized that German and European integration were parallel processes. The existence of the European framework made it possible for Germany's neighbors to accept the unification of 1990 as not posing an immediate threat.

"Strong" states in this setting are characterized domestically by (1) a stable institutional setting, which generates legitimacy, (2) agreement over distribution, and (3) internationally by an acceptance of the status quo and an unwillingness to change the international distribution of power.

We might take a contemporary example of how strong states are better able to deal with international economic issues. When formerly communist countries begin the process of adaptation to the international economy and the "market," those states with a vigorous sense of historic community, such as Hungary or Poland, face a much easier task than states such as U.S.S.R. or Russia or Armenia or Yugoslavia, where there is little or no agreement over national institutions. Such institutions are essential in inducing people to accept a temporary sacrifice for an eventual greater communal good. Their absence not only made economic reform much harder in the extreme cases of the U.S.S.R. and Yugoslavia: it actually ensured that their attempts at economic reform would tear the state apart.

The nation here provides not so much a functional setting for an economic process, but rather creates legitimacy by all sorts of emotional, sentimental, historical, institutional, legal, procedural and noneconomic ties. It is not *for* any particular use: rather it *is*. This simple national existence as a well of political legitimacy makes it possible for its citizens to tolerate the always unpredictable and frequently disappointing outcomes of market processes. But if anyone were to argue that this is *why* the nation should exist, they would be making a profound mistake. If this were merely a functional reason, it would never be accepted by the nation's citizens. The nation is in this vision not a provider of anything but instead a comfortable and secure cushioning and a reassurance that there is a community of experiencing. In the midst of great uncertainty perhaps this knowledge alone can make tolerable the life of *homo oeconomicus*.

Stable state structures, with the ability to command loyalty, existed before the advent of modern nationalism. They continue to provide a focus of legitimacy after the demise of the nation as a meaningful player in the economic game.[33] The nation in this view is a way of describing a civic society. This sort of nation is not incompatible with economic rationality; and it is not destabilizing to international politics.

Simon Kuznets argued that the characteristics of better social integration and in consequence an easier handling of the consequences of disruptive change could give to small states political advantages that might compensate them for their purely economic disadvantages relative to large countries. "Small nations, because of their smaller populations and hence possibly greater homogeneity and closer internal ties, may find it easier to make the social adjustments needed to take advantage of the potentialities of modern technology and economic growth—the terms defined most broadly. The task may prove much harder for the larger countries because the ties that bind their larger populations may be far weaker and thus provide a less secure basis for acceptance, by consent, of social changes which, while in the short run hurting some groups and benefiting others, may be indispensable for adequate growth of the economy as a whole." [34]

It may be possible to plot the course of a vicious and a virtuous circle that may emerge out of the current relationship between nationalism and "economic forces."

In the vicious cycle, disillusionment with the international economy leads to a demand to strengthen national forces against the intrusions of internationalism; expectations about what national governments can do in response are increased; actual performance is criticized as being inadequate and ineffective; the path is clear for more extravagant demagoguery and greater intolerance in domestic politics, and to the disintegration of civil society. At the same time, the economic community is also destroyed.

In the virtuous cycle, concerns of global efficiency and integration into international markets lead to an acceptance that there are limits on what a national government can do; the government is in this way in part relieved from the pressure of demands to perform. It is easier to build up legitimacy, and demagoguery becomes less effective as a strategy of political conduct.

What will determine whether states embark on the vicious or the virtuous cycle? It would be erroneous simply to adopt, as a matter of unreflected prejudice, one of the two positions sketched out at the opening of this chapter. It is as misleading to be relentlessly pessimistic about the pains of modernization, as to be exuberantly optimistic about its benefits. There are, it is suggested, two key issues at stake: acceptance of an international orientation in economics; and recognition that the capacity of governments to act in the context of a nation-state are limited. It is not widely enough seen that acceptance of these two principles will make nation-states more legitimate as the focus for other sorts of non-economic political activity. The creation of this kind of legitimacy is an important task for politicians, and they do it best at a national, not an international level. It is not all a question of economics, but it also makes for better economics. After all, we might remember, man does not live by bread alone.

## Notes

1. Some classic accounts are: J.D. Hammond, "The Industrial Revolution and Discontent," *Economic History Review* 2, 1930, 215–28; Eric J. Hobsbawm, *The Age of Revolution 1789–1848,* London: Weidenfeld and Nicolson, 1962.
2. This was, for instance, the thesis of Thorstein Veblen's account of *Imperial Germany and the Industrial Revolution,* New York: B.W. Huebsch, 1918. It is taken up in many recent works: for an example see Hans-Ulrich Wehler, *Bismarck und der Imperialismus*, Cologne: Kiepenheuer & Witsch 1969.
3. See the literature on mercantilism. The classic study is Eli Heckscher, *Mercantilism*, London: G. Allen & Unwin, 1935.
4. As an influential example of the latter, see Paul Lovejoy, *Transformations in Slavery: A History of Slavery in Africa,* Cambridge: Cambridge University Press, 1983. For a modern study of the difficulty of introducing market economics, see (ed.) Joan M. Nelson, *Fragile Coalitions: The Politics of Economic Adjustment,* New Brunswick N.J.: Transaction Publishers, 1989.
5. See the analysis of the origins of this way of thinking: Albert O. Hirschman, *Shifting Involvements: Private Interest and Public Action*, Princeton: Princeton University Press, 1982.
6. Norman Angell, *The Great Illusion: A Study of the Relation of Military Power in Nations to their Economic and Social Advantage,* London: William Heinemann, 1910. Michael Doyle, "Kant, Liberal Legacies and Foreign Affairs," *Philosophy and Public Affairs* 1983. Francis Fukuyama, *The End of History and the Last Man,* London: Hamish Hamilton, 1992.
7. See J. Barrington Moore, Jr., *The Social Origins of Dictatorship and Democracy.*
8. One of the major intellectual concerns of authors who link nationalism and modernization is the denial of the reality of early modern patriotism: e.g., Eric Hobsbawm, *Nations and Nationalism since 1780: Programme, Myth, Reality*, Cambridge: Cambridge University Press, 1990, p. 175.
9. Quoted in Harold James, *A German Identity 1770–1990,* London: Weidenfeld & Nicolson, 1989, p.38.
10. Judith Shklar, *Men and Citizens: A Study of Rousseau's Social Theory,* Cambridge: Cambridge University Press, 1969.

11. "Die moderne Nationalität," *Neue Zeit* V, 1887, quoted in Anthony Smith, *Theories of Nationalism,* London: Duckworth 1983, p.74.

12. "Marxism and the National Question" (1913), in J.V. Stalin, *Marxism and the National and Colonial Question,* London: Lawrence and Wishart, 1936, p. 7.

13. Karl W. Deutsch, *Nationalism and Social Communication,* New York, 1966. Ernest Gellner, *Nations and Nationalism,* Oxford: Basil Blackwell, 1983. Also Smith, *Theories,* pp. 40–64.

14. Max Weber, *Nationalitäten und Eisenbahnpolitik,* Vienna 1876, p. 5. Eugene Weber, *Peasants into Frenchmen: The Modernization of Rural France 1870–1914,* Stanford: Stanford University Press, 1976.

15. Kent R. Greenfield, *Economics and Liberalism in the Risorgimento: A Study of Nationalism in Lombardy,* Baltimore: Johns Hopkins Press 1934, 1965, p. 283.

16. Quoted in Denis Mack Smith, *Italy,* Ann Arbor: University of Michigan Press, 1969, p. 23.

17. Heinrich von Treitschke, *Politik: Vorlesungen gehalten an der Universität zu Berlin,* Leipzig 1899, I, p.367.

18. Ludwig August von Rochau, *Grundsätze der Realpolitik,* Heidelberg: J.C.B. Mohr, 1869.

19. Theodore von Laue, *Sergei Witte and the Industrialization of Russia,* New York, 1963.

20. W. W. Rostow, *The Stages of Economic Growth: A Non-Communist Manifesto,* Cambridge: Cambridge University Press, 1971, pp. 34–5; W. W. Rostow, *Politics and the Stages of Growth,* Cambridge: Cambridge University Press, 1971, p. 64.

21. Jakob Riesser, *The German Great Banks and their Concentration in Connection with the Economic Development of Germany,* Washington, D.C.: National Monetary Commission, 1911, pp.11–12 (from the German text of 1906).

22. Quoted in Fritz Fischer, *Griff nach der Weltmacht,* Düsseldorf: Droste Verlag, 1961, p. 124.

23. Rosa Luxemburg, *Die industrielle Entwicklung Polens,* Leipzig 1898; 'Was Wollen Wir?' (1906), in Rosa Luxemburg, *Gesammelte Werke* II, Berlin: Dietz Verlag, 1972, p.51.

24. Mancur Olson, *The Rise and Decline of Nations: Economic Growth, Stagflation and Social Rigidities,* New Haven: Yale University Pressm, 1982. Olson's model is particularly applicable, as he noted, to twentieth-century democracies; but the best case for his model, the Weimar Republic, had a peculiarly unstable institutional setting.

25. David Marquand, *Ramsay MacDonald,* London: Jonathan Cape, 1977, p. 721.

26. Harry Dexter White: radio script of 10 April 1946.

27. J. Keith Horsefield (ed.), *The International Monetary Fund 1945–1965, Twenty Years of International Monetary Cooperation, Volume III Documents,* Washington, D.C.: IMF, 1969, pp. 19 and 72–3.

28. House of Commons Standing Committee on Banking and Commerce, Testimony, December 1945, p. 7.

29. Horsefield, p.21. For a criticism of the imposition of domestic redistributive concerns on the international order, see Wilhelm Röpke, *International Order and Economic Integration,* Dordrecht: D. Reidel, 1959.

30. Quoted in Alan S. Milward, *The Reconstruction of Western Europe 1945–51,* London: Methuen, 1984, p. 321.

31. Quoted in Jean Lacouture, *De Gaulle: The Ruler 1945–1970,* New York: Norton, 1992, p. 345.

32. Quoted in Henry R. Nau, *The Myth of America's Decline: Leading the World Economy into the 1990s*, New York: Oxford University Press, 1990, p. 162.
33. See on this the arguments of Robert B. Reich, *The Work of Nations*, New York: Knopf, 1991.
34. Simon Kuznets, "Economic Growth of Small Nations," in (ed.) E.A.G. Robinson, *Economic Consequences of the Size of Nations: Proceedings of a Conference Held by the International Economic Association*, London: Macmillan, 1960, p. 28.

# 3

# From Competitive Interests, Perceived Injustice, and Identity Needs to Collective Action: Psychological Mechanisms in Ethnic Nationalism

*Assaad E. Azzi*

A look at events in the contemporary world reveals an increase in the frequency and intensity of conflict between ethnocultural groups that are part of a larger social category, notably the "nation-state." In most developing countries, in Eastern Europe, as well as in Western countries, the revival of ethnic affiliation and identification and the emergence (or resurgence) of ethnic nationalism are becoming a potent challenge to the legitimacy of existing international boundaries and a precursor of intergroup hostility and violence. What are the sources of this nationalism? Is the promotion of a distinct ethnic identity a sufficient motive for individuals to organize, support or participate in organized collective action? Or, are there rational motives related to material self-interest that lead individuals to act on behalf of their ethnic group? The main purpose of the present chapter is to demonstrate the contribution of social psychological theory and research to the development of a global understanding of nationalism and ethnic group conflicts by delineating the processes and mechanisms which connect individual-level variables to group-level and institutional variables.[1]

The chapter is divided into three sections. The first reviews past and current theories and research which shed light on three psychological motives assumed to potentiate a readiness on the part of individual members of a group to initiate or support collective confrontation with another group: (1) the rational pursuit of group competitive interests; (2) the perceived injustice of existing systems for distributing scarce resources; and (3) the need for a positive and distinct identity. The second section consists of a critical analysis of how these motives manifest themselves in ethnic nationalism. The third section deals with the mechanisms that mediate between individual motives and organized collective action, which is the form in which ethnic nationalism is most frequently expressed.

## Some Definition Issues

Nationalism, which consists of a collective claim to "nationhood," entails a challenge to existing structures of intergroup relations and a desire to either disengage from an interdependent relationship with other groups or achieve hegemony over them. Psychologically, the claim to nationhood implies a claim of "groupness" which, as suggested in other chapters of this volume, is typically articulated in an ideology which (a) makes more or less explicit a subjective definition and legitimization of the group and its boundaries based on historic, territorial, linguistic, religious, or cultural interdependence among its members, (b) propagates a message of ingroup distinctiveness and intergroup differentiation, and (c) advances territorial claims.

Underlying the social definition of national groups and their boundaries is the psychological process of categorical differentiation.[2] Research in psychology during the past two decades has revealed the central role played by this process in people's representations of the physical and social worlds which surround them. Given the large amount and complexity of the information that impinges on the human senses and given human memory and processing-capacity limitations, the process of categorical differentiation provides a simplified means of processing information by reducing its size and classifying it in as few categories as possible. For instance, despite the physical differences between chairs which make each of them a distinct object, our concept of "chair" does not always attend to these differences but rather consists of a set of features that chairs share and which make them distinct from other objects. The process of categorizing objects or people entails the *maximization of differences between members of different categories (differentiation) and the minimization of differences among members of the same category (homogenization).* It is not difficult to see how this process would operate in the social construction of national categories.

The fact that categorization involves an *accentuation* of differences and similarities implies that group identities are, at least in part, socially "constructed." This, however, does not mean that categorical representations, and groups themselves for that matter, are the product of pure imagination, as has been argued by a number of anthropologists.[3] On the contrary, it is probably the case that the social-construction process starts with existing differences between social categories. These differences could be physical (e.g., skin color, height, facial features), institutional (different religious, social, or political institutions), linguistic, territorial, and so forth. Sometimes, there are subtle sociocultural differences (in the customs, norms, and rules which regulate everyday social interaction and communication). In the absence of explicit social constructions, these existing differences may contribute to feelings of group belonging and intergroup differences without necessarily becoming part of elaborate cognitive or collective representations of the group. People may feel that they are Basques, Sinhalese, or Slovaks merely by sharing and taking for granted the values, customs, and institutions of these communities. This form of identification is different from the one generated by the social construction processes which are embodied in nationalist ideologies. Nationalism involves a social construction process whereby the *existing differences between social categories are endowed with psychological significance such that the categories become part of a collective cognitive "representation" in which the group now appears to be a perceptual "unit" differentiated from other units.*[4] The factors which affect the transition from one form of identification to the other will be discussed later in the chapter.

Given this definition, the question arises whether nationalism necessarily entails intergroup conflict. Our working definition of intergroup conflict is that it is an overt collective confrontation initiated by one or more parties (i.e., social groups and/or their representatives) with the aim of achieving, promoting, or preserving particular group interests. This definition implies that conflict should be distinguished from concepts like ethnocentrism, prejudice, and stereotyping, concepts that social psychologists often use as if they were synonymous with conflict. Whereas these concepts are used to refer to intrapsychic states, feelings, cognitions, and beliefs which may causally mediate conflict, establishing whether these processes are necessary for intergroup conflict is a matter for empirical investigations rather than a matter of definition. It is possible that these psychological states are important sources of conflict but that they are neither necessary nor sufficient to bring about conflict. Indeed, they may be consequences as much as determinants of conflict.[5]

Because it challenges existing structures of intergroup relations, nationalism carries seeds of intergroup conflict. It is the aim of this chapter to provide insights into how the social psychological mechanisms which generally mediate intergroup conflict manifest themselves in the determination of nationalist conflicts.

## Conditions for the Initiation of Intergroup Conflict: Realistic and Competitive Interests

One can discern two general approaches across various disciplines to the study of motives which mediate intergroup conflict, in general, and ethnic conflict, in particular. One approach emphasizes the motive of pursuing and maximizing "rational" or realistic interests; the other approach underscores the role of symbolic motives rooted in affective ties, emotional or expressive needs, and group identification and attachment.[6] After reviewing social psychological versions of these approaches, the point will be made that they are not mutually exclusive.

*Incompatible Realistic Interests and Conflict*

According to realistic conflict theory[7] individuals and groups are rational actors whose actions are driven by the motive to maximize their self-interest. Given this premise, the theory argues that conflict between groups arises as a function of the *objective* structure of relations between them: if the relations are competitive, then conflict is inevitable; conflict is avoided or resolved through the creation of a cooperative structure of relations. Competition and cooperation are defined as incompatibility and compatibility of group "realistic" (or material) goals, respectively. Two groups are said to have *incompat-*

*ible* goals when the goals of one can only be achieved at the expense of the other's goals. In this zero-sum situation, the groups' relations are competitive and conflictual. Superordinate or compatible goals mean that the goals of one group can only be achieved if the goals of the other are also achieved. Therefore, they necessitate cooperative relationships for their achievement. According to realistic conflict theory, the psychological consequences of goal incompatibilities (which are themselves objectively/socially determined) manifest themselves in the form of an increase in (1) the perception of threat to the ingroup, (2) the feelings of hostility toward the outgroup which is perceived to be the source of threat, (3) ingroup solidarity, (4) the salience of ingroup identity, (5) the tightening of group boundaries, (6) negative stereotyping of the outgroup, and (7) ethnocentric behavior.[8]

Criticisms of realistic conflict theory gained ground with accumulating experimental findings showing that some symptoms of conflict—notably ethnocentric behavior in the form of an ingroup-favoring bias in the evaluation of group performance and attributes, or in the allocation of resources—take place under cooperative situations or when no explicit competition is present.[9] Such findings were interpreted by some authors as indicating that competitive interdependence is not necessary for intergroup conflict, and that the salience of the ingroup-outgroup categorization in itself is sufficient to produce some conflict symptoms, namely ethnocentric behavior.[10] This explanation of ethnocentrism—i.e., that it is due to salient categorization rather than to competitive interests—has been interpreted to imply that conflict could be resolved only when individuals interact with each other as individuals and not as members of different categories.[11] According to this view, unless it abolishes group boundaries, cooperation is unlikely to lead to the reduction of conflict. But some recent findings are inconsistent with this conclusion; these findings show that the introduction of superordinate goals which imply the dissolution of intergroup boundaries could increase rather than decrease the likelihood of ethnocentric behavior.[12]

The possibility that social-categorization effects were confounded with goal interdependence, and that the latter may not be necessary for ethnocentrism to occur, led Tajfel and his colleagues[13] to design a paradigm that separates these effects: the "minimal group paradigm" (MGP). In the typical MGP study, subjects are divided into two arbitrary groups (on the basis of preferences for paintings, a random toss of a coin, and so forth) and then asked to allocate rewards between pairs of individuals by checking on matrices specifically designed for the MGP studies. In addition, face-to-face interaction is not allowed, and individuals are only identified by their group membership (thus keeping their individual identities anonymous). The groups are therefore "minimal" in the sense that there is no history of interdependence within or between groups. The results of studies using MGP were, though not very strong, consistent across experiments[14]: given a distribution between an ingroup member and an outgroup member, and given alternative choices on the response matrices (maximum ingroup profit, maximum difference between ingroup and outgroup, fairness, and maximum joint profit), the dominant choice of subjects is maximum difference. The counterintuitive finding emphasized by researchers is that subjects choose to maximize the difference between ingroup and outgroup even if this choice sacrifices the ingroup's absolute monetary gain.

Although they challenge major tenets of realistic conflict theory, the findings of these studies do not warrant the conclusion that a competitive structure of relations is not necessary for conflict to occur. There are reasons for the difficulty of dismissing a primary role of a competitive structure in intergroup conflict in light of the reviewed literature. Most minimal group studies have investigated conditions for the occurrence of "ingroup favoritism" and not for the occurrence of "intergroup conflict." Thus, these studies may warrant the conclusion that salient categorization may be sufficient to produce ethnocentrism in the form of an ingroup favoritism in resource allocation, but do not warrant the conclusion that a salient categorization per se is sufficient to produce intergroup conflict. To equate conflict with ingroup favoritism is misleading, especially since the measures of ingroup favoritism in experimental and field studies sometimes show a positive evaluation of the ingroup which is not necessarily accompanied by a derogation of the outgroup.[15] The conclusive criticism of realistic conflict theory, which could be firmly made on the basis of this literature, is that *subjective* and *symbolic* interdependence should also be considered as potential mediators of conflict behavior.

An important shortcoming of realistic conflict theory is its emphasis on the "objective" structure of relations. While such emphasis is by no means misleading, it has ignored the role that group members themselves play in the definition of group goals and, consequently, in the determination of the structure of intergroup relations. It merely considers group goals and individuals' consent to such goals as given.[16] This conception implies three assumptions that are not elaborated in the theory: (1) that the incompatible goals are *unambiguous* and recognized by members of the rival groups, (2) that these goals are the most important or salient and that they *rank first* within a repertoire of group goals, and (3) that these goals are held and ranked *consensually* by group members. The importance of the processes mediating goal definition is underscored by the possibility that subjective and objective definitions of goals and also of the payoffs (i.e., costs and benefits) implied by the pursuit of these goals, may not coincide.[17] It is especially under such conditions that it is necessary to consider the subjective component of group goals.[18]

Yet, even subjective competitive interdependence may not be sufficient to produce intergroup conflict. As will be discussed later, a group or its leaders not only have to define their goals and their rank order, they also have to select among alternative *means* to achieve these goals—direct, open, or violent confrontation being only some of them. In addition, the forging of a consensus with regard to group goals in large social groups is not to be taken for granted. Usually, the initiation of a conflict takes place through complex mobilization efforts which are undertaken by a numerically small network of group members who, at the time, may represent only a minority viewpoint within the group. The multiplicity of goals, their hierarchical sorting, the multiplicity of the means to achieve any goal, and the forging of consensus around group goals and the appropriate means to achieve them, are all conditions that have been ignored in realistic conflict theory. These processes will be discussed in greater detail in the third section of the chapter which deals with the processes mediating collective action.

## Resource Deprivation, Perceived Injustice, and Conflict

A problematic assumption implicitly made in realistic conflict theory is the symmetry of the relationship between the two parties.[19] Such an assumption ignores the power structure that often exists between groups. The *degree of dependence* of group A on group B may not be the same as that of group B on group A, especially when the two groups are part of a common superordinate unit such as the "nation-state."

The degree of dependence may vary not only with regard to goals, but also with regard to the resources available to achieve these goals.[20] In the context of superordinate social units with a centralized organization and authority, established power differences between groups provide the dominant group with a greater control not only over the resource-distribution process[21] but also over the ideology which legitimizes it.[22] Under such circumstances, members of subordinate and disadvantaged groups *may* or *may not* engage in a conflict aimed at achieving, improving, or maximizing their share. How could realistic conflict theory account for situations where the status quo deprives certain groups of the resources they (presumably) want, and yet these groups do not act to change the status quo? Relative deprivation and justice research suggest that the tendency to engage in goal-oriented confrontational action is a function of the perceived illegitimacy or injustice of existing distribution systems. In contrast to realistic conflict theory which conceives of conflict as symmetrical (i.e., bilaterally initiated), relative deprivation and justice theories conceive of conflictual behavior (e.g., riots, revolutions) as initiated unilaterally by individuals and aggregates who feel that they are deprived of what they believe they are entitled to.

Relative deprivation theories focus particularly on the psychological processes that mediate between the asymmetries in status and power between groups and the outbreak of collective and political violence. These theories implicitly or explicitly assume that collective violence is, at least in part, the product of (1) the *aggregation of individual feelings* of deprivation, frustration, and anger, and (2) situational *triggering events*. Such a conception implies that the larger the number of individuals experiencing (independently and without coordination) similar feelings of deprivation, and the greater the number of grievances accumulating, the greater the likelihood that a triggering event will lead to the emergence of collective violence. The feeling of relative deprivation itself is conceived as the outcome of *psychological comparisons*, and the various theories propose different comparison processes, depending on the form of deprivation produced. Theories of personal or *egoistic deprivation*[23] argue that relative deprivation is the outcome of an intra-individual comparison; the specific units which are compared vary from theory to theory: past and present outcomes,[24] actual and expected outcomes,[25] or actual and deserved outcomes.[26] The theories share the assumption that increases in the discrepancy between the two comparison units produce feelings of relative deprivation and dissatisfaction, thus increasing the potential for political violence. Theories of *fraternal deprivation*[27] argue that intra-individual comparison processes which lead to egoistic deprivation are not sufficient to produce *collective* political violence; they also argue that fraternal deprivation, which results from comparing outcomes of one's own group to the outcomes of another group, is a necessary mediator of such violence. Indeed, research shows that fraternal deprivation, compared to egoistic deprivation, is a better predictor of participation in riots,[28] voting for black mayoralty candidates by white Americans,[29] militancy and support for violent protests among black Americans,[30] support for Quebec nationalism by French-speaking Canadians,[31] and the attitudes of Muslims towards Hindus in India.[32]

Yet, feelings of fraternal deprivation may not be sufficient to compel individuals to engage in collective action. A number of recent studies suggest that individuals who perceive that their group is subject to discrimination—thus presumably experiencing fraternal deprivation—may deny that they themselves are subject to discrimination.[33] Such findings raise the possibility that, even when they believe that their group is deprived and is subject to discrimination, individuals may still believe that there exist means for individual upward mobility which could bypass group discrimination. Consider the implications of such a belief for intergroup conflict: people who believe that personal deprivation and group deprivation are independent of each other may not be willing to participate in collective action. If this is true, then collective action is more likely when both egoistic and fraternal deprivations are subjectively high, or when group interest is perceived to be intimately related to self-interest, than when one is perceived to be high and the other low or when they are perceived to be independent. A positive subjective relationship between personal and group deprivation is most likely to be induced through mobilization processes. Such processes have been neglected in the relative deprivation literature[34] and will be discussed in the section on collective action.

It is reasonable to argue that, in general, relative deprivation theories assume the primacy of material resource deprivation rather than deprivation of symbolic resources as the motive for participation in collective political action. Indeed, most studies of relative deprivation[35] use economic indicators or measures of economic deprivation to make inferences about the presence of relative deprivation; very few, if any, address identity or cultural grievances, the kinds of grievances which are explicitly aired in many ethnocultural conflicts.[36]

Furthermore, although earlier versions of the theory which were influenced by frustration-aggression theory[37] emphasized emotional motives (frustration, anger) and the spontaneity and impulsiveness of collective violence, recent formulations[38] have added emphasis on "rational" mediating processes, such as the perception of deserved outcomes and the assignment of responsibility to the source of deprivation. Yet, none of these formulations gives sufficient attention to (a) the processes that make individuals judge that a gap, a deprivation, or an unrealized aspiration is *unjust* or *illegitimate*; nor to (b) the rational justifications for participating in collective action.[39] For an answer to (a) we have to turn to justice theories. The answer to (b) will be discussed in the section on collective action.

According to justice theories, perceived injustice is mediated by two processes: social comparison of values (e.g., outcomes and/or inputs), and a psychological formula used to assess the "fairness" of the values included in a comparison. The dominant social psychological approach to justice, equity theory,[40] argues that justice and fairness are determined by the calculation of a ratio of inputs (i.e., contributions, investments, costs) to outcomes (i.e., rewards, benefits) for one individual and comparing it to the ratio of another individual. Although the mathematical formulae provided to capture this cognitive process differ slightly from one author to another, they all assume the operation of a principle of proportionality (i.e., an individual's outcomes should be proportional to his or her contributions).

In line with a realistic approach, most equity and justice theories assume that *self-interest* plays a major role in the selection of the comparison party, the inputs and outcomes to be compared, the quality of feelings experienced, and the kind of behavioral reaction elicited. Thus, a party which is advantaged by a disproportional and inequitable outcome would experience feelings of guilt which motivate equity-restoring actions such as cognitively de-emphasizing the value of her outcome or increasing the value of her contribution. In contrast, the disadvantaged party usually experiences feelings of anger, and would be compelled to restore equity behaviorally (by demanding compensation, or decreasing his future contribution) or, if this is impossible or costly, cognitively (by distorting the perceived values of inputs and outcomes).

Notwithstanding the richness of these formulations, the principle of proportionality assumed by equity theorists to underlie justice perceptions and judgments has been found to be only one among several distributive principles that produce a sense of justice or injustice. Accumulating research indicates that equality, need, and other *normative* principles that are not reducible to a proportionality formulation are used in various contexts and for various resources.[41] Moreover, *distributive* justice is only one among many processes which determine perceived injustice; another, no less important process, is *procedural* justice.[42]

The procedural elements in the distribution of resources are usually related to the process through which the distribution decision is made. Procedural justice research suggests that procedural components are at least as important as the evaluation of outcomes and inputs in determining perceived justice,[43] particularly in the legal domain,[44] and in the political domain.[45] One crucial procedural element is *participation* in the decision-making process. Research indicates that participation in the distribution decision process affects the evaluation of the decision's fairness, independent of the effect of outcome evaluations. For instance, individuals participating in a legal decision-making process find verdicts more just than those who are not given the opportunity to participate.[46] Researchers[47] make a distinction between two types of participation or control: (1) process control (i.e., participation through the presentation of one's viewpoint) and (2) decision control (i.e., control over the decision outcome). The former could be achieved through the opportunity to "voice" one's viewpoint, which is a highly valued right in Western democracies.[48] The latter could be achieved through voting rights. Tyler[49] argues that process control or "voice" is sufficient to produce perceptions of outcomes as just, even in the party who is disadvantaged by the decision. He also proposes a group-value model of procedural justice which essentially argues that membership in and identification with a legal-political system leads individuals and citizens to accept the system's formalized procedures and, by implication, to accept (unconditionally) decision outcomes produced by such procedures. However, it is possible that a necessary condition for these effects is that the parties involved believe that they are being *equally* treated.[50]

Unlike realistic conflict or relative deprivation theories, there is nothing in justice theories that defines the resources or the procedures over which people compete as necessarily being "material." Indeed, some researchers[51] explicitly distinguish between material and nonmaterial resources (e.g., status, love, information). In addition, the distinction between distributive and procedural justice contrasts the "outcome-oriented" distributive concerns to the more "expressive" procedural concerns.[52] These distinctions echo those made by sociologists and political scientists between tangible and nontangible resources.[53] This distinction allows for the possibility that some of the interests that people pursue are symbolic, in the sense that their value is abstract and psychological rather than discrete and measurable. The need to achieve a positive or distinct social identity, emphasized by psychologists,[54] social scientists, and historians,[55] is a symbolic interest which appears to be dominant in ethnic nationalism.

## Conditions for the Initiation of Conflict: Identity and Symbolic Interests

*Social Identity Needs and Conflict*

In an attempt to account for ethnocentrism in intergroup behavior, Tajfel and his colleagues developed "social identity theory".[56] The theory's major argument states that a need for a positive social identity mediates between intergroup categorization and an individual's ethnocentric behavior. A salient social categorization creates a dependency between an individual's social identity in the situation and his or her category membership. In such circumstances, the individual could achieve a positive social identity through a *positive differentiation* between his or her group and the salient outgroup. The mere salience of ingroup-outgroup categorization is, according to the theory, sufficient to activate the need for positive differentiation. Thus, in the minimal groups which are created in experimental studies and which lack any preexisting identity value, the salience of social categories is assumed to activate a need in individuals to define their group's identity positively relative to the outgroup. In studies where the two groups are not minimal but rather preexist the salience-activating experimental situation (e.g., ethnic groups, gender), preexisting differences between the groups (e.g., power or status differences) may affect the degree of activation of the need for positive differentiation. In general, given the association between a group's status and the valence of its identity (i.e., low status confers a negative social identity), members of low status groups have a stronger need to achieve a positive social identity than members of high status groups.

Social identity theory specifies a number of *means* that members of low status groups can use to achieve a positive social identity: (1) ethnocentric individual behavior or evaluation; (2) individual exit from the negatively valued group and assimilation into a positively valued group; (3) a collective redefinition of the ingroup's attributes in positive terms; (4) definition of new attributes on which the ingroup can be differentiated positively from the outgroup; (5) changing the comparison outgroup; and (6) engaging in collective action to change the status quo and eliminate the (socioeconomic and political) bases for the ingroup's negative identity. According to the theory, the choice of one or more of these means is a function of social mobility beliefs and of the perceived legitimacy and stability of the existing differences between the groups. If social mobility across group boundaries (i.e., leaving the low status group and joining the high status group) is perceived to be possible, then individual exit is a likely choice. If it is perceived to be impossible (or if it is not a cognitively available option), and the existing status quo is perceived to be legitimate and stable, then cognitive collective reconstructions of the group's identity are likely (e.g., reevaluation of the group's attributes in a more positive light such as "Black is beautiful," definition of new attributes, or a change in the comparison outgroup), the alternative being passive acceptance of the group's negative social identity. But if social mobility is perceived to be impossible *and* the status quo illegitimate and unstable, then collective action is likely. As for high status groups, the theory predicts that their members would experience a need for positive differentiation if they perceive their superiority to be threatened, illegitimate, or unstable. They can achieve this need through any of the above means.[57]

Social identity theory's emphasis on the role of perceived illegitimacy in the mediation of collective action brings it close to the relative deprivation and justice approach. Yet, the two approaches emphasize different motives, the former emphasizing social identity needs and the latter feelings stemming from resource deprivation. They also differ in the kinds of processes they choose to include or exclude. On the one hand, social identity theory does not specify the processes that produce the perceived illegitimacy, nor those that define and mediate collective action; indeed, very little research has been carried out to explore the conditions under which perceived illegitimacy arises and the various identity-boosting options are selected. With few exceptions,[58] most research driven by the theory focuses on investigating the conditions for ingroup favoritism in resource allocation or trait evaluation, which is only one of the identity-boosting options. Thus, although research deriving from social identity theory provides insights into the dynamics of some forms of ethnocentric behavior, it provides little information about the dynamics of conflict, and the role that perceived injustice and feelings of deprivation play in this process.[59] On the other hand, although the research on distributive and procedural justice is extensive and crosses the boundaries of behavioral disciplines, most of it focuses on justice in interpersonal relations and relatively little attention is given to investigate the distributive and procedural justice principles that operate in the regulation of intergroup relations, or how perceived injustice arises in such relations.

A number of studies suggest that justice principles are sometimes used in a strategic manner, indirectly producing ingroup favoritism under certain conditions and outgroup favoritism under others.[60] The fact that both ingroup and *outgroup* favoritism could be the outcomes of strategic motives is consistent with one of the explanations suggested by Taylor et al.[61] for the personal/group discrimination discrepancy—that is, individuals acknowledge the existence of discrimination against their group but deny that they are personally subject to discrimination: instead of reflecting a *denial* of personal discrimination, this discrepancy may be produced by an *exaggeration* of the discrimination against the ingroup. The "strategic behavior" approach is also supported by some findings on intergroup perceptions and attributions: despite social identity theory's prediction that individuals would dissociate themselves from their group if it is ascribed negative traits, a number of studies have found that they also dissociate themselves from "positive" group traits[62]; it seems that this effect obtains especially when these traits are viewed with resentment or envy by members of powerful outgroups). Indeed, one of the means provided in social identity theory to achieve a positive social identity—that is, exit from one group and assimilation into another—may be mediated by outgroup favoritism and, perhaps, ingroup derogation. Although research has not explicitly addressed this possibility, other lines of research suggest that members of disadvantaged groups may display outgroup favoritism,[63] and that differences within and between immigrant groups in the desire for assimilation may translate into differences in their members' perceptions of discrimination.[64]

## Symbolic/Cultural Values and Conflict

The distinction between symbolic and realistic motives has also surfaced in survey research on racial attitudes in the United States. Research in the last two decades has unveiled two paradoxically contradictory attitude trends. On the one hand, a decline in the racist attitudes of white Americans has been consistently observed in the last three decades while, on the other hand, they are strongly opposed to the implementation of affirmative-action policies (e.g., desegregation and school busing). Such contradictory attitudes have been interpreted as reflecting a new form of racism, called "symbolic racism".[65] Symbolic racism is a disguised form of racism rooted in a cultural conflict of values[66]: on the one hand, white Americans value fairness and equality in opportunities but, on the other hand, they have learned racist attitudes during their socialization. Critics of this approach argue that opposition to policies stems from a perception of a realistic conflict between whites and blacks; in particular, argues this approach, the collective violence and demands by black political movements may be viewed by whites as a threat to their interests.[67] Other critics point out that these survey results have only dealt with *attitudes* and not with behavior. When *behaviors* are measured (e.g., participation in and support of anti-busing organizations), self-interest but not symbolic racial attitudes emerges as the main predictor, while racial attitudes would still predict anti-busing *attitudes*.[68] It is worth noting that this research deals with the reactions of one party (whites) to the changes implemented as a result of a conflict initiated by another party (blacks). These findings do not therefore provide information on whether the initiation of the conflict (by blacks and the civil rights movement in this case) was based on realistic or symbolic concerns. It is likely that both realistic grievances and symbolic needs played an important role in the conflict behavior of black Americans[69] but that symbolic concerns are at the root of the reaction by whites to black demands. Indeed, according to Ueda (chapter 4), American administrations have generally adhered to an historical tradition of staying out of involvement in programs of ethnocultural maintenance or group socioeconomic advancement; but, since the civil rights movement, minority leaders have increasingly emphasized demands for the recognition of the "corporate" status of ethnic minorities along with demands for the recognition of equal cultural status. It is likely that white Americans' symbolic racism which has been observed to emerge after the civil rights movement may be a reaction to what they consider a violation, by Afro-American and other cultural affirmation movements, of the long-held laissez-faire tradition with regard to ethnic group relations.

A different, anthropological approach to the role of cultural and symbolic values stresses the potential institutional and value incompatibilities that emerge when different cultural groups are brought together within a superordinate political, legal, and economic entity.[70] Similar in form to realistic conflict theory, the basic premise of this approach is that conflict is inevitable when groups with *incompatible cultural institutions* or values are grouped together in a common society. Under these circumstances, the preservation of the inclusive unit would necessarily imply the subordination (cultural, economic, and political) of one group to another. The only difference with realistic conflict theory is the focus on value and institutional incompatibilities which, in the early work by Furnivall, were assumed to be related to economic incompatibilities. In the work by Smith, however, cultural incompatibilities are assumed to emerge and lead to conflict independent of economic incompatibilities. Critics of this latest version point out that, without their coincidence with economic incompatibilities, it is not possible to predict exactly when and how group differences in cultural values lead to conflict.[71] Indeed, some anthropologists have argued that cultural diversity in itself (i.e., in the absence of economic disparities) is equally likely to produce symmetrical or asymmetrical power relationships[72] and, thus, unlikely to always lead to conflict relationships.

Another, sociological line of research contrasts the cultural identity roots of ethnic conflict with their instrumental rational roots.[73] Proponents of the instrumental (i.e., rational choice) approach emphasize the adaptive fluctuating nature of group identities and the fuzziness of boundaries between groups.[74] Thus, ethnocultural identities become salient and potent when the material and status needs of ethnic group members could be achieved through collective ethnic action.[75] Otherwise, individuals may choose to act individually or on the basis of other group identities (e.g., occupation, class). Other social scientists contend that contemporary ethnic conflicts (especially in non-Western countries) erupt when traditional "primordial" identities and cultural values are threatened by emerging economic and political pressures for modernization.[76]

### Realistic and Identity Interests in Ethnic Nationalism and Conflict

As the previous review suggests, realistic and symbolic motives have often been described by social psychologists and other social scientists as mutually exclusive motives for intergroup conflict. Yet, a close look at contemporary intergroup conflicts suggests that conflicts could involve material interests, identity interests, or both. Moreover, the two kinds of interests may be interdependent in determining intergroup conflict. This interdependence will be gradually made clear in the following sections. The next section is an attempt to specify (1) the particular realistic (distributive and procedural) justice concerns and (2) the particular identity interests that arise in the relationships between ethnocultural groups that are part of a superordinate category.

### Distributive and Procedural Concerns in Ethnic Group Relations

Taken together, the realistic conflict, relative deprivation, and justice approaches suggest that intergroup conflict could be produced either by the perception that existing systems of distributing resources are unjust and discriminative, or by the perception that group interests are threatened or that their achievement is thwarted by the actions of another group. The question that remains unanswered in this literature concerns the particular criteria or principles which people consider to be just for the allocation of resources between groups, and the violation of which would lead to perceived injustice and produce the potential for collective discontent. Given the lack of empirical research in social psychology on the specific distributive and procedural justice principles that are implemented by some groups (or claimed by others) for the distribution of resources between groups, we turn to observations and comparative analyses of ethnic conflicts in the contemporary world[77] in order to make inferences about such principles.

The following is a tentative (and non-exhaustive) list of distributive principles that appear to underlie ethnic group demands: (1) self-determination[78] (e.g., Baltic republics in the former Soviet Union; Palestinians in Israel, Ibos in Nigeria during the Biafra war, Swiss cantons, Quebec in Canada); (2) the right of indigenous people, which implies ownership of a territory (e.g., Malay claims in Malaysia; Maori claims in New Zealand; claims by North American native groups); (3) homeland rule, meaning that a group has a right to rule the land that constitutes its only home (e.g., Jews in Israel, Sinhalese in Sri Lanka); (4) majority rule (e.g., the African National Congress in South Africa); (5) proportional representation in the civil service and governmental positions (proportionality can be assessed on the basis of group size, status, prestige, and so on; e.g., Shiites in Lebanon); (6) parity which implies equal representation, bilingualism, and so on (e.g., Belgium); (7) need (e.g., special consideration and affirmative action programs in, e.g., the United States, India, Malaysia); (8) proportional contribution or equity (at the individual level) with the specification of a minimum (or maximum) for each group, or with a guarantee of equal opportunities (at the group level); (9) on the basis of proportional contribution at the group level (e.g., greater representation for the group which contributed most to the formation, maintenance, progress, and prosperity of the superordinate unit; e.g., Maronites in Lebanon); (10) according to a definition of what is required for the common good (e.g., sovereignty and unity of the nation; national security; preservation of the distinctive constituent cultures); (11) on the basis of reciprocity or alternation (e.g., presidency rotated among the principal constituent groups in, for example, the former Yugoslavia).

In general, and in contrast to interpersonal justice principles, intergroup procedural and distributive principles are not likely to be the products of cultural evolution. Instead, they are the products of active confrontations[79] and negotiations between groups, which typically take place when new institutions are being formed.[80] An analysis of the inherent compatibilities and incompatibilities among these (and other) principles is necessary for the elaboration of specific hypotheses regarding the likelihood of conflict between groups over their implementation. An inherent incompatibility between two principles for which two groups have divergent preferences would lead to the prediction of an imminent conflict between them. Consider, for instance, the potential incompatibilities between the equity and need principles. Whereas equity implies that outcomes should be allocated in proportion to contributions, the need principle prescribes an allocation in proportion to needs. Disagreements between groups over which of these two principles are common, particularly when the groups differ in socioeconomic status because, under these conditions, one group would claim more of the outcome on the basis of its greater contributions (e.g., in the form of taxes) while the other claims more of the outcome on the basis of its greater needs.[81]

Another analysis would be required to investigate the factors that determine the selection or promotion of a particular principle by members of a group. For instance, group preferences may depend on the nature of the resource (e.g., political representation, economic resources, cultural symbols such as language of education and religious holidays), the level of receipt (i.e., individual versus group), the nature of the recipients (the type of groups involved, e.g., gender, racial, religious, ethnolinguistic), the goal priorities of the group, the value placed on the maintenance of a distinct group identity, and the perceived justice of the procedures used to determine the distributive principle.

An important way in which groups may diverge in their preferences for justice principles is when one group emphasizes individual-level justice while another places a higher value on group-level justice. The allocation principles implied by each of these levels are, under certain conditions, incompatible. Thus, because the rise or imposition of modern nation-state institutions has been associated with the diffusion of a secular individualistic ideology, demands by ethnic groups for the implementation of group-level justice are incompatible with the individual-level justice principles promoted by this ideology. For instance, giving an indigenous group priority in acceding government positions may violate the principle of meritorious entitlement to top political decision-making positions, a violation which may be resented by the skilled members of "immigrant" communities (e.g., Malay versus Chinese in Malaysia).

Regardless of the particularities of conflicts—in terms of the particular resource at issue, and the particular historical, cultural, and sociopolitical context—the nature of the demands and claims made by ethnic groups in conflict are generally rooted in procedural concerns. Ethnic claims focus on the degree of group political participation and representation, the elimination of discriminatory practices and institutions, the institution of group rights, the recognition of the group's distinct culture, language or religion, and so forth. The procedural basis of group claims is related to the fact that conflicts almost always take place between groups which differ in political power and that this power inequality is essentially a *procedural inequality*—that is, one group has greater power and control over major resources as well as the distribution process.[82]

This is especially the case in the context of the nation-state system in which ethnic groups are asymmetrically interdependent.[83] Indeed, according to Dandeker (chapter 1), both nation-state and ethnic nationalisms have generally been associated with violence precisely because they involve claims for exclusive territorial sovereignty (which means exclusive control over the governance of the territory). Another reason why political representation is a predominant issue in ethnic conflicts stems from the fact that the degree of political representation each group gains (e.g., in executive and legislative branches of government) would determine the power and control the group has over decision making regarding the distribution of most other resources and, ultimately, over its fate as a distinctive social and cultural unit. Indeed, the degree of group representation in decision-making bodies determines whether a group is included in or excluded from the decision-making process.[84] In contrast to the procedural issue of individual participation, discussed earlier, the phenomenological meaning of *group* participation is thus inseparable from the *degree of representation*— that is, the number of representatives—that the group has in the decision-making process.

This implies that, in intergroup relations, "voice" may not be sufficient and "decision control" may be necessary to produce the perception of power distributions at the superordinate level as just. Concerns for group representation are especially likely to predominate in the context of majority-minority relations.[85] Here, the use of an electorally based "majority rule" system implies the exclusion of minorities from the decision-making process. Similarly, the implementation of proportional representation in government in association with a "majority vote" decision rule deprives minorities of "decision control".[86] Both of these systems produce procedural inequalities: a majority group with decision control and a minority group with no decision control. Indeed, research shows that minority group members express preferences for the equal allocation of political representation whereas majority group members display preferences for its proportional allocation.[87] These differences between majority and minority groups reflect a differential emphasis on individual- versus group-level justice. Thus, majority rule and proportional representation are both premised on an ideology which emphasizes individual-level justice whereas equal representation aims at achieving group-level justice.

In general, however, the degree of control that a group possesses is not only a function of the numbers of representatives it has in decision-making bodies. It is also a function of the decision rule used in these decision-making bodies.[88] Of particular relevance here are two decision rules documented in group decision-making research: unanimity and majority vote.[89] Unanimity implies that a decision is made only after all participants in the decision-making process have agreed and reached consensus. Consequently, every participant has "decision control." Majority vote, which may vary from one decision-making body to another as to what constitutes an appropriate majority, does not require a consensus and implies that a decision could be made at the expense of a minority opposition. Although, in principle, *individual* participants under majority vote have equal control (because they have equal voting rights), *representatives* of a minority group have practically less decision control than representatives of a majority group. Thus, proportional representation in decision-making bodies combined with the use of a majority decision rule in the decision-making process, while consistent with the principles of individual-level justice, violates group-level justice by creating procedural inequality between majority and minority groups. A mathematical model describing the "distribution of control" between ethnic groups as a function of group representation and decision rule has been proposed by Azzi and Jost[90] who also provide experimental evidence that individuals who are assigned to a minority-group judge the combination of proportional representation and majority vote as unjust whereas individuals who are assigned to a majority group see it as just. They also show that procedures requiring a unanimous vote are perceived as just, regardless of the representation principle and of the size of group membership. These findings are consistent with research findings from the jury decision-making literature which show that participants usually express greater satisfaction with a unanimity-based process than with a majority-rule process and that this is especially so for participants who hold minority positions in the decision-making group.[91] There is also some experimental evidence that unanimity rule is generally seen as more fair than majority rule in small groups (especially those dealing with judgmental issues[92]).

In general, procedural concerns regarding group representation in

decision-making bodies are more likely to predominate within decision-making bodies representing a heterogeneous population (i.e., composed of more than one group) than within superordinate decision-
making bodies representing a homogeneous population, especially when
the constituent groups differ in size. Several additional factors could
be suggested which may affect the emergence of procedural justice
concerns in intergroup relations, such as the degree to which the decision is relevant to the vital interests of one or all groups concerned,
and whether these interests are material or symbolic.

## Individual Identity Needs and Group Identity Interests

As suggested earlier, a deeper understanding of collective action
necessitates the clarification of the differences and connections between individual motives and group interests. Nowhere is this distinction as crucial as in the analysis of identity interests. The crucial
questions here are: How do group identity interests get defined? Are
they the mere aggregation of similar individual identity needs? Do
group identity interests always coincide with their individual members' identity needs?

But prior to the discussion of this problem, it is important to raise a
more elementary question with regard to identity needs, namely whether
the fundamental need is to achieve a *distinct* or a *positively distinct*
social identity. According to social identity theory, the fundamental
individual identity need is the achievement of a *positively distinct*
social identity. However, according to Mummenday and Simon,[93] individuals can be satisfied by achieving a *distinct* social identity through
an emphasis on *different* but not necessarily *better* attributes. Many
studies, cited earlier, provide findings that are consistent with the last
position: namely, that a positive evaluation of the ingroup does not
necessarily entail a negative evaluation of the outgroup.[94] If anything,
existing research does not allow any conclusion about which is *the*
fundamental identity motive, nor how many such motives there are. It
is possible that each of the various motives (i.e., ingroup favoritism,
seeking difference but not positive difference, outgroup favoritism,
and so forth) is important in a particular context.

Returning to the question concerning the correspondence between
individual identity needs and group identity interests, one can draw
from social identity theory two (contrasting) *individual* identity orien-

tations which have implications for the strength of individuals' desire to maintain a distinctive *group* identity: (1) an individual *assimilation* orientation which implies a strong identification with an outgroup or a superordinate category and, hence, a weak desire to promote the distinctiveness of the ingroup's identity; and (2) an orientation aimed at the *reaffirmation* of the ingroup's identity. The first orientation is behaviorally expressed through individual mobility across group boundaries (i.e., exit), whereas the second is expressed through participation in collective attempts to change the definition of the ingroup's identity.

Clearly, the individual assimilation orientation is incompatible with the promotion of the group's distinct identity. In analyzing the conditions which affect individuals' inclination towards one or the other identity orientation, social identity theory implicitly assumes that individuals' concern for their own social identity overrides their concern for the group's identity. The arguments that the theory proposes to link social mobility and social change beliefs to the choice of means to achieve positive differentiation imply that an assimilation orientation (in the form of exit) is the natural individual inclination which, only when constrained, would give place to the reaffirmation orientation. This implicit assumption limits the theory's ability to account for why many people for whom social mobility is possible, still refuse to assimilate and instead explicitly promote demands for either integration or separation (e.g., French-speaking Canadians; Sikhs in India[95]). The theory's limitations basically stem from its focus on individuals' concern for their own social identity and not on their concern for their group's identity. The two forms of concerns may be related but are essentially distinct.

A more refined taxonomy of identity orientations is provided by Berry.[96] Berry proposes four possible identity orientations, the determination of which depends on whether or not members of a group (1) want to maintain their distinct *group* identity and (2) want to have positive relationships with the outgroup(s). An affirmative answer to both questions produces an *integration* orientation. A negative answer to both questions is rare and produces *marginal* groups.[97] A desire to maintain a distinct group identity without positive relations with the outgroup produces a *separation* orientation. Finally, a desire to have a positive relation with the outgroup without maintaining a distinct group identity produces an *assimilation* orientation. As to the determinants of these identity orientations, Berry emphasizes the initial conditions of contact between groups (i.e., whether contact is voluntary or involuntary). Other determinants could be derived from observations of ethnic conflicts. These include factors such as the degree of institutionalization of the group's culture, the prevailing ideology (e.g., individualistic), the group's numerical size, its relative position in the power structure, its geographical dispersion or concentration within a particular territory, its "degree of indigenousness," and so on.

In contrast to social identity theory, Berry's model explicitly deals with individuals' concerns with the group's identity. However, like social identity theory, it does not provide an explanation of how explicitly articulated group-identity goals would emerge from individual identity orientations. Presumably, both theories assume that the aggregation of similar individual orientations would produce group-identity demands. But such an assumption suffers from the same problem that plagues realistic conflict theory, namely the problem of consensus-building. This problem is central because of the potential for incompatibilities between individual-identity orientations and group-identity interests. Take, for instance, an assimilation orientation. Looking at the numerous ethnic conflicts which are raging around the world, it is almost impossible to find one conflict which features explicit collective demands for assimilation. In contrast, integration and separatism are clearly articulated group goals in many ethnic conflicts. It is worth analyzing the cultural and ideological factors that make assimilation an essentially individualistic orientation.

An assimilation orientation emerges especially in cultural groups with individualistic ideologies which emphasize individual citizenship and deemphasize ethnic group identification (as is illustrated, in chapter 4, in Ueda's analysis of ethnic relations in the United States); it is unlikely to emerge in cultural groups with a less individualistic ideology, unless forced or coerced by a dominant group. An individualistic ideology provides individuals with the freedom to move out of an ethnic group and into a large and, sometimes, culturally amorphous superordinate category. Indeed, an individualistic ideology, by definition, emphasizes *individual* achievement and success. Its psychological implication is a high degree of achievement motivation associated with a belief that there should not be an upper limit for upward mobility. Given an upper ceiling for upward mobility within low status groups, exit from such groups and/or assimilation into a high status group may become the only or the fastest ways to fully accede to the resources available at the superordinate level. Under such circumstances, members of low status groups would perceive the upper limit of mobility within their own group as an illegitimate constraint on a legitimate desire for upward mobility and would perceive cross-group mobility as a potential legitimate alternative. In contrast, individuals in less individualistic cultures may accept upper limits on upward mobility, and may even seek stability at a certain level in the social hierarchy; alternatively, they may collectively seek to disengage their group from the superordinate unit. Consequently, for members of subordinate groups in these cultures, cross-group mobility may not be a cognitively available, socially sanctioned, or legitimate alternative.

Thus, an individual assimilation orientation is likely when (1) individuals believe that there should be no upper ceiling for their upward mobility, (2) they perceive an upper ceiling on upward mobility within the ingroup, (3) this ceiling is lower than that which is perceived in the outgroup, and (4) cross-group mobility is a cognitively available, socially unconstrained, and legitimate alternative. Conditions (1) and (4) are more likely to be present in individualistic cultures than in less individualistic ones. Therefore, an assimilation orientation is more likely in the former than in the latter.

In addition to demonstrating the intimate interplay between realistic and identity motives, this analysis shows how an assimilation orientation stands in contrast to *group* identity interests. Indeed, under conditions where assimilation is likely to emerge, *intragroup differences* in identity orientations are also likely to emerge: those group members who possess the necessary skills (e.g., language fluency, education, training) to compete for the superordinate resources are more likely to have an assimilation orientation than those who lack such skills.[98] Given intra-group differences in individual capabilities to compete for upward social mobility, assimilation is unlikely to be a consensual choice leading up to an articulation of a formal group demand. Furthermore, an assimilation orientation is likely to deprive the group of highly skilled and resourceful individuals and, consequently, reduce the likelihood of collective action[99] as well as increase the likelihood of *intragroup conflict*.

Another individual orientation which could not become a group orientation is *marginality*. It is reasonable to argue that this is a result of situational factors rather than a personal or collective choice. Thus, it could even result when the answers to Berry's two questions are positive (i.e., desire to maintain group identity and to have positive relations with the outgroup). In this case, for instance, marginality may be produced by the outgroup's not allowing the ingroup to preserve its distinct identity nor to achieve integration. It follows that only *integration* and *separation* could be explicitly articulated as group demands.

An additional identity orientation should be differentiated from "integration". Whereas Berry[100] defines integration as the desire to maintain a distinct group identity associated with a desire for a positive contact with the outgroup, he does not deal with the cultural implications of the desired positive contact. Members of some groups may not simply want to have positive relations with another group or a superordinate group but may also want to adopt some of the cultural values and customs of that group. The outcome would be a mixture of cultural values which reflects a desire to retain *some* of the ingroup's cultural values or symbols while replacing the rest with values taken from the other group's culture. Such an identity orientation may be called *biculturalism*. Whether biculturalism could be conceived as a personal or collective "choice" as opposed to being the evolutionary product of sociostructural conditions[101] is an empirical question to be investigated.

Both individual and group identity orientations are constrained by sociopolitical and socioeconomic factors. In social psychology, social identity theory acknowledges the role of such factors by introducing social mobility and social change beliefs as important mediators of identity choices. Berry's model introduces factors such as the conditions of initial contact. In other social sciences, various analyses have been proposed with regard to economic and cultural interdependence and their implications for the maintenance of distinct group identities. In particular, Gordon[102] makes a distinction between cultural and structural pluralism. *Cultural pluralism* is a feature of national societies which allow various groups to maintain their distinctive cultural institutions and symbols. *Structural pluralism* features a socioeconomic segregation between groups, which may or may not imply the maintenance of cultural distinctiveness. In this analysis, cultural pluralism is not necessarily incompatible with socioeconomic integration. Nevertheless, dominant political ideologies in modern nation-states tend to assume that socioeconomic integration could only be achieved through cultural assimilation.

This assumption concurs with the arguments presented in self-categorization theory, which is a recent elaboration on social identity theory.[103] Turner argues that there are three levels of categorization: personal, group, and human. Personal categorization implicates personal characteristics which distinguish the self from other individuals. Group categorization involves ingroup-outgroup comparisons and hence attempts to define the distinctiveness of the ingroup in the constellation of other social groups. Human categorization transcends both personal and group categorizations in that similarities among human individuals across groups are emphasized and distinctions are made between the human species and other species. The theory also argues that there is a functional antagonism between the salience of one level of categorization and another. The functional antagonism among these levels means that the salience of one level of categorization necessarily decreases the salience of the others. Thus, the salience of group categorization produces an accentuation of intragroup similarities and intergroup differences which reduces or inhibits the perception of intragroup differences (which would apply if personal categorization were salient) or intergroup similarities (which would apply if human categorization were salient). Presumably, the principle of functional antagonism applies to any hierarchically nested set of categories and may, therefore, apply to the relationship between ethnic identities and superordinate "nation-state" identities.

It is possible to derive from Turner's analysis the implication that ethnic identities and superordinate national identities should be mutually exclusive, in the sense that only one could be salient or strong at a time. This position is upheld by many social scientists[104] and politicians who assume that the process of nation building entails the eradication of ethnocultural or "primordial" identifications and their replacement by civic identification with the superordinate state,[105] or that the process of globalization of world society entails the end of the "nation-state" itself.[106]

It is possible that the functional antagonism between ethnic identity and the "nation-state" identity stems from the conception of the two identities as lying on opposite ends of a hypothetical psychological continuum such that if one is strong the other should be weak. Our analysis, in contrast, proposes that the two identities are best conceived as lying on two separate psychological continua, each ranging from weak to strong. The conception of nested identities as lying on separate scales allows for precise predictions of identity orientations. To illustrate, consider that the continua range from 1 (weak) to 10 (strong). Suppose that individual A is at point 3 for the superordinate identity and point 8 for the ethnic identity, individual B is at points 8 and 8 (respectively), individual C at points 8 and 3, and individual D at points 3 and 3. The knowledge of these individuals' positions on the two scales allows for the prediction of their group identification. Thus, individual A is more likely than the others to support a separatist ethnic movement, individual B is more likely than the others to be bicultural, individual C is more likely to exit the ingroup and assimilate into the superordinate group, and individual D is more likely to be marginal. According to this conception, one condition for collective action and ethnic nationalism would be a stronger identification with an ethnic group than with the superordinate category. The important point here is that when the two levels of identification are placed on separate scales, the possibility for strong (or weak) identification *at both levels* arises. Thus, an individual can strongly identify with both ethnic and superordinate group.[107]

It is important, at this point, to emphasize that the antagonism between the two levels of identification may not be inherent in the cognitive structure which mediates the categorization process but may instead be the product of political ideologies and structures which pit the two against each other. Indeed, as suggested by other chapters in this volume and by the early discussion of the definition of nationalism, *explicit collective representations* of the two types of identity (ethnic and nation-state) appear to emerge at particular points in history as a function of the genesis of particular political and economic structures. James (this volume) provides an insight into the economic changes which brought about early nationalisms (e.g., in Germany, Russia, Japan). Both Dandeker and Ueda document the view that the development of the "nation-state" associated with a civic culture requires a divorce between nationality and ethnic culture. But it is important to note that this divorce did not always involve a fusion or merger of the constituent groups into one superordinate culture.[108] Rather, it frequently meant a process of homogenization (through mass education and communication) whereby members of certain groups (notably subordinate groups) had to assimilate into the dominant group whose culture came to define the superordinate unit's culture. Interestingly, *ethnic* nationalisms appear to carry the same requirements, as illustrated by the hegemonic anti-minority attitudes and policies which are looming in the newly emerging states in Eastern Europe (e.g., Lithuania, Georgia, Croatia). These two recent units of political organization and identification (i.e., the nation-state and the ethnic group) have created a social "discourse" of categorization which made group identities explicit cognitive entities to be defined unambiguously along territorial and cultural dimensions.[109]

It is possible that the processes of intragroup homogenization and intergroup differentiation which are manifest in "nation-state" and ethnic nationalisms are causally associated with the *hegemonic* inclinations of these nationalisms. For instance, the emerging ethnic nationalisms in Eastern Europe which are fueled by a quest for national freedom, group rights, and self-determination are nevertheless hegemonic towards the "non-national" groups which are caught up in their enclaves. This hegemonic tendency may be related to the need to homogenize and, hence, legitimize the corporate status of the nationalist group. Indeed, both James and Dandeker (this volume) suggest that early nationalisms (e.g., German, French, Russian, Japanese), which were associated with political violence, were also accompanied by these two processes.

To sum up, although the need to diminish subcategorical distinctions is likely to arise from the processes of categorical differentiation which are built into human mental structures, this need appears to be greatly amplified by the explicit categorizations which are produced by nationalist discourse. It is the superimposition of the social constructive process of categorization on the cognitive process of categorical differentiation which is probably responsible for the extreme and violent forms in which homogenization and differentiation processes are manifest in nationalism.

## Conditions for Intergroup Conflict:
## From Individual Motives to Collective Action

### The Social Recognition of Collective Actors

As suggested by the preceding discussion, demands for the recognition of groups as legitimate political actors with corporate status are an integral part of nationalist agendas. But the widespread ideological assumption that ethnic identities and superordinate "nation-state" identities are functionally antagonistic poses obstacles to these nationalist demands.

One obstacle stems from the implication that individuals rather than groups would be perceived as legitimate political actors.[110] Superordinate identification is likely to be associated with the beliefs that the similarities among individuals across ethnic groups outweigh the differences among them and that therefore, individuals should relate to the superordinate structure as individual citizens and not as members of groups. Such beliefs detract from the legitimacy of group-based collective action and, consequently, restrains individuals from joining in such action. There is also an indirect way in which the absence of social recognition of the corporate status of ethnocultural groups may restrict the chances of collective action. The absence of such recognition (especially for low-status and minority groups) affects individuals' identity orientations and, hence, their readiness to endorse or participate in collective action. Given that the cultural values and identity symbols of dominant groups (e.g., language, lifestyle, customs, moral values) are more likely than those of subordinate groups to be incorporated in the identity and culture defined for the superordinate unit, members of non-dominant groups would actually feel stronger pressures than members of dominant groups to undergo cultural and identity changes if they desire to affirm their superordinate identification and/or to have access to scarce resources (e.g., political and civil service positions) available in the superordinate bureaucracy. Because these identity dilemmas may produce intragroup differences in identity orientations, they would constitute an important obstacle to the building of a group consensus around group goals which is necessary for collective action to occur.

The legitimization of individual actors as opposed to group actors also affects people's beliefs about the causes of successful or failed individual attempts at social mobility. In particular, it directs individuals' causal explanations for their successes and failures more towards personal than situational or institutional factors. Thus, given that members of low status groups are more likely to fail than members of high status groups, the prevailing ideology would direct their causal explanations of the failure more to personal deficits (e.g., lack of ability) than to institutional obstacles (e.g., discrimination; lack of opportunity). Such attributions in turn are likely to decrease their achievement motivation, especially if they believe that the personal deficits are stable and uncontrollable (hence not easily modifiable through learn-ing or training). Attributions to personal causes are also likely to de-crease individuals' readiness to initiate or participate in collective ac-tion because such action requires the cognition that something in ex-isting institutions must be changed in order to promote their upward social mobility.

*Efficacy Beliefs in Individual versus Collective Action*

One means to counter these ideological obstacles to collective ac-tion would be for group leaders to set in motion differential beliefs in the relative efficacy of individual versus collective actions. By con-vincing individuals that collective action is likely to yield better out-comes than individual attempts at social mobility, group leaders may increase the chances of successful mobilization. This, however, is not an easy task because of the complexity of efficacy beliefs. We can specify at least three types of efficacy beliefs which play a crucial role in determining individuals' readiness to act individually versus en-dorse collective action.

First, individuals may have a strong or weak belief in *collective efficacy*. A strong collective efficacy belief means that (1) collective action is likely to yield at least some of the outcomes desired by the group, (2) other members of the group are willing to participate in the action, and (3) the group possesses the resources (e.g., wealth, arms, resilience) to withstand potential counterattacks by the outgroup. The strength of collective efficacy beliefs is, therefore, affected by the perceived power of the outgroup.[111] It is also a function of the particu-lar course of action proposed by the group leaders: leaders and group members are likely to estimate the efficacy of a particular course of action relative to the efficacies of alternative courses of action.[112]

Second, individuals may have a strong or weak belief in *individual self-efficacy*. A strong belief in individual self-efficacy means that the individual could make it on his or her own. Such a belief predisposes individuals to choose to exit their group and assimilate into the domi-nant group. In contrast, a weak belief constrains the choice of exit, although it does not necessarily imply that the individual will auto-matically decide to initiate or support collective action. For this to occur, the third type of efficacy belief is required.

The third type involves beliefs in *participatory self-efficacy*. A strong belief means that the individual's participation is seen as having a potential incremental effect on collective action. In other words, group members should believe that their individual participation would make a difference. This, along with the belief in collective efficacy (which implies that other members of the group will also participate), is a necessary condition for collective action. Without it, even strong beliefs in collective efficacy may not be sufficient to produce participation, for a preponderance of weak beliefs in participatory self-efficacy may produce *free-riding*.

The previous analysis suggests that, in order to counter individualistic obstacles to group mobilization, group leaders need to (1) emphasize the legitimacy of the group's "corporate" status, (2) pull individual members away from an exit choice by weakening their individual self-efficacy beliefs, (3) strengthen their collective efficacy beliefs by convincing them that collective action is necessary and efficient and that other members are ready to join, and (4) induce the belief that one's individual participation is necessary for the success of the collective action.

*Intragroup Organization as a Resource for Mobilization*

The social construction of ethnic group goals and the determination of the best course of action to achieve them are likely to involve complex social influence processes. These are probably more complex than the processes mediating consensus formation in small decision-making groups.[113] Nevertheless, a conceptual distinction between organized subgroups and their mass constituency provides an easy solution to the problem. Group goals are usually defined by small groups of "representatives." One could study the decision-making process through which a small group of representatives defines group goals separately from the processes of influence and persuasion that take place between these organized subgroups and their mass constituency. The decision-making dynamics of these small groups of representatives may not be identical to the dynamics found in the small groups which are the focus of social psychological research.[114] With few exceptions,[115] the experimental small group does not usually represent a larger constituency. Intergroup negotiation researchers[116] have pointed out that the group behavior of individuals who are representatives of groups is different in many respects from the behavior of individuals who are not group representatives.

The importance of small groups of representatives or "social move-ment organizations," emphasized by a number of researchers in vari-ous fields,[117] stems from the fact that the formulation of group goals and the means to achieve them requires a capacity to collect relevant information about the issues affecting the group, the position and means of the outgroup, and the potential costs and benefits of various courses of action. Given that a high degree of uncertainty surrounds individu-als' pursuit of such information,[118] coordination and the pooling of resources become crucial conditions for the selection of goals and means. Organized groups are crucial in gathering and articulating the relevant information for the definition of group goals, and in providing or activating utilitarian and normative justifications for the choice of particular courses of collective action—notably, for political violence.[119]

The conception of collective action as instigated by organized groups or "social movement organizations" stands in contrast to the concep-tion implicit in relative deprivation theories - i.e., that collective action is a spontaneous action potentiated by the aggregated feelings of dep-rivation (across time and individuals) and elicited by "triggering" events. The former fits what Eckstein[120] calls an "inherency" approach which emphasizes the rational, purposeful aspect of collective action, whereas the latter fits what Eckstein calls a "contingency" approach, which emphasizes the emotional, affective, spontaneous, and "non-agentic" aspect of collective behavior.[121] Yet, this contrast need not imply that the two approaches to collective action are mutually exclusive. Indeed, collective action initiated in intergroup conflicts may take different forms which could be readily categorized into organized and non-organized.[122] *Organized* collective action is elicited and coordinated by a relatively small group of individuals who define the group's goals and interests as well as the means to achieve them. *Non-organized* collective action emerges "spontaneously" in particular crowd situa-tions and does not feature the emergence of clear demands nor the specification of consensual group goals. In the absence of an orga-nized group, a crowd of individuals which gathers in a particular place at a particular time (e.g., the people who engaged in the spring 1992 Los Angeles riots) is unlikely to elaborate well-articulated group goals, engage in a temporally continuous and ideologically coherent collec-tive action, and sustain influence attempts to mobilize other group members for the collective action.[123] All these outcomes necessitate coordination and organization which are unlikely to spontaneously emerge in a crowd. Given this distinction, it could be argued that "triggering" events may be required to elicit non-organized collective action precisely because of the absence of group organization with well-articulated ideological (or moral) definition of its goals. The conceptual distinction between organized and non-organized collective action suggests that the two approaches (inherency versus contingency) should not be viewed as mutually exclusive, but as complementary[124]— for instance, the inherency model providing a better account of organized action, while the contingency model providing a better account of non-organized action.

To summarize, the importance of socially organized action for goal definition and means selection flows from the following assumptions: (1) incompatibility of interests between groups presupposes that these interests have been determined and some degree of consensus among group members regarding these interests has developed; (2) the choice of one form of collective action (e.g., democratic negotiations, civil disobedience, political violence) implies some degree of consensus among group members as to its costs and benefits and, hence, to its efficacy *relative to alternative courses of action*, (3) consensus among group members with regard to these issues cannot emerge "spontaneously" in non-organized and large social categories; and (4) the consensus is likely to be reached through processes of social influence between a relatively small number of individuals (leaders), who formulate and propose particular interests, and their constituency.

These assumptions do not imply that crowd behavior which emerges in the context of a non-organized collective action is necessarily anomic. On the contrary, as pointed out by Reicher,[125] many collective events which implicate crowds (e.g., riots) cannot be adequately explained without reference to a confrontation between two identifiable groups: the rioters and the police (the latter usually acting on behalf of a social category that is different from the rioters'). According to Reicher, participants in a riot cannot view themselves as an anonymous crowd, at least not to each other, nor as an unidentifiable group; rather, they view themselves as a "group" sharing the same identity, an identity which is almost always activated by the ingroup-outgroup categorization made salient by authority or police actions. It follows that, although coordination and planning may be absent, members of the crowd may act in accordance with norms which spontaneously emerge in the present situation as a function of a salient intergroup categorization; these norms may play an important role in defining a relatively narrow range of targets for political violence, as a function of situational interactional factors,[126] or which derive from past actions in similar situations.[127]

The dynamics of collective action are complicated by the potential for intra-group disagreements. *Schisms* within groups are likely to emerge with regard to the definition and rank ordering of group goals and, more so, with regard to the means to achieve these goals. Means, more than goals, have behavioral implications and, consequently, are likely to feature highly salient costs. The choice of means, especially within tightly organized "conflict groups," may fluctuate over the course of conflict. Schisms are likely to start with the emergence of an extremist faction, especially under conditions where various means used by moderate factions do not lead to social change.[128] However, one should not rule out the possibility that schisms may also start in the reverse order: moderate factions may emerge (sometimes by splitting from extremist factions), especially if a protracted struggle using extreme means has not led to any change, if the costs of the prevailing means reach a point that exceeds the level which group members are willing to sustain, or if there are signals from the outgroup that it is willing to compromise.

## The Dynamics of Mobilization and Collective Action

Having defined group goals and the means to achieve them, group representatives would have to mobilize their constituency if collective action is to be initiated. Given that conflict involves the overt confrontation between two groups, and that each group consists of the mass constituency and an organized leadership (sometimes more than one), the social influence processes which mediate its occurrence could be categorized as taking place between: (1) each organized group and its constituent population; (2) rival organized groups within a group, if any; (3) the organized representatives of the two groups; (4) each organized group and the constituency of the other group; and (5) the two constituencies. The present analysis will be limited to the first and third forms of influence processes—that is, where the source of influence is a non-dominant organized group initiating a conflict and the targets are, on the one hand, its constituency, and on the other, the organized group in power.[129] These influence processes are best captured, in social psychology, by theories of minority influence developed by Moscovici[130] and Mugny,[131] and, in the social sciences, by ethnic and resource mobilization theories.[132] These theories, briefly reviewed in the following sections, provide relevant insights into the conditions under which minority opposition groups could have an impact on their constituents and on members of the outgroup, thus instigating collective action.

At the core of Moscovici's[133] theory of minority influence is the distinction between active and passive minorities. A passive minority resists the influence of a disagreeing majority through nonconformity. The conditions for its resistance are well documented in social psychology.[134] In view of the earlier analysis of identity orientations, one can argue that a passive minority (e.g., who accepts a negative identity or a state of deprivation and subordination) is likely to become marginalized in the larger society. In contrast, an "active' minority not only resists majority influence but, according to Moscovici, also provides a well-defined alternative point of view. Thus, rather than being a passive resistor, an active minority is committed to confront the majority, defend its own views against the majority's and, ultimately, replace the majority's views with its own.

According to Moscovici,[135] although majorities may possess resources which make them generally more powerful and influential than minorities,[136] numerical minorities can have influence by using particular behavioral strategies (e.g., presenting their message with persistence, unanimity, and autonomy). Moscovici also argues that the impacts of active minorities and majorities are mediated by different processes. Individuals who face a numerical majority displaying an opinion or judgment different from their own become concerned more with the "deviant" aspect of their own responses than with the validity of the majority's arguments.[137] Consequently, they engage in a superficial validation process through which they compare their responses to the majority's response without the consideration of arguments or counterarguments. Their major concern is to reduce their disagreement with the majority. Therefore, majority influence is likely to produce conformity—i.e., public compliance which is not necessarily accompanied by an internalization of the majority's position. In contrast, individuals exposed to an active disagreeing minority, who promotes its position in a consistent manner and who displays internal cohesion and unanimity, are likely to engage in attempts to convince the minority to change its position. Consequently, they are likely to engage in a validation process that focuses on the content of the minority's position and which may potentially lead to their internalization of the minority's position. Thus, generally speaking, majority influence is more likely to produce public compliance (or conformity) and less likely to produce internalization than minority influence.[138] Another difference between the two types of influence concerns the time at which the impact is felt. Thus, while the majority's influence is felt at the time of exposure, that of the minority is likely to be latent and delayed.

Of special relevance to intergroup conflict is Mugny's 1982 model which extends Moscovici's formulations to include three distinct parties: the minority, the established authority or power, and the "population" or silent majority. He thus places the process of minority influence in the political context of power relations between groups. In this model, the active minority is competing with the established power to win the support of the population. Mugny argues that a *rigid* style of confrontation with the established power, combined with a *flexible* style of influence towards the population increases the impact of the minority. He also provides an analysis and some evidence about the ways in which a minority can overcome the numerous ideological obstacles that the established power can use to diminish or eliminate its impact.[139] Research inspired by Mugny's model shows that the influence of an active minority is a function of whether or not it shares the same category membership as its target; in general, a greater impact on ingroup members is found when the boundaries between the ingroup and outgroup are made salient.[140] However, the same strategy decreases its impact on outgroup members. A series of experimental findings show that a minority which differs from the majority both in category group membership and in opinion has less impact on majority members than a minority which differs from the majority only in opinion.[141] More recent studies have, however, yielded inconsistent findings. For instance, while some studies have found minorities to have a greater impact on ingroup than on outgroup members,[142] other studies have shown the opposite pattern.[143] One problem in comparing these studies stems from the different and inconsistent experimental operations of the main concepts.

The most important reason for these inconsistent findings is probably the conceptual confounding of two distinct processes[144]: the impact of an ingroup minority on an outgroup (this is a question about intergroup influence), and the impact of an ingroup minority on the ingroup constituency (intra-group influence). Turner suggests a refinement of Mugny's 1982 model by proposing a distinction between two populations: one that shares the same category membership with the established power, the other with the minority. Thus, whereas one population is an ingroup for the active minority, the other constitutes its outgroup.

In any case, the theories and research on minority influence need to pay more attention to a hitherto neglected factor which may play an important role in ethnic group mobilization, namely the specific claims or positions advanced by the source of influence. Thus, as suggested in an earlier section, it is possible that a minority's demands for corporate recognition would cast the conflict as an intergroup one rather than as a conflict between a numerical minority versus a numerical majority viewpoint. Turner's analysis suggests that such categorical casting of the conflict may aid in the group's mobilization effort (influence on the ingroup's constituency) because it appeals to loyalty feelings and also because it implies that the active minority's demands would not be seen as self-interested but as representative of the interests of a constituent population. The dominant group, in this case, would have a vested interest in defusing such a categorical definition of the conflict and in emphasizing loyalty to the common superordinate group. Such a strategy may be instrumental to the dominant group because it would cast the minority group's leaders as dissenters rather than representatives of the collective interests of a social category. Indeed, Mugny[145] shows that any majority strategy which "psychologizes" the active minority (i.e., makes it look like a bunch of deviants or crazies) reduces its chances to have an impact on its targets.

The conditions that lead to the formation of an active organized minority have not been the focus of interest in the minority influence literature. The formation of an active organized minority which challenges the existing status quo is usually the result of the actions of individuals who possess the necessary skills, resources, and commitment to mobilize members of their *social category* and make them behave as a *group*.[146] It is usually elite members of a social category who form the organized group.[147] The self-interests of the individual founders of the organized group may be an important motive for their involvement in its formation.[148] The aspirations of elite members of subordinate groups are more likely to be oriented towards careers in the political bureaucracy than towards economic entrepreneurship.[149] Given such aspirations, and given the scarcity and importance of the desired positions, they are likely to experience group-based discrimination and a ceiling for their upward mobility which is lower than that for members of the dominant group. Consequently, they may "disidentify" with the dominant group's culture and values[150] and shift their commitment from attempts to assimilate to attempts at the promotion of their ethnic group's goals and the mobilization of the group's members for collective action. This they do through the articulation of an explicit ideology that attributes the social "immobility" (in contrast to social mobility) of members of their group to discrimination by the outgroup and to the injustice of the status quo.[151] From a rational choice perspective, the incentives here may be both symbolic and economic: symbolic goods (e.g., group identity and status) are public goods, available to all members of the group, and may be crucial for the mobilization process, whereas material incentives—that is, non-public goods—may help to maintain the commitment of the group elites or representatives,[152] especially given that active and committed representatives expose themselves to higher personal risks and costs than their followers.[153]

In initiating mobilization processes, a committed and organized minority has to overcome the obstacles which impede individual participation in collective action. These obstacles, which have been the focus of rational choice analyses, derive from, among other facts: (1) the possibility that causal connections between institutional factors and individual outcomes may not be immediately salient to individuals, (2) the fact that discrimination may not be perceived nor attributed to institutionalized systems,[154] (3) the possibility that individual constituents may be uncertain about the number of other members of their group who are willing to participate in collective action,[155] (4) the fact that individuals may not perceive that the achievement of group interests is relevant to their self-interest, (5) the fact that individuals' endorsement of group goals may often be at odds with the achievement of their short-term self-interests,[156] and (6) the fact that individuals may not possess enough resources to gather the appropriate information which is required to produce strong collective efficacy beliefs.

Given these obstacles, the organized group has to decide on the strategy to use for mobilization and persuasion. The preceding analysis suggests that an emphasis on the value of the group's distinct identity and a sharpening of group boundaries is one strategy which may increase the likelihood of individual participation in collective action. The research on justice and relative deprivation suggests another strategy: an emphasis on the "moral" aspect (i.e., injustice) of the group's material interests. A pure emphasis on the "rational-material" interests of the group, which is implied by realistic conflict theory, may be neither sufficient nor necessary.[157] Yet, such a strategy may be efficient in the mobilization of particular segments of the ingroup's population. In general, one could argue that the efficiency of any mobilization strategy is a function of the characteristics of the targeted segment of the population. One basic population characteristic is the strength of identification with the ethnic category relative to the superordinate category. For instance, individuals who have a stronger identification with the superordinate category than with their ethnic category (i.e., displaying an assimilation orientation) may not be affected by slogans about the importance of their distinct ethnic identity. Yet these individuals could be mobilized if they are persuaded that the maintenance or achievement of their self-interest is contingent on the achievement of group interests. An emphasis on identity grievances may be more effective for individuals whose identification with their ethnic category is stronger than their identification with the superordinate category. For these individuals, increasing the salience of ingroup-outgroup categorization and ingroup identification may lead to the "depersonalization" of their self-interest and may, consequently, produce the sense that the immediately important self-interest *is* the group's interest.[158]

An additional effective mobilizing strategy is to simplify the ideology that justifies the choice of particular goals or courses of action. The efficiency of this strategy stems from the complexity of social causations and the limited capacity of individuals to grasp them.[159] Casting the problem in terms of an ingroup-outgroup polarized dichotomy is one such simplification strategy.[160] Exaggerating the divergence between ingroup and outgroup would easily channel constituents' attributions of existing disadvantages or threats to the outgroup rather than to their personal inabilities or to the ingroup's deviant characteristics.[161] It would also lead to greater confidence that other ingroup members will not free-ride,[162] thus strengthening their willingness to put aside their short-term self-interest in order to pursue common collective interests.[163] Directly blaming the outgroup is another simplifying strategy which could increase the subjective interdependence between self-interest (or egoistic deprivation) and group interest (or fraternal deprivation). Moreover, given the perceived advantage it has in informational resources, the organized minority could raise ingroup members' subjective probabilities of the collective action's success.[164]

Mobilization processes may also involve the use of coercive violence against both ingroup and outgroup members, as suggested by Laitin.[165] Sometimes, as in Lebanon and Sri Lanka, violence is used by radical factions as a means to punish ingroup members who display signs of moderation or compromise with an outgroup. Successful violent acts against prominent outgroup members could increase a group's recruitment success, as has been documented for the Basque terrorist group ETA. In either case, according to Laitin, the violence has the effect of increasing the costs of accepting the status quo. Laitin also proposes that guerilla groups sometimes use an "action-repression-action spiral" strategy consisting of violent actions which aim at provoking the authorities to retaliate, which then galvanizes support for the guerilla group. Moreover, and as illustrated by Dandeker (see chapter 1), the use of violence may play an important role in the creation and crystallization of political and community boundaries.

Finally, it should be added that mobilization to participate in violent collective action may involve a different set of incentives than mobilization for nonviolent action. In most cases where groups are in a state of civil war, recruitment into the militia groups may be facilitated by the possibility that these groups may provide opportunities for quick and easy upward social mobility.

## Conclusion

The purpose of this chapter is to show how the analysis of psychological mechanisms could be integrated with group-level analyses in order to facilitate a global understanding of intergroup conflict, in general, and ethnic nationalism, in particular. The review of social psychological work suggests that goal incompatibility is a necessary determinant of intergroup conflict. This conclusion, however, does not imply that groups could be viewed, like individuals are, as motivated to maximize their interests. This is so for the simple reason that a group is made up of individuals who may not have the same level of motivation to act on behalf of group interests. The definition of group goals does not ensure that individual members of the group will automatically act to maximize them. The willingness of individuals to engage in collective confrontational action on behalf of group goals is a function of complex social psychological processes related to (1) whether the established structure of relations between groups, which often involves differential access to resources, is perceived as just or unjust, (2) the degree of interdependence which is perceived to exist between individual interests and group interests, and (3) the strength of individuals' identification with a group relative to their identification with a more inclusive superordinate group.

The processes mediating the perception of established systems of resource allocation as just or unjust have been examined by justice research, and the relationship between such perceptions and collective action has been addressed in relative deprivation research. Although both approaches suggest that individuals may engage in conflictual action when they perceive that they are deprived of what (they believe) they deserve, neither approach specifies the particular distributive and procedural principles that make individuals believe that their *group* is deprived of what it deserves. On the basis of comparative case analyses of ethnic conflicts and of constitutional systems in multiethnic societies, a number of such principles were proposed. One fundamental issue—in that it underlies a variety of group distributive and procedural concerns—has to do with the establishment of groups (in contrast to individuals) as legitimate recipients of resources and loci for political identification and action. Political representation and the recognition of the rights of distinct groups are two of the most salient group concerns in ethnic nationalism. Indeed, they are associated with the most intense, violent, and intractable conflicts. Yet, they are among the least researched phenomena in the social sciences and are completely absent in psychology.

These concerns stem from the importance individuals place upon preserving and promoting a distinct social identity. Social identity theory and research have provided a wealth of knowledge on the conditions that activate this identity need, in addition to important conceptual insights as to the means that individuals use in order to achieve and satisfy this need. Survey research on racial attitudes has also suggested the role symbolic needs and interests play in shaping such attitudes. Some anthropological and sociological approaches to ethnic group relations have also emphasized the importance of group identity motives. Nevertheless, none of these approaches deals with the processes that link individual identity needs with the emergence of group identity demands. The review suggests that some individual identity needs are incompatible with the maintenance of group identity, and that the relationship between the two is a function of the strength of individuals' identification at various levels of group categorization.

The strength of identification itself is a function of sociopolitical and socioeconomic factors. Political ideologies play an important role in defining the individual-group relationships at various levels of categorization. A dominant ideology associated with the "nation-state" system confers more legitimacy on the individual's identification with the superordinate level (i.e., the nation-state) than on his or her identification with a subordinate ethnocultural group. Combined with the effects of socioeconomic factors, political ideologies create the conditions for a complex relationship among material interests and identity interests, at the individual and group levels. Incompatibilities among material and identity interests may arise within groups, thus producing the potential for intragroup schisms in defining goal priorities. They may also arise between groups producing the potential for conflict.

The interplay between realistic and identity motives is also evident in the processes that mediate the mobilization of group members for collective action. The review suggests that the activation of identity and/or justice concerns plays an important role both in determining the willingness of some individuals to initiate and in persuading others to participate in a confrontational collective action on behalf of group goals. Initiating and sustaining collective action requires the emergence of an organized, committed, consistent, and active minority of ingroup members who have the relevant information and resources to define group goals and the priorities among them, to assess the efficiency of, and select among various courses of action for the achievement of these goals, and to articulate the ideology through which they persuade individual members of the group to support and/or participate in collective action. Their attempts at mobilization of their constituents are likely to succeed if they convince them that collective action is more efficient than individual action in producing desired outcomes, and if they also persuade them that their own individual participation has an incremental effect on the collective action's chances of success.

In conclusion, it is worth noting that the analysis presented in this chapter does not place any evaluative connotation on the concepts of conflict and nationalism. Whereas conflict, in general, and nationalism, in particular, have been generally viewed as "negative," undesirable phenomena,[166] the present analysis suggests that they can be either a constructive or destructive process.[167] They are constructive to the extent that they bring about social change[168] or they constitute the only means through which threatened groups express their feelings, goals, and demands. They are also constructive to the extent that they reduce the ideological ambiguities regarding the status of various groups within superordinate entities, for instance, through the specification and clarification of systems and principles that would regulate the relations between the groups.[169] They are destructive to the extent that they entail a cycle of violence which could escalate to a degree where the conflict becomes intractable, and its costs outweigh its benefits.

# Notes

1. Social psychological research on intergroup relations in the past two decades (for reviews, see Brewer and Kramer 1985; Hamilton 1981; Hogg and Abrams 1988; Messick and Mackie 1989; Stephan 1985; Stroebe, Kruglanski, Bar-Tal, and Hewstone 1988; Tajfel 1982a; Taylor and Moghaddam 1987) has focused on the investigation of the cognitive processes underlying some phenomena in intergroup relations, for example, stereotyping (e.g., Cantor, Mischel, and Schwartz 1982; Hamilton 1981; Hamilton, Dugan, and Trolier 1985; Jussim, Coleman, and Lerch 1987; McCauley, Stitt, and Segal 1980), racial attitudes (e.g., Dovidio and Gaertner 1986; Kinder and Sears 1981, 1985; Sears 1988), the cognitive mediators and consequences of categorization (e.g., Linville, Fisher and Salovey 1989; Rothbart, Dawes, and Park 1984; Taylor, Fiske, Etkoff, and Ruderman 1978; Wilder 1981, 1986) and the effects of social categorization on the evaluation of social groups and the allocation of rewards (e.g., Brewer 1979; Diehl 1990; Tajfel 1982a; Turner 1981, 1987). An unfortunate consequence of this focus has been a sharp decline in research investigating the sources of conflict behavior between groups from their high levels in the 1960s (e.g., Blake, Shepard, and Mouton 1964; Deutsch 1973; Levine and Campbell 1972; Rabbie and Wilkens 1971; Sherif, Harvey, White, Hood, and Sherif 1961, 1988; Sherif and Sherif 1953; Wilson and Kayatani 1968; Wilson and Miller 1961). The only exception to this trend is research on relative deprivation which has seen an upsurge in recent years (e.g., Crosby 1976, 1982; Gurr 1980; Olson, Herman and Zanna 1986; Vanneman and Pettigrew 1972). It is, however, important to note that the current interest in cognitive processes is premised on the assumption that intergroup perceptions and representations are important factors in the determination of intergroup relations although very little research, if any, has investigated the causal links between these cognitive processes and inter-

group conflict. Potential mechanisms that mediate between some of these cognitive processes and conflict are discussed later in the chapter.

2. Bruner 1957; Tajfel 1959, 1981; Turner et al. 1987.

3. E.g., Anderson 1983; Leach 1957.

4. The distinction between these two types of identification is parallel to the distinction made by George Herbert Mead (1934) between the "I" and the "me" components of the self. The "I" is that part of the self which is involved in action without being aware of itself. The "me" is that part of the self which comes into being when one reflects about the self; it is an "object," a representation which could be cognitively molded, shaped, and imaged. The "me," in contrast to the "I," is a product of social communication and discourse precisely because it is an object which could be represented cognitively and linguistically.

5. Sherif et al. 1961, 1988. It is worth noting the difference between this definition and the widely accepted definition (in social psychology) derived from Sherif et al. 1961, 1988: "Whenever individuals belonging to one ingroup interact, collectively or individually, with another group or its members in terms of their group identification, we have an instance of intergroup relations" (1988, p. 21). Unlike Sherif's definition, the definition proposed here differentiates between the situation where members of two groups interact individually and where they interact collectively. Collective action requires some degree of consensus among group members whereas individual actions do not. It follows that when individuals are acting individually their behavior may not be representative of the group and may even be unacceptable to other group members. For instance, a soldier who kills an enemy during a battle may be praised, but one who kills an enemy when his or her leaders are sitting at the negotiations table and accidentally initiates or escalates a conflict may be tried or fired. Indeed, it is a common occurrence in many ethnic conflicts that radical factions within a group use violence in order to prevent the success of negotiations initiated by other factions (e.g., Sri Lanka, Lebanon). Given these possibilities, we find unacceptable a definition which considers a situation in which an individual confronts an outgroup member as being an "intergroup" conflict when other ingroup members do not support such action.

6. Examples of the former approach include realistic conflict theory and game theory (Campbell 1965; LeVine and Campbell 1972; Sherif 1966; Simmel 1955; Coser 1956, 1967; Rabbie and Horwitz 1969; Wilson and Kayatani 1968; Blake, Shepard, and Mouton 1964), relative deprivation theories (Gurr 1970; Runciman 1966; Vanneman and Pettigrew 1972; Crosby 1976), uneven development theories (Bonacich 1972; Furnivall 1948; Hechter 1978), rational choice models (Hechter, Friedman, and Applebaum 1982; Hechter 1987; Banton 1983, 1987; Blalock and Wilken 1979; Blalock 1967, 1989) and justice theories (Austin 1986; Walster, Berscheid, and Walster 1973; Deutsch 1985; Folger 1986). Examples of the latter include social identity theory and self-categorization theory (Tajfel and Turner 1986; Turner et al. 1987; Hogg and Adams 1988), symbolic politics theory (Kinder and Sears 1981; McConahay 1986; Sears 1988), and models of ethnic conflicts which emphasize the role of cultural identity (Horowitz 1985; A.D. Smith, 1981).

7. Sherif 1966; Sherif, Harvey, White, Hood and Sherif 1961, 1988; Sherif and Sherif 1953; Simmel 1955; Coser 1956, 1967; Campbell 1965; LeVine and Campbell 1972.

8. LeVine and Campbell 1972.

9. See Doise, Csepeli, Dann, Gouge, Larsen, and Ostell 1972; Ferguson and Kelley 1964; Kahn and Ryen 1972; Rabbie, Benoist, Oosterbaan, and Visser 1974; Rabbie, Schot, and Visser 1989; Rabbie and Wilkens 1971; Ryen and Kahn 1975.
10. Brewer 1979; Tajfel and Turner 1986; Turner 1981.
11  Cf. Brewer and Miller 1984.
12. Brown 1978, 1988; Brown and Wade 1987; Deschamps and Brown 1983.
13. Tajfel, Flament, Billig, and Bundy 1971.
14. See Allen and Wilder 1975; Billig and Tajfel 1973; Doise et al. 1972; Doise and Sinclair 1973; Tajfel et al. 1971; Turner 1975, 1978; for reviews see Billig 1976; Brewer 1979; Brown 1988; Diehl 1990; Hogg and Abrams 1988; Tajfel 1982a; and Turner 1981.
15. Brewer 1979, 1986; Brewer and Campbell 1976.
16. Billig 1976; Taylor and Moghaddam 1987.
17. Cf. Blalock and Wilken 1979, pp. 29–30; Kelley and Thibaut 1978.
18. LeVine and Campbell 1972.
19. Billig 1976.
20. Blalock 1967, 1989; Blalock and Wilken 1979; Tilly 1978.
21. Cook and Hegtvedt, 1986.
22. Billig 1976; Cohen 1986.
23. Crosby 1976; Davis 1959; Gurr 1970.
24. Davis 1959.
25. Gurr 1970.
26. Crosby 1976.
27. Runciman 1966; Vanneman and Pettigrew 1972; Walker and Pettigrew 1984.
28. Caplan 1970.
29. Vanneman and Pettigrew 1972.
30. Abeles 1976; Dibble 1981.
31. Dubé and Guimond 1986.
32. Tripathi and Srivastava 1981.
33. Crosby 1982; Nagata and Crosby 1990; Taylor, Wright, Moghaddam, and Lalonde 1990.
34. Kinder and Sears 1985.
35. See Runciman 1966; Gurr 1970; Crosby 1982; Martin and Murray 1984; Muller 1980.
36. Horowitz 1985; McCready 1983; Montville 1990; Oberschall 1973; D. Rothchild 1986; A.D. Smith 1981; Tajfel 1982b; Williams 1982.
37. Berkowitz 1962; Freud 1930; Dollard, Doob, Miller, Mowrer, and Sears 1939.
38. Crosby 1976, 1982; Gurr 1970; Muller 1980.
39. Muller 1980.
40. Adams 1965; Berkowitz and Walster 1976; Homans 1961; Walster, Berscheid, and Walster 1973; Walster, Walster and Berscheid 1978.
41. Deutsch 1975, 1985; Foa and Foa 1980; Reis 1986; Schwinger 1980, 1986.
42. Folger 1977; Lerner 1975; Leventhal 1980; Lind and Tyler 1988.
43. Folger 1977; Barrett-Howard and Tyler 1986.
44. Thibaut and Walker 1975; Austin and Tobiasen 1984.
45. Tyler 1984.
46. LaTour 1978; Walker, LaTour, Lind, and Thibaut 1974.
47. Thibaut and Walker 1975; Lind and Tyler 1988.
48. Lane 1988.
49. Tyler 1989, 1990; Lind and Tyler 1988.

50. Azzi, in press.
51. E.g., Foa and Foa 1980; Törnblom et al. 1985; Reis 1986.
52. Folger, 1986; Lind and Tyler, 1988.
53. E.g., Horowitz 1985; Oberschall 1973; D. Rothchild 1986.
54. Tajfel and Turner 1986.
55. Bourdieu 1979; Horowitz 1985; A.D. Smith 1981.
56. Hogg and Abrams 1988; Tajfel 1974, 1981; Tajfel and Turner 1986; Turner 1975, 1981, 1987.
57. Giles and Johnson 1981; Hogg and Abrams 1988; Tajfel 1981; Tajfel and Turner 1986. Conceptually, if the high-status group is a numerical minority and the threat is serious (e.g., threat of genocide), then exit (individual and *collective*) may occur. An example of collective exit is the religious conversion of Christian minorities in the Balkans and the Near East under muslim Arab and Ottoman regimes. An additional option for a high-status minority (and, potentially, for low status groups) is to physically leave the superordinate unit (e.g., mass emigration, or separation into an autonomous or independent political unit), thus retaining their positive group identity.
58. E.g., Blair and Azzi 1992; Ellemers 1991; Skevington 1980; Wright, Taylor, and Moghaddam 1990.
59. See Tajfel 1984, and Walker and Pettigrew 1984, for conceptual attempts.
60. Van Knippenberg 1978; van Knippenberg and van Oers 1984.
61. Taylor et al. 1990.
62. Hewstone and Ward 1985; Jaspars and Waernen 1982.
63. Clark and Clark 1947; Corenblum and Annis 1992; Vaughan 1964.
64. Nagata and Crosby 1990; Robinson 1984.
65. Sears 1988; Kinder and Sears 1981; McConahay 1986.
66. Cf. Myrdal 1944.
67. Bobo 1983, 1988.
68. Citrin and Green 1990.
69. See Sears and McConahay 1973.
70. Furnivall 1948; M.G. Smith 1965, 1986.
71. Horowitz 1985.
72. See Jenkins, 1986.
73. See McKay 1982; Meadwell 1989.
74. See Barth 1969; LeVine and Campbell 1972.
75. Banton 1983; Hechter 1987; Oberschall 1973.
76. See Esman and Rabinovich 1988; Geertz 1973; Horowitz 1985; McKay 1982; Montville 1990; J. Rothchild 1981; Shils 1957.
77. The following analysis was influenced by readings of general analyses of ethnic group relations by social scientists (especially Horowitz 1985; and Lijphart 1977) and case or comparative analyses which cover a wide range of methods and geographical areas (Amirahmadi 1987; Barth 1969; Ben-Dor 1983; Boucher, Landis and Clark 1987; Coleman and Rusberg 1964; Demaine 1984; Dutter 1990; Esman 1977; Esman and Rabinovich 1988; Glazer and Moynihan 1975; Goldman and Wilson 1984; Hechter 1975; Hunter 1966; Karklins 1986; Kuper and M.G. Smith 1969; Lim 1985; Milne 1981; Montville 1990; Naidu 1980; Paden 1980; D. Rothchild and Olorunsula 1983; J. Rothchild 1981; Schermerhorn 1978; Simpson and Yinger 1985; A.D. Smith 1981; Sugar 1980; Tiryakian and Rogowsky 1985; van den Berghe 1965, 1967, 1981; Williams 1982).
78. Claims for the implementation of the principle of self-determination aim at reducing a group's dependence on other groups regarding the distribution of

resources. It is probably the principle which is most strongly associated with nationalism, in general, and ethnic nationalism, in particular, because it implies the articulation of an ideology which defines group boundaries along *territorial* dimensions. These claims are bound to promote a belief of common fate among ingroup members which, according to research on group dynamics (Cartwright and Zander 1968; Festinger 1950; Thibaut and Kelley 1959), is likely to produce and sharpen psychological group boundaries as well as a consensual definition of the group. Nevertheless, it is not clear from social psychological research whether a subjective definition of group boundaries necessarily implies that these boundaries ought to be territorial. It is possible that such implication is not psychological but rather ideological stemming from the close association in Western political ideologies between "nationhood" and "territorial/political sovereignty" (see Dandeker, chapter 1; and following section in this chapter). Nevertheless, one psychological process which may potentially underlie the "territorial" implications of self-determination claims may be that the psychological definition and legitimization of distinct categorical boundaries is facilitated by the delineation of "visible" physical boundaries.

79. Cf. Moscovici 1976.
80. Cf. Leventhal et al. 1980.
81. See Törnblom 1988, for a similar analysis regarding incompatibility-induced conflict in interpersonal relationships.
82. Blalock 1989; Cohen 1986; Cook and Hegtvedt 1986; Tilly 1978.
83. Horowitz 1985.
84. Azzi, in press; McDonald and Engstrom 1991.
85. Azzi, in press.
86. Cf. Lijphart 1977.
87. Azzi, in press; Azzi and Jost 1992.
88. Azzi and Jost 1992; Lijphart 1977, 1984.
89. Davis 1980; Falk 1981; Hare 1980; Hastie, Penrod and Pennington 1983; Saks 1977.
90. Azzi and Jost 1992.
91. Saks 1977; Hastie et al. 1983.
92. Kaplan and Miller 1987; Miller 1989.
93. Mummenday and Simon 1989.
94. E.g., see Brewer 1979; Brewer and Campbell 1976.
95. See Williams 1982, for separatist cases.
96. Berry 1984.
97. See Fordham 1988, and Robinson 1984, for case analyses.
98. Taylor and McKirnan 1984.
99. Cf. Giles and Johnson 1981; Taylor and McKirnan 1984.
100. Berry 1984.
101. See Giles and Johnson 1981; Haarmann 1987; Jones 1986; Yinger 1981, 1986.
102. Gordon 1964, 1981.
103. Turner et al. 1987.
104. E.g., Geertz 1975; Gellner 1987.
105. This position is evident in the ways in which the political representation of ethnic groups is dealt with in legal and constitutional systems. Analyses of the forms of political representation in multicultural societies (e.g., Lijphart 1977, 1990; Horowitz 1985, 1990, 1991) suggest that, while formal principles for the distribution of political representation are almost universally included in written and unwritten political documents in democratic societies, the representation of

ethnic or cultural groups is not always addressed in these documents. Indeed, in many plural (i.e., multicultural) and democratic societies such principles are absent, unspecified, or explicitly shunned. This lack of specification could be attributed to individualistic political ideologies which are especially pronounced in the case of *ascriptive* groups, notably ethnocultural groups (V. van Dyke 1977). In this ideology (which, in large part, has been spread by Western colonialism; see Kedourie 1988), individuals rather than groups are considered the legitimate loci of rights (May 1987). Indeed, according to such ideologies, citizenship rights are formally given to individuals qua individuals, not to individuals as members of groups, nor to groups qua groups (although, ironically, the deprivation of rights is sometimes based on group membership). By the same token, the individual's citizenship is promoted as the focus of his or her identity vis-à-vis the state; identification of individuals with constituent ascriptive groups is considered to be "primordial" and should, at most, be subordinate to their identification with the superordinate political entity (cf. Geertz 1973, chapter 10; Horowitz 1985, chapter 4). This is clearly illustrated in Ueda's description in this volume of the policies of American governments in the early twentieth century at the height of an immigration wave from Europe. These policies aimed at encouraging the strong civic education of new immigrants, requiring them to learn English, and so forth, with the expectation that the acquisition of citizenship rights should loosen ethnic identification. Nevertheless, his analysis also shows that not all ethnic groups were subjected to the same treatment and allowed to merge into the dominant national culture. Ueda contrasts the relatively harmonious integration of European minorities with that of non-Western immigrants: policymakers believed that the latter are less capable than the former of exercising citizenship and, hence, of being incorporated into the American national culture.

106. Hobsbawm 1990; see Dandeker, ch. 1, this volume.
107. Because, in self-categorization theory, the functional antagonism between different levels of categorization is specifically linked to salience mechanisms, the concept of "category salience" should probably be distinguished from the concept of "strength of identification" (the two terms seem to be confounded in the theory). Thus, one could argue that while "category salience" activates the social identity connected with the salient category, "strength of identification" determines the *threshold* for the activation of a particular category as well as the potential emotional and behavioral consequences of its activation. The stronger the identification with a group, the lower the threshold for the activation of a category and its identity and the higher the emotional value attached to that identity. In addition, strength of identification has a direct effect on the potential for collective action that mere category salience does not. Thus, the stronger the identification, the more likely will the individual choose to remain in the group and engage in collective action (even under conditions where upward mobility through individual exit is possible). But when the identification is weak, individuals are likely to undertake actions that will affirm their *disidentification* with the ingroup, *especially* when the category connected with that identity is salient.
108. Haarmann 1987.
109. This analysis suggests that there may be a qualitative difference in how individuals experience group memberships before and after the creation of explicit, territorial and formal boundaries. The process of "nation-building" (and also of ethnic nationalism) involves a process of explicit definition of the cultural iden-

tity of the group (i.e., *identity* among members and *distinctiveness* from non-members) which, as argued earlier, involves the accentuation of existing inter-group cultural differences and their investment with psychological (emotional) value and "objective" meaning. In contrast, identification in "pre-nationalist" societies did not necessarily involve legal, formal, and explicit definitions of categorical boundaries. Indeed, it is unlikely that individuals in these societies represented themselves as members of coherent and unified cultural entities; rather, they probably saw themselves as belonging to one locale in a constella-tion of locales (villages, towns, regions) which were self-governing but which had informal networks of trade, exchange, and social relationships which made boundaries between them fuzzy at best (Leach 1957). Gellner (1987), in his discussion of Renan's (1882) analysis of what a nation is, sums it up as follows: "Traditional man . . . lacked any concept of 'culture' . . . He knew the gods of his culture, but not the culture itself. In the age of nationalism, all this is changed twice over; the shared culture is revered *directly* and not through the haze of some token, and the entity so revered is diffuse, internally undifferentiated, and insists that a veil of forgetfulness should discreetly cover obscure internal differ-ences" (p. 10).

110. It should be noted, however, that groups which are formed on the basis of acquired rather than ascribed characteristics (e.g., political parties; departments within an institution; professional groups) are likely to be perceived as legiti-mate actors (Lijphart 1977), although not without controversy (see May 1987; J.M. van Dyke 1977). By the same token, a set of individuals perceived as an "aggregate" (e.g., the jury) is likely to be perceived as a more legitimate actor than a set of individuals which is perceived as a group.

111. Blalock 1989; Tilly 1978.

112. Tilly 1978.

113. E.g., Davis 1980; Stasser, Kerr, and Davis 1989.

114. E.g., Davis 1980; Stasser, Kerr, and Davis 1989.

115. E.g., Janis 1982.

116. Stephenson 1978, 1981, 1984.

117. McCarthy and Zald 1977; Oberschall 1973; Olzak 1989; Tilly 1978.

118. See Blalock and Wilken 1979, pp. 442–450; Tilly 1978.

119. Muller 1980.

120. Eckstein 1980.

121. For a similar distinction, see Tilly 1978.

122. Oberschall 1973.

123. Killian 1984; Oberschall 1973.

124. Tilly 1978.

125. Reicher 1982, 1984, 1987, 126. E.g., Hare 1985.

127. Naidu 1980; Tilly 1978.

128. Blalock 1989.

129. The research on minority influence, which is reviewed in this chapter, does not distinguish between influence aimed at the outgroup's constituency and that which is aimed at its leaders.

130. Moscovici 1976, 1980, 1985.

131. Mugny 1982; for a review, see Paicheler 1988; Turner 1991.

132. E.g., McCarthy and Zald 1977; Oberschall 1973; Tilly 1978.

133. Moscovici 1976.

134. For reviews, see Allen 1975; Moscovici 1985.

135. Moscovici 1980.

136. See Latané and Wolf 1981.
137. In this case, the individual who is a target of the majority's influence attempt constitutes a "passive" minority. Presumably, when this minority consists of more than one individual, their concern with their "deviance" would stem from the fact that they do not coordinate with, nor provide support to each other or, in other words, that they do not respond to the influence attempt as a "group" but merely as individuals.
138. Although Moscovici does not deal extensively with the conditions under which majority views and norms may be "internalized," it is important to note that the relative stability of social orders implies a certain degree of internalization of prevailing norms and values. Such internalization is not always the product of coercive pressures by a "majority." Rather, it is most probably the product of long-term socialization processes and of recurrent social communication processes which produce "social representations" that are shared by members of a culture (Farr and Moscovici 1984).
139. Mugny 1982; for a review, see Paicheler 1988.
140. E.g., Mugny, Kaiser, Papastamou, and Pérez 1984.
141. Nemeth and Wachtler 1973; Maass, Clark, and Haberkorn 1982; for a review, see Maass and Clark 1984.
142. E.g., Clark and Maass 1988; Mugny, Kaiser, Papastamou, and Pérez 1984.
143. Martin 1988; Pérez and Mugny 1987; Volpato, Maass, Mucchi-Faina, and Vitti 1990.
144. Turner 1991.
145. Mugny 1982.
146. For distinctions between social categories and groups see Campbell 1958, and Rabbie and Horwitz 1988.
147. A.D. Smith 1982; Taylor and McKirnan 1984; Taylor and Moghaddam 1987.
148. But it is not the only one; see Toch 1965.
149. Horowitz 1985; A.D. Smith 1982.
150. Steele, 1988.
151. Deutsch 1985; Taylor and Moghaddam 1987.
152. Banton 1983; Hechter 1987.
153. Banton 1987; Oberschall 1973.
154. Blalock and Wilken 1979.
155. Gamson 1975; Klandermans 1984.
156. Blalock 1989; Dawes 1980; Hechter 1987; Olson 1971; Wilke, Messick, and Rutte 1986.
157. Toch 1965.
158. Turner et al. 1987.
159. Blalock 1989.
160. Blalock 1989; Martin, Scully, and Levitt 1990.
161. Taylor and McKirnan 1984.
162. Kramer and Brewer 1984, 1986.
163. Messick and Brewer 1983.
164. Hechter et al. 1982; Banton 1987.
165. Laitin.
166. E.g., Gurr 1980.
167. Billig 1976; Deutsch 1973; Taylor and Moghaddam 1987.
168. Moscovici 1976.
169. Horowitz 1985; Lijphart 1977; Montville 1990.

# References

Abeles, R. 1976. "Relative Deprivation, Rising Expectations, and Militancy," *Journal of Social Issues* 32, 119–137.

Adams, J. S. 1965. "Inequity in Social Exchange," in L. Berkowitz (ed.), *Advances in Experimental Social Psychology*, 267–299. New York: Academic Press.

Allen, V.L. 1975. "Social Support for Non-Conformity," in L. Berkowitz (ed.), *Advances in Experimental Social Psychology*, vol. 8, 1–43. New York: Academic Press.

Allen, V. L. and D. A. Wilder. 1975. "Categorization, Belief Similarity, and Group Discrimination," *Journal of Personality and Social Psychology* 32, 971–977.

Amirahmadi, H. 1987. "A Theory of Ethnic Collective Movements and Its Application to Iran," *Ethnic and Racial Studies* 10, 363–391.

Anderson, B. 1983. *Imagined Communities: Reflection on the Origin and Spread of Nationalism*. London: Verso.

Austin, W.G. and J.M. Tobiasen. 1984. "Legal Justice and the Psychology of Conflict Resolution," in R. Folger (ed.), *The Sense of Injustice: Social Psychological Perspectives*, 227–274. New York: Plenum Press.

Austin, W.G. 1986. "Justice in Intergroup Conflict," in S. Worchel and W. G. Austin (eds.), *The Psychology of Intergroup Relations*, 152–175. Chicago: Nelson-Hall.

Azzi, A. (in press). "Procedural Justice and the Allocation of Power in Intergroup Relations: Studies in the United States and South Africa," *Personality and Social Psychology Bulletin*.

Azzi, A. and J.T. Jost. 1992. "Votes without Power: Distribution of Control and Procedural Justice in Majority-Minority Relations," Social/Personality Technical Report no. 5, Yale University. (Manuscript submitted for publication.)

Banton, M. 1983. *Racial and Ethnic Competition*. Cambridge: Cambridge University Press.

Banton, M. 1987. *Racial Theories*. Cambridge: Cambridge University Press.

Barrett-Howard, E. and T.R. Tyler. 1986. "Procedural Justice as a Criterion in Allocation Decisions," *Journal of Personality and Social Psychology* 50, 296–304.

Barth, F., ed. 1969. *Ethnic Groups and Boundaries*. Bergen: Universitetsforlaget.

Ben-Dor, G. 1983. *State and Conflict in the Middle East*. New York: Praeger.

Berkowitz, L. 1962. *Aggression: A Social Psychological Analysis*. New York: McGraw-Hill.

Berkowitz, L. and E. Walster, eds. 1976. *Advances in Experimental Social Psychology*, vol. 9. New York: Academic Press.

Berry, J.W. 1984. "Cultural Relations in Plural Societies: Alternatives to Segregation and their Sociopsychological Implications," in N. Miller and M.B. Brewer (eds.), *Groups in Contact: The Psychology of Desegregation*, 11–27. New York: Academic Press.

Billig, M. 1976. *Social Psychology and Intergroup Relations*. London: Academic Press.

Billig, M. and H. Tajfel. 1973. "Social Categorization and Similarity in Intergroup Behavior," *European Journal of Social Psychology* 3, 27–52.

Blair, I. and A. Azzi. 1992. *Antecedents of Collective Action: Group Permeability and Ingroup Identification*. Paper presented at the Centennial Convention of the American Psychological Association, Washington, D.C.

Blake, R.R., H.A. Shepard, and J.S. Mouton. 1964. *Managing Intergroup Conflict in Industry*. Houston: Gulf.

Blalock, H.M. 1967. *Toward a Theory of Minority Group Relations*. New York: Wiley.

————. 1989. *Power and Conflict: Toward a General Theory*. Newbury Park, CA: Sage.

Blalock, H.M. and P.H. Wilken. 1979. *Intergroup Processes: A Micro-Macro Perspective*. New York: Free Press.

Bobo, L. 1983. "Whites' Opposition to Busing: Symbolic Racism or Realistic Group Conflict," *Journal of Personality and Social Psychology* 45, 1196–1210.

————. 1988. "Group Conflict, Prejudice, and the Paradox of Contemporary Racial Attitudes," in P. Katz and D. Taylor (eds), *Towards the Elimination of Racism: Profile in Controversy*. New York: Plenum.

Bonacich, E. 1972. "A Theory of Ethnic Antagonism: The Split Labor Market." *American Sociological Review* 37, 547–59.

Bornstein, G., L. Crum, J. Wittenbraker, K. Harring, C. Insko, and J. Thibaut. 1983. "On the Measurement of Social Orientations in the Minimal Group Paradigm," *European Journal of Social Psychology* 13, 321–350.

Boucher, J., D. Landis, and K.A. Clark, eds. 1987. *Ethnic Conflict: International Perspectives*. Newbury Park, CA: Sage.

Bourdieu, P. 1979. *La distinction: critique sociale du jugement*. Paris: Les Editions de Minuit.

Branthwaite, A., S. Doyle, and N. Lightbown. 1979. "The Balance between Fairness and Discrimination," *European Journal of Social Psychology* 9, 149–163.

Branthwaite, A. and J.E. Jones. 1975. "Fairness and Discrimination: English versus Welsh," *European Journal of Social Psychology* 5, 323–338.

Brewer, M. B. 1979. "Ingroup Bias in the Minimal Intergroup Situation: A Cognitive-Motivational Analysis," *Psychological Bulletin* 86, 307–324.

————. 1986. "The Role of Ethnocentrism in Intergroup Conflict," in S. Worchel and W.G. Austin (eds.), *Psychology of Intergroup Relations*, 88–102. Chicago: Nelson-Hall.

Brewer, M.B. and D.T. Campbell. 1976. *Ethnocentrism and Intergroup Attitudes: East African Evidence*. New York: Halsted Press.

Brewer, M. B. and R.M. Kramer. 1985. "The Psychology of Intergroup Attitudes and Behavior," *Annual Review of Psychology* 36, 219–243.

Brewer, M.B. and N. Miller. 1984. "Beyond the Contact Hypothesis: Theoretical Perspectives on Desegregation," in N. Miller and M.B. Brewer (eds.), *Groups in Contact: The Psychology of Desegregation*, 281–302. New York: Academic Press.

Brewer, M.B. and M. Silver. 1978. "Ingroup Bias as a Function of Task Characteristics," *European Journal of Social Psychology* 8, 393–400.

Brown, R. 1978. "Divided we Fall: An Analysis of Relations between Sections of a Factory Workforce," in H. Tajfel (ed.), *Differentiation between Social Groups: Studies in the Social Psychology of Intergroup relations*. London: Academic Press.

————. 1988. *Group Processes: Dynamics within and between Groups*. Oxford: Blackwell.

Brown, R. and G. Wade. 1987. "Superordinate Goals and Intergroup Behavior: The Effect of Role Ambiguity and Status on Intergroup Attitudes and Task Performance," *European Journal of Social Psychology* 17, 131–142.

Bruner, J. 1957. "On Perceptual Readiness." *Psychological Review* 64, 123–51.

Caddick, B. 1980. "Equity Theory, Social Identity, and Intergroup Relations," *Review of Personality and Social Psychology* 1, 219–245.

Campbell, D.T. 1958. "Common Fate, Similarity and other Indices of the Status of Aggregates of Persons as Social Entities," *Behavioral Science* 3, 14–25.

————. 1965. "Ethnocentrism and other Altruistic Motives," in D. Levine (ed.), *Nebraska Symposium on Motivation*, vol. 13. Lincoln, NE: University of Nebraska Press.

Cantor, N., W. Mischel, and J. Schwartz, J. 1982. "Social Knowledge: Structure, Content, Use, and Abuse," in A. H. Hastorf and A. M. Isen (eds.), *Cognitive Social Psychology*, 33–72. New York: Elsevier/North Holland.

Caplan, N. 1970. "The New Ghetto Man: A Review of Recent Empirical Studies," *Journal of Social Issues* 26, 59–73.

Cartwright, D. and A. Zander, eds. 1969. *Group Dynamics: Research and Theory*. New York: Harper & Row.

Citrin, J. and Green, D.P. (1990). "The Self-Interest Motive in American Public Opinion," *Research in Micropolitics* 3, 1–28.

Clark, K.D. and M.P. Clark. 1947. "Racial Identification and Preference in Negro Children," in T.M. Newcomb and E.L. Hartley (eds.), *Readings in Social Psychology*. New York: Holt, Rinehart and Winston.

Clark, R.D., III and A. Maass. 1988. "Social Categorization in Minority Influence: The Case of Homosexuality," *European Journal of Social Psychology* 18, 347–364.

Clark, M. 1984. "Record Keeping in Two Types of Relationships," *Journal of Personality and Social Psychology* 47, 549–557.

Cohen, R.L. 1986. "Power and Justice in Intergroup Relations," in H.W. Bierhoff, R.L. Cohen and J. Greenberg (eds.), *Justice in Social Relations*, 65–86. New York: Plenum Press.

Coleman, J.S. and C.G. Rusberg, eds. 1964. *Political Parties and National Integration in Tropical Africa*. Berkeley: University of California Press.

Commins, B. and Lockwood, J. 1979. "The Effects of Status Differences, Favored Treatment, and Equity on Intergroup Comparisons," *European Journal of Social Psychology* 9, 281–289.

Cook, K.S. and K.A. Hegtvedt. 1986. "Justice and Power: An Exchange Analysis," in H.W. Bierhoff, R.L. Cohen, and J. Greenberg (eds.), *Justice in Social Relations*, 19–41). New York: Plenum.

Corenblum, B. and R.C. Annis. 1992. "Development of Racial Identity in Minority Children." Paper presented at the Centennial Convention of the American Psychological Association, Washington, D.C.

Coser, L. 1956. *The Functions of Social Conflict*. New York: Free Press.

————. 1967. *Continuities in the Study of Social Conflict*. New York: Free Press.

Crosby, F. 1976. "A Model of Egoistical Relative Deprivation," *Psychological Review* 83, 85–113.

————. 1982. *Relative Deprivation and Working Women*. New York: Oxford University Press.

Davis, J. 1959. "A Formal Interpretation of the Theory of Relative Deprivation," *Sociometry* 22, 280–296.

Davis, J.H. 1980. "Group Decision and Procedural Justice," in M. Fishbein (ed.), *Progress in Social Psychology*. Hillsdale, NJ: Erlbaum.

Dawes, R.M. 1980. "Social Dilemmas," *Annual Review of Psychology* 31, 169–193.

Demaine, H. 1984. "Furnivall Reconsidered: Plural Societies in Southeast Asia in the Post-Colonial Era," in C. Clarke, D. Ley, and C. Peach (eds.), *Geography and Ethnic Pluralism*. London: Allen & Unwin.

Deschamps, J.C. and R.J. Brown. 1983. "Superordinate Goals and Intergroup Conflict," *British Journal of Social Psychology* 22, 189–195.

Deutsch, M. 1973. *The Resolution of Conflict*. New Haven: Yale University Press.

———. 1975. "Equity, Equality, and Need: What Determines which Value Will Be Used as the Basis of Distributive Justice?" *Journal of Social Issues* 31, 137–149.

———. 1985. *Distributive Justice: A Social-Psychological Perspective*. New Haven: Yale University Press.

Diab, L. 1970. "A Study of Intragroup and Intergroup Relations among Experimentally Produced Small Groups," *Genetic Psychology Monographs* 82, 49–82.

Dibble, U. 1981. "Socially Shared Deprivation and the Approval of Violence: Another Look at the Experience of American Blacks during the 1960s," *Ethnicity* 8, 149–168.

Diehl, M. 1990. "The Minimal Group Paradigm: Theoretical Explanations and Empirical Findings," in W. Stroebe and M. Hewstone (eds.), *European Review of Social Psychology*, vol. 1. New York: Wiley.

Doise, W., G. Csepeli, H.D. Dann, G.C. Gouge, K. Larsen, and A. Ostell. 1972. "An Experimental Investigation into the Formation of Intergroup Representations," *European Journal of Social Psychology* 2, 202–204.

Doise, W. and A. Sinclair. 1973. "The Categorization Process in Intergroup Relations," *European Journal of Social Psychology* 3, 145–157.

Dollard, J.L., L. Doob, N. Miller, O. Mowrer, and R. Sears. 1939. *Frustration and Aggression*. New Haven: Yale University Press.

Doms, M. 1983. "The Minority Influence Effect: An Alternative Approach," in W. Doise and S. Moscovici (eds.), *Current Issues in European Social Psychology*, vol. 1. Cambridge: Cambridge University Press.

Doms, M. and E. Van Avermaet. 1980. "Majority Influence, Minority Influence and Conversion Behavior: A Replication," *Journal of Experimental Social Psychology* 16, 283–292.

———. 1985. "Social Support and Minority Influence: The Innovation Effect Reconsidered," in S. Moscovici, G. Mugny, and E. van Avermaet (eds.), *Perspectives on Minority Influence*, 53–74. Cambridge: Cambridge University Press.

Dovidio, J. and S.L. Gaertner, eds. 1986. *Prejudice, Discrimination, and Racism*. Orlando, FL: Academic Press.

Dubé, L. and S. Guimond. 1986. "Relative Deprivation and Social Protest: The Personal-Group Issue," in J.M. Olson, C.P. Herman, and M.P. Zanna (eds.), *Relative Deprivation and Social Comparison*. Hillsdale, NJ: Lawrence Erlbaum.

Dutter, L.E. 1990. "Ethnic Political Behavior in the Soviet Union," *Journal of Conflict Resolution* 34, 311–334.

Eckstein, H. 1980. "Theoretical Approaches to Explaining Collective Political Violence," in T.R. Gurr (ed.), *Handbook of Political Conflict: Theory and Research*. New York: Free Press.

Ellemers, N. 1991. *Identity Management Strategies: The Influence of Socio-Structural Variables on Strategies of Individual Mobility and Social Change*. Ph.D. diss., Rijksuniversiteit Groningen, The Netherlands.

Esman, M.G., ed. 1977. *Ethnic Conflict in the Western World*. Ithaca, NY: Cornell University Press.

Esman, M.G. and I. Rabinovich. 1988. *Ethnicity, Pluralism, and the State in the Middle East*. Ithaca, NY: Cornell University Press.

Falk, G. 1981. "Unanimity versus Majority Rule in Problem-Solving Groups: A Challenge to the Superiority of Unanimity," *Small Group Behavior* 12, 379–399.

Farr, R. and S. Moscovici, eds. 1984. *Social Representations*. Cambridge: Cambridge University Press.

Ferguson, C.K. and H.H. Kelley. 1964. "Significant Factors in Overevaluation of Own Group's Product," *Journal of Abnormal and Social Psychology* 69, 223–228.

Festinger, L. 1950. "Informal Social Communication," *Psychological Review* 57, 271–82.

———. 1954. "A Theory of Social Comparison Processes," *Human Relations* 7, 117–140.

Foa, E.B. and U.G. Foa. 1980. "Resource Theory: Interpersonal Behavior as Exchange," in K.J. Gergen, M.S. Greenberg, and R.H. Willis (eds.), *Social Exchange: Advances in Theory and Research.* New York: Plenum.

Folger, R. 1977. "Distributive and Procedural Justice: Combined Impact of 'voice' and Improvement on Experienced Inequity," *Journal of Personality and Social Psychology* 35, 137–150.

———. 1986. "A Referent Cognitions Theory of Relative Deprivation," in J.M. Olson, C.P. Herman, and M.P. Zanna (eds.), *Relative Deprivation and Social Comparison.* Hillsdale, NJ: Lawrence Erlbaum.

Fordham, S. 1988. "Racelessness as a Factor in Black Students' School Success: Pragmatic Strategy or Phyrric Victory," *Harvard Educational Review* 58, 54–84.

Freud, S. 1930. *Civilization and its Discontents.* London: Hogarth Press.

Furnivall, J.S. 1948. *Colonial Policy and Practice: A Comparative Study of Burma and Netherlands India.* Cambridge: Cambridge University Press.

Gamson, W. 1975. *Strategy of Social Protest.* Homewood, IL: Boxwood.

Geertz, C. 1973. *The Interpretation of Cultures.* New York: Basic Books.

Gellner, E. 1987. *Culture, Identity, and Politics.* Cambridge: Cambridge University Press.

Giles, H. and P. Johnson. 1981. "The Role of Language in Ethnic Group Relations," in J.C. Turner and H. Giles (eds.), *Intergroup Behavior.* Chicago: University of Chicago Press.

Glazer, N. and D.P. Moynihan, eds. 1975. *Ethnicity: Theory and Experience.* Cambridge: MA: Harvard University Press.

Goethal, G.R. and J.M. Darley. 1987. "Social Comparison Theory: Self-Evaluation and Group Life," in B. Mullen and G.R. Goethals (eds.), *Theories of Group Behavior.* New York: Springer-Verlag.

Goldman, R.B. and A.J. Wilson, eds. 1984. *From Independence to Statehood: Managing Ethnic Conflict in Five African and Asian States.* London: Frances Pinter.

Gordon, M. 1964. *Assimilation in American Life.* New York: Oxford University Press.

———. 1981. "Models of Pluralism: The New American Dilemma," *Annals of the American Academy of Political and Social Science* 454, 178–88.

Greenberg, J. 1983. "Equity and Equality as Clues to the Relationship between Exchange Participants," *European Journal of Social Psychology* 13, 195–196.

Gurr, T.R. 1970. *Why Men Rebel.* Princeton: Princeton University Press.

———. 1980. "Introduction," in T.R. Gurr (ed.), *Handbook of Political Conflict: Theory and Research.* New York: Free Press.

Haarmann, H. 1987. *Language in Ethnicity: A View of Basic Ecological Relations.* Berlin: Mouton de Gruyter.

———, ed. 1981. *Cognitive Processes in Stereotyping and Intergroup Behavior.* Hillsdale, NJ: Erlbaum.

Hamilton, D. L., P.M. Dugan, and T.K. Trolier. 1985. "The Formation of Stereotypic Beliefs: Further Evidence for Distinctiveness-Based Illusory Correlations," *Journal of Personality and Social Psychology* 48, 5–17.

Hare, A.P. 1980. "Consensus versus Majority Vote: A Laboratory Experiment," *Small Group Behavior* 11, 131–143.

———. 1985. *Social Interaction as Drama: Applications from Conflict Resolution.* Beverly Hills: Sage.

Hastie, R., S. Penrod, and N. Pennington. 1983. *Inside the Jury*. Cambridge, MA: Harvard University Press.

Hechter, M. 1975. *Internal Colonialism: The Celtic Fringe in British National Development, 1536–1966*. Berkeley: University of California Press.

————. 1978. "Group Formation and the Cultural Division of Labor," *American Journal of Sociology* 84, 293–318.

————. 1987. *Principles of Group Solidarity*. Berkeley: University of California Press.

Hechter, M., D. Friedman, and M. Appelbaum. 1982. "A Theory of Ethnic Collective Action," *International Migration Review* 16, 412–434.

Hewstone, M. and C. Ward. 1985. "Ethnocentrism and Causal Attribution in Southeast Asia," *Journal of Personality and Social Psychology* 48, 614–623.

Hobsbawm, E.J. 1990. *Nations and Nationalism since 1780*. Cambridge: Cambridge University Press.

Hogg, M.A. and D. Abrams. 1988. *Social Identifications: A Social Psychology of Intergroup Relations and Group Processes*. London: Routledge.

Homans, G. C. 1961. *Social Behavior: Its Elementary Forms*. New York: Harcourt, Brace & World.

Horowitz, D.L. 1985. *Ethnic Groups in Conflict*. Berkeley: University of California Press.

————. 1990. "Making Moderation Pay: The Comparative Politics of Ethnic Conflict Management," in J.V. Montville (ed.), *Conflict and Peacemaking in Multiethnic Societies*. Lexington, MA: D.C. Heath.

————. 1991. *A Democratic South Africa? Constitutional Engineering in a Divided Society*. Cambridge, MA: Harvard University Press.

Hunter, G. 1966. *Southeast Asia: Race, Culture and Nation*. London: Oxford University Press.

Janis, I. 1982. *Groupthink: Psychological Studies of Policy Decisions and Fiascoes*. Boston: Houghton Mifflin.

Jaspars, J. and S. Warnaen. 1982. "Intergroup Relations, Ethnic Identity and Self-Evaluation in Indonesia," in H. Tajfel (ed.), *Social Identity and Intergroup Relations*. Cambridge: Cambridge University Press.

Jenkins, R. 1986. "Social Anthropological Models of Inter-Ethnic Relations," in J. Rex and D. Mason (eds.), *Theories of Race and Ethnic Relations*. Cambridge: Cambridge University Press.

Jones, J.M. 1986. "Racism: A Cultural Analysis of the Problem," in J. Dovidio and S.L. Gaertner (eds.), *Prejudice, Discrimination, and Racism*. Orlando: FL: Academic Press.

Jussim, L., L.M. Coleman, and L. Lerch. 1987. "The Nature of Stereotypes: A Comparison and Integration of Three Theories," *Journal of Personality and Social Psychology* 52, 536–546.

Kahn, A. and A.H. Ryen. 1972. "Factors Influencing the Bias towards One's Own Group," *International Journal of Group Tensions* 2, 33–50.

Kaplan, M.F. and C.E. Miller. 1987. "Group Decision Making and Normative vs. Informational Influence: Effects of Type of Issue and Assigned Decision Rule," *Journal of Personality and Social Psychology* 53, 306–313.

Karklins, R. 1986. *Ethnic Relations in the USSR: The Perspective from Below*. Boston: Allen & Unwin.

Kedourie, E. 1988. "Ethnicity, Majority, and Minority in the Middle East," in M.J. Esman and I. Rabinovich (eds.), *Ethnicity, Pluralism, and the State in the Middle East*. Ithaca, NY: Cornell University Press.

Kelley, H.H. and J. Thibaut. 1978. *Interpersonal Relations: A Theory of Interdependence*. New York: Wiley.

Killian, L.M. 1984. "Organization, Rationality and Spontaneity in the Civil Rights Movement," *American Sociological Review* 49, 770–83.

Kinder, D.R. and D.O. Sears. 1981. "Prejudice and Politics: Symbolic Racism versus Racial Threats to the Good Life," *Journal of Personality and Social Psychology* 40, 414–431.

Kinder, D.R. and D.O. Sears. 1985. "Public Opinion and Political Action," in G. Lindzey and E. Aronson (eds.), *Handbook of social psychology*, vol. 2, 659–742. New York: Random House.

Klandermans, B. 1984. "Social-Psychological Expansions of Resource Mobilization Theory," *American Sociological Review* 49, 770–83.

Kramer, R.M. and M.B. Brewer. 1984. "Effects of Group Identity on Resource Use in a Simulated Commons Dilemma," *Journal of Personality and Social Psychology* 46, 1044–57.

———. 1986. "Social Group Identity and the Emergence of Cooperation in Resource Conservation Dilemmas," in H. Wilke, D. Messick, and C. Rutte (eds.), *Experimental Social Dilemmas*. Frankfurt: Peter Lang.

Kuper, L. and M.G. Smith, eds. 1969. *Pluralism in Africa*. Berkeley: University of California Press.

Lane, R.E. 1988. "Procedural Goods in a Democracy: How One is Treated versus What One Gets," *Social Justice Research*, 2, 177–192.

Lansberg, I. 1984. "Hierarchy as a Mediator of Fairness: A Contingency Approach to Distributive Justice in Organizations," *Journal of Applied Social Psychology* 14, 124–135.

Latané, B. and S. Wolf. 1981. "The Social Impact of Majorities and Minorities," *Psychological Review* 88, 438–453.

LaTour, S. 1978. "Determinants of Participant and Observer Satisfaction with Adversary and Inquisitorial Modes of Adjudication," *Journal of Personality and Social Psychology* 36, 1531–1545.

Lech, E.R. 1957. *Political Systems of Highland Burma*. London: Athlone.

Lerner, M.L. 1975. "The Justice Motive in Social Behavior: Introduction," *Journal of Social Issues* 31, 1–19.

Leung, K. and M.H. Bond. 1984. "The Impact of Cultural Collectivism on Reward Allocation," *Journal of Personality and Social Psychology* 47, 793–804.

Leventhal, G.S. 1980. "What Should Be Done with Equity Theory? New Approaches to the Study of Fairness in Social Relationships," in K.G. Gergen, M.S. Greenberg, and R.H. Willies (eds.), *Social Exchange: Advances in Theory and Research*, 27–55). New York: Plenum Press.

Leventhal, G.S., J. Karuza, Jr., and W.R. Fry. 1980. "Beyond Fairness: A Theory of Allocation Preferences," in G. Mikula (ed.), *Justice and Social Interaction*. New York: Springer-Verlag.

Leventhal, G.S., and D.W. Lane. 1970. "Sex, Age, and Equity Behavior," *Journal of Personality and Social Psychology* 15, 312–316.

LeVine, R.A. and D.T. Campbell. 1972. *Ethnocentrism: Theories of Conflict, Ethnic Attitudes, and Group Behavior*. New York: Wiley.

Lijphart, A. 1977. *Democracy in Plural Societies: A Comparative Exploration*. New Haven, CT: Yale University Press.

———. 1984. *Democracies: Patterns of Majoritarian and Consensus Government in Twenty-one Countries*. New Haven, CT: Yale University Press.

————. 1990. "The Power-Sharing Approach," in J.V. Montville (ed.), *Conflict and Peacemaking in Multiethnic Societies*. Lexington, MA: Lexington Books.

Lim, M.H. 1985. "Affirmative Action, Ethnicity and Integration: The Case of Malaysia." *Ethnic and Racial Studies* 8, 250–276.

Lind, E.A. and T.R. Tyler. 1988. *The Social Psychology of Procedural Justice*. New York: Plenum Press.

Linville, P.W., G.W. Fischer, and P. Salovey. 1989. "Perceived Distributions of the Characteristics of Ingroup and Outgroup Members: Empirical Evidence and a Computer Simulation," *Journal of Personality and Social Psychology* 57, 165–188.

Maass, A. and R.D. Clark, III. 1983. "Internalization versus Compliance: Differential Processes underlying Minority Influence and Conformity," *European Journal of Social Psychology* 13, 197–215.

————. 1984. "Hidden Impact of Minorities: Fifteen Years of Minority Influence Research," *Psychological Bulletin* 95, 428–450.

Maass, A., R.D. Clark, III , and G. Haberkorn. 1982. "The Effects of Differential Ascribed Category Membership and Normal on Minority Influence," *European Journal of Social Psychology* 12, 89–104.

Mackie, D.M., L.T. Worth, and A.G. Asuncion. 1990. "Processing of Persuasive Ingroup Messages," *Journal of Personality and Social Psychology* 58, 812–822.

Major, B. and J.B. Adams. 1983. "Role of Gender, Interpersonal Orientation, and Self-Presentation in Distributive-Justice Behavior," *Journal of Personality and Social Psychology* 45, 598–608.

Major, B. and K. Deaux. 1982. "Individual Differences in Justice Behavior," in J. Greenberg and R.L. Cohen (eds.), *Equity and Justice in Social Behavior*, 43–76. New York: Academic Press.

Martin, R. 1988. "Ingroup and Outgroup Minorities: Differential Impact upon Public and Private Response," *European Journal of Social Psychology* 18, 39–52.

Martin, J. and A. Murray. 1983. "Distributive Injustice and Unfair Exchange," in D.M. Messick and K.S. Cook (eds.), *Equity Theory: Psychological and Sociological Perspectives*, 169–202. New York: Praeger.

————. 1984. "Catalysts for Collective Violence: The Importance of a Psychological Approach," in R. Folger (ed.), *The Sense of Injustice: Social Psychological Perspectives*, 95–139. New York: Plenum Press.

Martin, J., M. Scully, and B. Levitt. 1990. "Injustice and the Legitimation of Revolution: Damning the Past, Excusing the Present, and Neglecting the Future," *Journal of Personality and Social Psychology* 59, 281–290.

May, L. 1987. *The Morality of Groups: Collective Responsibility, Group-Based Harm, and Corporate Rights*. Notre Dame, IN: University of Notre Dame Press.

McCarthy, J.D. and M.N. Zald. 1977. "Resource Mobilization and Social Movement: A Partial Theory," *American Journal of Sociology* 82, 1212–41.

McCauley, C., C.L. Stitt, and M. Segal. 1980. "Stereotyping: From Prejudice to Prediction," *Psychological Bulletin* 87, 195–208.

McConahay, J.B. 1986. "Modern Racism, Ambivalence, and the Modern Racism Scale," in J.F. Dovidio and S.L. Gaertner (eds.), *Prejudice, Discrimination, and Racism*. Orlando, FL: Academic Press.

McCready, W., ed. 1983. *Culture, Ethnicity, and Identity: Current Issues in Research*. New York: Academic Press.

McDonald, M.D. and R.L. Engstrom. 1991. "Minority Representation and City Council Electoral Systems: A Black and Hispanic Comparison," in A.M. Messina, L.R.

Fraga, L.A. Rhodebeck, and F.D. Wright (eds.), *Ethnic and Racial Minorities in the Advanced Industrial Democracies*. Westport, CT: Greenwood Press.

McKay, J. 1982. "An Exploratory Synthesis of Primordial and Mobilizational Approaches to Ethnic Phenomena," *Ethnic and Race Relations* 5, 395–420.

Mead, G.H. 1934. *Mind, Self, and Society*. Chicago: University of Chicago Press.

Meadwell, H. 1989. "Cultural and Instrumental Approaches to Ethnic Nationalism," *Ethnic and Racial Studies* 12, 309–28.

Messé, L.A., R.W. Hymes, and R.J. MacCoun. 1986. "Group Categorization and Distributive Justice Decisions," in H.W. Bierhoff, R.L. Cohen, and J. Greenberg (eds.), *Justice in Social Relations*. New York: Plenum.

Messick, D.M. and M.B. Brewer. 1983. "Solving Social Dilemmas: A Review," in L. Wheeler and P. Shaver (eds.), *Review of Personality and Social Psychology*. Beverly Hills: Sage.

Messick, D.M. and D. Mackie. 1989. "Intergroup Relations," *Annual Review of Psychology* 40, 45–81.

Miller, C.E. 1989. "The Social Psychological Effects of Group Decision Rules," in P.B. Paulus (ed.), *Psychology of Group Influence*. Hillsdale, NJ: Lawrence Erlbaum.

Mills, J. and M.S. Clark. 1982. "Exchange and Communal Relationships," in L. Wheeler (ed.), *Review of Personality and Social Psychology*, vol. 3. Beverly Hills: Sage.

Milne, R.S. 1981. *Politics in Ethnically Bipolar States*. Vancouver: University of British Columbia Press.

Montville, J., ed. 1990. *Conflict and Peacemaking in Multiethnic Societies*. Lexington, MA: D.C. Heath.

Moscovici, S. 1976. *Social Influence and Social Change*. London: Academic Press.

———. 1980. "Toward a Theory of Conversion Behavior," in L. Berkowitz (ed.), *Advances in Experimental Social Psychology*, vol. 13, 209–239. New York: Academic Press.

———. 1985. "Social Influence and Conformity," in G. Lindzey and E. Aronson (eds.), *Handbook of Social Psychology*, vol. 2, 347–412. New York: Random House.

Moscovici, S., E. Lage, and M. Naffrechoux. 1969. "Influence of a Consistent Minority on the Responses of a Majority in a Color Perception Task," *Sociometry* 32, 365–379.

Moscovici, S. and B. Personnaz. 1980. "Studies in Social Influence 5: Minority Influence and Conversion Behavior in a Perceptual Task," *Journal of Experimental Social Psychology* 16, 270–282.

Mugny, G. 1975. "Negotiations, Image of the Other and the Process of Minority Influence," *European Journal of Social Psychology* 5, 209–228.

———. 1982. *The Power of Minorities*. London: Academic Press.

———. 1984. "Compliance, Conversion and the Asch Paradigm," *European Journal of Social Psychology* 14, 353–368.

Mugny, G., C. Kaiser, S. Papastamou, and J. Pérez. 1984. "Intergroup Relations, Identification and Social Influence," *British Journal of Social Psychology* 23, 317–322.

Muller, E.N. 1980. "The Psychology of Political Protest and Violence," in T.R. Gurr (ed.), *Handbook of Political Conflict: Theory and Research*. New York: Free Press.

Mummendey, A. and B. Simon. 1989. "Better or Different? Part 3: The Impact of Importance of Comparison Dimension and Relative Ingroup Size upon Intergroup Discrimination," *British Journal of Social Psychology* 28, 1–16.

Myrdal, G. 1944. *An American Dilemma: The Negro Problem and Modern Democracy*. New York: Harper.

Nagata, D. and F. Crosby. 1990. "Comparisons, Justice, and the Internment of Japanese Americans." Paper presented at the Thirteenth Annual Meeting of the International Society of Political Psychology, Washington, D.C.

Naidu, R. 1980. *The Communal Edge to Plural Societies: India and Malaysia.* Sahibabad, India: Vikas.

Nemeth, C. 1985. "Compromising Public Influence for Private Change," in S. Moscovici, G. Mugny, and E. van Avermaet (eds), *Perspectives on Minority Influence*, 75–90. Cambridge: Cambridge University Press.

———. 1986. "Differential Contributions of Majority and Minority Influence," *Psychological Review* 93, 23–32.

Nemeth, C., M. Swedlund, and B. Kanki. 1974. "Patterning of Minority's Responses and their Influence on the Majority," *European Journal of Social Psychology* 4, 53–64.

Nemeth, C. and J. Wachtler. 1973. "Consistency and Modification of Judgment," *Journal of Experimental Social Psychology* 9, 65–79.

———. 1983. "Creative Problem Solving as a Result of Majority vs. Minority Influence," *European Journal of Social Psychology* 13, 45–55.

Ng, S.H. 1981. "Equity Theory and the Allocation of Rewards between Groups," *European Journal of Social Psychology* 11, 439–444.

———. 1984. "Power and Intergroup Discrimination," in H. Tajfel (ed.), *The Social Dimension: European Developments in Social Psychology*, 179–206. Cambridge: Cambridge University Press.

———. 1986. "Equity, Intergroup Bias and Interpersonal Bias in Reward Allocation," *European Journal of Social Psychology* 16, 239–255.

Oberschall, A. 1973. *Social Conflict and Social Movements.* Englewood Cliffs, NJ: Prentice-Hall.

Olson, J.M., C.P. Herman, and M.P. Zanna, eds. 1986. *Relative Deprivation and Social Comparison.* Hillsdale, NJ: Lawrence Erlbaum.

Olson, M. 1971. *The Logic of Collective Action.* Cambridge: Harvard University Press.

Olzak, S. 1989. "Analysis of Events in the Study of Collective Action," *Annual Review of Sociology* 15, 119–41.

Paden, J.N., ed. 1980. *Values, Identities, and National Integration: Empirical Research in Africa.* Evanston, IL: Northwestern University Press.

Paicheler, G. 1988. *The Psychology of Social Influence.* Cambridge: Cambridge University Press.

Pepitone, A.P. and H. Triandis. 1988. "On the Universality of Social Psychological Theories," *Journal of Crosscultural Psychology* 18, 471–498.

Pérez, J. and G. Mugny. 1987. "Paradoxical Effects of Categorization in Minority Influence: When Being an Outgroup is an Advantage," *European Journal of Social Psychology* 17, 157–169.

Personnaz, B. 1981. "Study in Social Influence Using the Spectrometer Method: Dynamics of the Phenomena of Conversion and Covertness in Perceptual Responses," *European Journal of Social Psychology* 11, 431–438.

Platow, M.J., C.G. McClintock, and W.B.G. Liebrand. 1990. "Predicting Intergroup Fairness and Ingroup Bias in the Minimal Group Paradigm," *European Journal of Social Psychology* 20, 221–40.

Rabbie, J.M., F. Benoist, H. Oosterbaan, and L. Visser. 1974. "Differential Power and Effects of Expected Competitive and Cooperative Intergroup Interaction on Intragroup and Outgroup Attitudes," *Journal of Personality and Social Psychology* 30, 46–56.

Rabbie, J.M. and M. Horwitz. 1988. "Categories versus Groups as Explanatory Concepts in Intergroup Relations," *European Journal of Social Psychology* 18, 117–123.

Rabbie, J.M., J.C. Schot, and L. Visser. 1989. "Social Identity Theory: A Conceptual and Empirical Critique from the Perspective of a Behavioural Interaction Model," *European Journal of Social Psychology* 19, 171–202.

Rabbie, J.M. and G. Wilkens. 1971. "Intergroup Competition and Its Effect on Intragroup and Intergroup Relations," *European Journal of Social Psychology* 1, 215–234.

Reicher, S. 1982. "The Determination of Collective Behaviour," in H. Tajfel (ed.), *Social Identity and Intergroup Relations*, 41–84. Cambridge: Cambridge University Press.

———. 1984. "The St. Paul Riot: An Explanation of the Limits of Crowd Action in Terms of a Social Identity Model," *European Journal of Social Psychology* 14, 1–21.

———. 1987. "Crowd Behavior as Social Action," in J.C. Turner, *Rediscovering the Social Group: A Self-Categorization Theory*, 171–202. Oxford: Basil Blackwell.

Reis, H. 1986. "Interest in Interpersonal Justice," in H.W. Bierhoff, R.L. Cohen, and J. Greenberg (eds.), *Justice in Social Relations*. New York: Plenum.

Renan, E. 188). "Qu'est-ce qu'une nation?" In *Oeuvres complètes de Ernest Renan*, tome 1. Paris: Calmann-Levy.

Robinson, V. 1984. "Asians in Britain: A Study in Encapsulation and Marginality," in C. Clarke, D. Ley, and C. Peach (eds.), *Geography and Ethnic Pluralism*. London: Allen & Unwin.

Rothbart, M., R. Dawes, and B. Park. 1984. "Stereotyping and Sampling Biases in Intergroup Perception," in J.R. Eiser (ed.), *Attitudinal Judgment*, 109–134. New York: Springer-Verlag.

Rothchild, J. 1981. *Ethnopolitics: A Conceptual Framework*. New York: Columbia University Press.

Rothchild, D. 1986. "Interethnic Conflict and Policy Analysis in Africa," *Ethnic and Racial Studies* 9, 66–86.

Rothchild, D. and V. Olorunsula, eds. 1983. *State versus Ethnic Claims: African Policy Dilemmas*. Boulder: Westview.

Runciman, W.G. 1966. *Relative Deprivation and Social Justice: A Study of Attitudes to Social Inequality in Twentieth-Century England*. Berkeley: University of California Press.

Ryen, A.H. and A. Kahn. 1975. "Effects of Intergroup Orientation on Group Attitudes and Proxemic Behavior," *Journal of Personality and Social Psychology* 31, 302–310.

Saks, M.J. 1977. *Jury Verdicts*. Lexington, MA: Heath.

Sampson, E.E. 1975. "On Justice as Equality," *Journal of Social Issues* 31, 45–63.

———. 1983. *Justice and the Critique of Pure Psychology*. New York: Plenum Press.

———. 1986. "Justice Ideology and Social Legitimation: A Revised Agenda for Psychological Inquiry," in H.W. Bierhoff, R.L. Cohen and J. Greenberg (eds.), *Justice in Social Relations*, 87–102. New York: Plenum Press.

Schermerhorn, R.A. 1978. *Comparative Ethnic Relations: A Framework for Theory and Research*. Chicago: University of Chicago Press.

Schwinger, T. 1980. "Just Allocations of Goods: Decisions among Three Principles," in G. Mikula (ed.), *Justice and Social Interaction*, 95–125. Bern: Huber.

———. 1986. "The Need Principle of Distributive Justice," in H.W. Bierhoff, R.L. Cohen, and J. Greenberg (eds.), *Justice in Social Relations*. New York: Plenum.

Sears, D.O. 1988. "Symbolic Racism," in P. Katz and D. Taylor (eds.), *Towards the Elimination of Racism: Profile in Controversy*. New York: Plenum.

Sears, D.O. and J.B. McConahay. 1973. *The Politics of Violence: The New Urban Blacks and the Watts Riot*. Boston, MA: Houghton Mifflin.

Sherif, M. and Sherif, C. W. 1953. *Groups in Harmony and Tension*. New York: Harper.

Sherif, M. 1966. *In Common Predicament: Social Psychology of Intergroup Conflict and Cooperation*. Boston, MA: Houghton Mifflin.

Sherif, M., O.J. Harvey, B.J. White, W.R. Hood, and C.W. Sherif. [1961] 1988. *Intergroup Conflict and Cooperation: The Robbers' Cave Experiment*. Middletown, CT: Wesleyan University Press.

Shils, E.A. 1957. "Primordial, Personal, Sacred and Civil Ties: Some Particular Observations of Sociological Research and Theory," *British Journal of Sociology* 8, 130–45.

Simmel, G. 1955. *Conflict and the Web of Group Affiliations*, translated by K.H. Wolff and R. Bendix. Glencoe, IL: The Free Press.

Simpson, G.E. and J.M. Yinger. 1985. *Racial and Cultural Minorities: An Analysis of Prejudice and Discrimination*. New York: Plenum.

Skevington, S. 1980. "Intergroup Relations and Social Change within a Nursing Context," *British Journal of Social and Clinical Psychology* 9, 201–213.

Smith, A. D. 1981. *The Ethnic Revival in the Modern World*. Cambridge: Cambridge University Press.

———. 1982. "Nationalism, Ethnic Separatism and the Intelligentsia," in C.H. Williams (ed.), *National Separatism*. Cardiff: University of Wales Press.

Smith, M.G. 1965. *The Plural Society in the British West Indies*. Berkeley: University of California Press.

———. 1986. "Pluralism, Race and Ethnicity in Selected African Countries," in J. Rex and D. Mason (eds.), *Theories of Race and Ethnic Relations*. Cambridge: Cambridge University Press.

Stasser, G., N.L. Kerr, and J.H. Davis. 1989. "Influence Processes and Consensus Models in Decision-making Groups," in P.B. Paulus (ed.), *Psychology of Group Influence*, 2d. ed. Hillsdale, NJ: Lawrence Erlbaum.

Steele, C. 1988. "The Psychology of Self-Affirmation: Sustaining the Integrity of the Self," in L. Berkowitz (ed.), *Advances in Experimental Social Psychology*, vol. 21, 261–302. New York: Academic Press.

Stephan, W. G. 1985. "Intergroup Relations," in G. Lindzey and E. Aronson (eds.), *Handbook of Social Psychology*, vol. 2, 599–658). New York: Random House.

Stephenson, G.M. 1978. "Interparty and Interpersonal Exchange in Negotiating Groups," in H. Brandstätter, J.H. Davis, and H. Schuler (eds.), *Dynamics of Group Decisions*. Beverly Hills: Sage.

———. 1981. "Intergroup Bargaining and Negotiation," in J.C. Turner and H. Giles (eds.), *Intergroup Behaviour*. Oxford: Blackwell.

———. 1984. "Intergroup and Interpersonal Dimensions of Bargaining and Negotiation," in H. Tajfel (ed.), *The Social Dimension: European Developments in Social Psychology*, vol. 2. Cambridge: Cambridge University Press.

Stroebe, W., A.W. Kruglanski, D. Bar-Tal, and M. Hewstone, eds. 1988. *The Social Psychology of Intergroup Conflict*. Berlin: Springer-Verlag.

Sugar, P., ed. 1980. *Ethnic Diversity and Conflict in Eastern Europe*. Santa Barbara: ABC-Clio.

Tajfel, H. 1959. "The Anchoring Effects of Value in a Scale of Judgments," *British Journal of Psychology* 50, 294–304.

————. 1974. "Social Identity and Intergroup Behaviour," *Social Science Information* 19, 65–93.

————. 1981. *Human Groups and Social Categories*. Cambridge: Cambridge University Press.

————. 1982a. "Social Psychology of Intergroup Relations," *Annual Review of Psychology* 33, 1–39.

————, ed. 1982b. *Social Identity and Intergroup Relations*. Cambridge: Cambridge University Press.

————. 1984. "Intergroup Relations, Social Myths and Social Justice in Social Psychology," in H. Tajfel (ed.), *The Social Dimension: European Developments in Social Psychology*, 695–715. Cambridge: Cambridge University Press.

Tajfel, H., C. Flament, M. Billig, and R.F. Bundy. 1971. "Social Categorization and Intergroup Behaviour," *European Journal of Social Psychology* 1, 149–177.

Tajfel, H. and J.C. Turner. 1986. "The Social Identity Theory of Intergroup Behavior," in S. Worchel and W. G. Austin (eds.), *The Psychology of Intergroup Relations*, 7–24. Chicago: Nelson-Hall.

Tanford, S. and S. Penrod. 1984. "Social Influence Model: A Formal Integration of Research on Majority and Minority Influence Processes," *Psychological Bulletin* 95, 189–225.

Taylor, S.E., S.T. Fiske, N.L. Etkoff, and A.J. Ruderman. 1978. "Categorical and Contextual Bases of Person Memory and Stereotyping," *Journal of Personality and Social Psychology* 36, 778–793.

Taylor, D.M. and D.J. McKirnan. 1984. "A Five-Stage Model of Intergroup Relations," *British Journal of Social Psychology* 23, 291–300.

Taylor, D.M. and F.M. Moghaddam. 1987. *Theories of Intergroup Relations: International Social Psychological Perspectives*. New York: Praeger.

Taylor, D.M., S.C. Wright, F.H. Moghaddam, and R.N. Lalonde. 1990. "The Personal/Group Discrimination Discrepancy: Perceiving My Group, but Not Myself, To Be a Target for Discrimination," *Personality and Social Psychology Bulletin* 16, 241–253.

Thibaut, J. and H.H. Kelley. 1959. *The Social Psychology of Groups*. New York: Wiley.

Thibaut, J. and L. Walker. 1975. *Procedural Justice: A Psychological Analysis*. Hillsdale, NJ: Erlbaum.

Tilly, Charles. 1978. *From Mobilization to Revolution*. Reading, MA: Addison-Wesley.

Tiryakian, E.A. and R. Rogowski, eds. 1985. *New Nationalisms of the Developed West*. Boston: Allen & Unwin.

Toch, H. 1965. *The Social Psychology of Social Movements*. New York: Bobbs-Merrill.

Törnblom, K.Y. 1988. "Positive and Negative Allocations: A Typology and Model for Conflicting Justice Principles," in E.J. Lawler and B. Markovsky (eds.), *Advances in Group Processes* 5, 141–168.

Törnblom, K.Y., D. Jonsson, and U.G. Foa. 1985. "Nationality, Resource Class, and Preferences among Three Allocation Rules: Sweden vs. USA," *International Journal of Intercultural Relations* 9, 51–77.

Tripathy, R.C. and R. Srivastava. 1981. "Relative Deprivation and Intergroup Attitudes," *European Journal of Social Psychology* 11, 313–18.

Turner, J. C. 1975. "Social Comparison and Social Identity: Some Prospects for Intergroup Behaviour," *European Journal of Social Psychology* 5, 5–34.

————. 1978. "Social Comparison, Similarity, and Ingroup Favoritism," in H. Tajfel (ed.), *Differentiation between Social Groups: Studies in the Social Psychology of Intergroup Relations*, 235–250). London: Academic Press.

———. 1981. "The Experimental Social Psychology of Intergroup Behaviour," in J. C. Turner and H. Giles (eds.), *Intergroup Behavior*, 66–101. Chicago, IL.: University of Chicago Press.

———. 1991. *Social Influence*. Buckingham: Open University Press.

Turner, J.C. with M.A. Hogg, P.J. Oakes, S. Reicher, and M.S. Wetherell. 1987. *Rediscovering the Social Group: A Self-Categorization Theory*. Oxford: Basil Blackwell.

Tyler, T. 1984. "Justice in the Political Arena," in R. Folger (ed.), *The Sense of Injustice: Social Psychological Perspectives*, 189–226. New York: Plenum Press.

Tyler, T.R. 1989. "The Psychology of Procedural Justice: A Test of the Group-Value Model," *Journal of Personality and Social Psychology* 57, 830–838.

———. 1990. *Why People Obey the Law*. New Haven, CT: Yale University Press.

Vaughan, G.M. 1964. "Ethnic Awareness in Relation to Minority-Group Membership," *Journal of Genetic Psychology* 105, 119–30.

van den Berghe, P.L. 1965. *South Africa: A Study in Conflict*. Middleton, CT: Wesleyan University Press.

———. 1967. *Race and Racism: A Comparative Perspective*. New York: Wiley.

———. 1981. *The Ethnic Phenomenon*. New York: Elsevier Press.

van Dyke, J.M. 1977. *Jury Selection Procedures*. Cambridge, MA: Ballinger.

van Dyke, V. 1977. "The Individual, the State, and Ethnic Communities in Political theory," *World Politics* 29, 350–57.

van Knippenberg, A.F.M. 1978. "Status Differences, Comparative Relevance and Intergroup Differentiation," in H. Tajfel (ed.), *Differentiation between Social Groups: Studies in the Social Psychology of Intergroup Relations*. London: Academic Press.

van Knippenberg, A.F.M. and H. van Oers. 1984. "Social Identity and Equity Concerns in Intergroup Perceptions," *British Journal of Social Psychology* 23, 351–61.

Vanneman, R.D. and T.F. Pettigrew. 1972. "Race and Relative Deprivation in the United States," *Race* 13, 461–486.

Volpato, C., A. Maass, A. Mucchi-Faina, and E. Vitti. 1990. "Minority Influence and Social Categorization," *European Journal of Social Psychology* 20, 119–132.

Walker, L., S. LaTour, E.A. Lind, and J. Thibaut. 1974. "Reactions of Participants and Observers to Modes of Adjudication," *Journal of Applied Social Psychology* 4, 295–310.

Walker, I. and T.F. Pettigrew. 1984. "Relative Deprivation Theory: An Overview and Conceptual Critique," *British Journal of Social Psychology* 23, 301–310.

Walster, E., E. Berscheid, and G.W. Walster. 1973. "New Directions in Equity Research," *Journal of Personality and Social Psychology* 35, 151–176.

Walster, E., G.W. Walster, and E. Berscheid. 1978. *Equity: Theory and Research*. Boston, MA: Allyn & Bacon.

Watts, B.L., L.A. Messé, and R.R. Vallacher. 1982. "Towards Understanding Sex Differences in Pay Allocations: Agency, Communion, and Reward Distribution Behavior," *Sex Roles* 8, 1175–1188.

Wilder, D. A. 1981. "Perceiving Persons as a Group: Categorization and Intergroup Relations," in D. Hamilton (ed.), *Cognitive Processes in Stereotyping and Intergroup Perception*, 213–257. Hillsdale, NJ: Erlbaum.

Wilder, D. 1986. "Social Categorization: Implications for Creation and Reduction of Intergroup Bias," *Advances in Experimental Social Psychology* 19, 292–355.

Wilke, H.A.M., D.M. Messick, and C.G. Rutte, eds. 1986. *Experimental Social Dilemmas*. Frankfurt am Main: Verlag Peter Lang.

Williams, C.H., ed. 1980. *National Separatism*. Cardiff: University of Wales Press.

Wilson, W. and N. Miller. 1961. "Shifts in Evaluations of Participants following Intergroup Competition," *Journal of Abnormal and Social Psychology* 63, 428–431.

Wilson, W. and M. Kayatani. 1968. "Intergroup Attitudes and Strategies in Games between Opponents of the Same or of a Different Race," *Journal of Personality and Social Psychology* 9, 24–30.

Wright, S.C., D.M. Taylor, and F.M. Moghaddam. 1990. "Responding to Membership in a Disadvantaged Group: From Acceptance to Collective Protest," *Journal of Personality and Social Psychology* 58, 994–1003.

Yinger, J.M. 1981. "Toward a Theory of Assimilation and Dissimilation," *Ethnic and Racial Studies* 4, 249–64.

———. 1986. "Intersecting Strands in the Theorization of Race and Ethnic Relations," in J. Rex and D. Mason (eds.), *Theories of Race and Ethnic Relations*. Cambridge: Cambridge University Press.

# 4

# Status Changes and Ethnic Conflict in Twentieth-Century America

*Reed Ueda*

The American polity accommodated marginal ethnic groups in the twentieth century by managing changes in status. The relations among groups were inescapably affected. By focusing on the historical social context in which status change and group relations interacted, this chapter shows how forms of status promoted tendencies toward intergroup discord, conflict, and violence. Changes in types of status influenced periodic trends toward a ranked ethnic order in which class and ethnicity were coincident, or an unranked ethnic order in which groups cut across class.[1] This inquiry reviews how a historic ranked order was created in the early-twentieth-century United States and moved toward an unranked order after World War II. It examines the historical roles in this transition of three major types of status—hierarchical differential status, universal liberal citizenship, and official group rights—and their effect on ethnic coexistence.

## The Differentiation of Ethnic Status and Group Inequality

In the early twentieth century, government created a structure of differentiated status that reinforced a ranked ethnic order. This process was reflected in the unfolding of four regional patterns of ethnic relations.[2] The historic federalism in the American polity formed the basic condition that gave rise to different local arrangements of ethnic relations. Principally shaped by the assimilation of the European immigrant population, the northern pattern expanded the republican ideal that government would relate to ethnic communities through universal citizenship and the liberal ideal of equal opportunity for individuals. The southern pattern was based on legal biracial segregation of whites and blacks. The western and territorial patterns rested on multiracial gradations among whites, Hispanics, American Indians, Asians, and Pacific Islanders. The southern, western, and territorial ethnic patterns embodied the conception of a polity of different status groups rather than one based on a unitary political community of homogeneous citizens.[3]

In the early twentieth century, government imposed inferior legal status on ethnic minority groups through policies that governed immigration, naturalization, segregation, and annexation. These status compartments often reinforced low socioeconomic position. They included aliens ineligible for citizenship, guestworkers, tribal citizens, territorial nationals, territorial citizens, and racial caste. This involved the elaboration of a status-divided society into a fully enfranchised white community and an array of status-deficit groups among black, Mexican, Asian, American Indian, and territorial peoples. Particularly in the southern, western, and territorial patterns, laws increasingly drew "a color line" depriving non-European minorities of equality of opportunity.[4] Prevailing ideas of the enduring dependency of non-Western peoples and their cultural indisposition to modernization were used to justify the legal segmentation of the ethnic order.[5] Racial minorities were placed on the margins of the central arena of nation building.[6]

The creation of a system of differentiated ethnic status came through a variety of mechanisms. Immigration and naturalization law admitted to American nationality peoples from Europe and Middle Eastern areas such as Armenia and Syria, officially treating these groups as a single white racial category. However, immigrants from outside northern and western Europe received lesser rights to admissions and indirectly diminished access to American nationality. Asian immigrants were the most restricted in admissions and completely barred from naturalization. In the South, the "Jim Crow" system of segregation and disfranchisement confined blacks to a legally ascribed inferior caste.[7] In the West and Pacific territories, the ban on naturalization of Asian immigrants placed the first generation in a status compartment of permanent alienage.[8] Although Mexicans had the opportunity to naturalize, American immigration policy induced mass alienage in the Mexican population by permitting unlimited transient labor migration and by recruiting Mexican guestworkers. Mexican Americans experienced the lowest rate of naturalization of all immigrant groups.[9] Guestworker programs produced the persistence and reentry of illegal aliens who had no American status at all.

The expansion of the United States beyond its continental limits posed new problems for the meaning of American nationality. The peoples inhabiting Alaska, Hawaii, the Philippines, Puerto Rico, and other possessions had to be included within a more complex framework of statutes. Congress made Alaska, acquired in 1867, and Hawaii, annexed in 1898, "incorporated territories" or areas in which the Constitution was effective. The inhabitants of these territories who formerly owed allegiance to another government became citizens of the United States upon incorporation of those territories. The political and civil status of the inhabitants of the Philippines and Puerto Rico, acquired by cession in 1898, posed more serious difficulties, because lawmakers and judges believed that these peoples were incapable of exercising citizenship.[10] In the *Insular Cases* of 1901–1903, the Supreme Court decided that the Philippines and Puerto Rico had never been incorporated by the United States but were "appurtenant thereto as a possession." The inhabitants of these regions were neither aliens nor U. S. citizens; they were U. S. "nationals" who owed allegiance to the United States government, were permitted to enter and leave the United States, and were entitled to its protection. These nationals soon became citizens of the territories in which they resided. In 1900 Congress made Puerto Rican inhabitants "citizens of Puerto Rico" and in 1902 it made Philippine inhabitants "citizens of the Philippine Islands." In 1917 Congress conferred American citizenship upon those persons made citizens of Puerto Rico by the act of 1900.[11] Inhabitants of the Virgin Islands were granted U. S. citizenship in 1927. Inhabitants of other unincorporated territories received less favorable treatment. Congress did not assign a positive status to indigenous inhabitants of Guam, Samoa, and the Panama Canal Zone. These people were considered simply "inhabitants of Guam, Samoa, or the Canal Zone entitled to the protection of the United States," with rights left unsecured.[12]

In the first half of this century, the high rate of alienage among

Asians and Mexicans exposed these groups to disadvantages in an age of growing distance between aliens and citizens.[13] Public policies restricting employment, welfare, residency, and property rights of aliens struck hard at Mexicans and Asians. Also, because unions excluded aliens from membership, Asian and Mexican immigrant workers failed to gain representation in industrial politics.[14]

The rights of Asian, Mexican, and Indian citizens for equal access to social and economic institutions remained limited. Asians in California and Hawaii and Mexicans in Texas were at various times segregated in separate public schools.[15] Although less consistently than southern blacks, Asians in California and Mexicans in Texas were excluded from public accommodations. The Dawes Severalty Act of 1887 provided for the naturalization of Indians who left tribal society, but most remained in reservations as members of a separate subject nation. Indians received general citizenship in 1924, but they were still identified with a tribal community and were geographically segregated.[16] Furthermore, public authorities acquiesced in private and customary discrimination against Asians, Mexicans, and Indians who had become citizens.

During the multiplication of differential ethnic status, government adhered to the historical tradition of staying out of the management of ethnic institutions and group life. This was a social policy of nonintervention parallel to the economic policy of laissez-faire. Government of institutions desisted from involvement in programs of ethnocultural maintenance or group socioeconomic advancement. (The major exception to this policy was the federal management of Indian reservations.) Ethnic nonintervention can be seen as a corollary to the historic republican tradition of the disestablishment of organized religion and its institutions.

In the early twentieth century, differential ethnic status was related to intergroup conflict in complex ways. It is well to remember that groups in the era had newly come into contact with each other and were from very different backgrounds. The newer groups in the nation were poorer than settled groups and culturally distant. Moreover, government's laissez-faire stance toward ethnic relations meant that it was willing to countenance socioeconomic inequality and customary discrimination. Officials did little to foster a racially inclusive civic consciousness. Under these conditions of intergroup encounter, differential ethnic status reinforced intolerance and social inequality.

Certain social conditions, however, mitigated the effects of differential status. The expansiveness of the American economy may have buffered the social inequality reinforced by the use of status to separate groups. In fact, socioeconomic niches existed for Asian groups who suffered from the most severe discrimination and status disadvantages so that they were actually able to gain independence and upward social mobility.

Furthermore, differential status may have actually reduced the potential for group conflict to reach more destructive or violent levels. By segregating ethnic and racial minorities in a time of intolerance, it avoided a single arena for racial competition in which whites might have been tempted to use more radical and harmful means to dominate minorities. This outcome seems to be particularly evident in the turn-of-the-century American south.[17] Differential status reinforced an equilibrium between social inequality and social order.

Nevertheless, the status system that supported a ranked ethnic order contributed to the potential for intergroup violence. Differentiated status turned groups against each other in defense of their hierarchical interests and position. Violent and destructive acts against outsiders were committed to enforce the rules of subordination and mores of racial supremacy.[18] In degrees that varied by local case, the need to express group hegemony underlay particular acts of violence. The outstanding example of recurrent and organized violence that expressed Anglo-Saxon Protestant supremacy was the Southern tradition of lynching blacks.[19] From 1882 to 1931, over 4,500 blacks died by lynching, mostly in the South.[20]

Immigrants were not immune from violent and fatal attacks. In 1899, a mob lynched five Sicilian storekeepers; in 1914, Leo Frank, a second-generation American Jew, was lynched by a mob in Georgia; in 1918, in southern Illinois, angry miners lynched a German alien. In West Frankfort, Illinois, a mob invaded an Italian neighborhood, beating people and burning buildings for three days during August 1920. Later in the 1920s, the Ku Klux Klan terrorized Italians and raided their homes in Herris, Illinois.[21] In the North, rioting against blacks occurred in large urban centers, notably in Chicago and East St. Louis after World War I.[22] In the West, sporadic assaults on Japanese and Mexicans took place.[23]

The episodes of intergroup violence in the early twentieth century had antecedents in nineteenth-century patterns of nativism and racial antagonism. Nativist riots broke out against Catholic immigrants in northern industrial cities and against the Chinese in the frontier communities of the West.[24] Mob attacks by whites against blacks occurred in the North and the Ku Klux Klan began to practice racial terror tactics after Reconstruction. Despite the criminality and destructiveness of these acts, the federal government declined to take an aggressive programmatic role to end them. By and large, the disorders were quelled through desultory efforts of the municipal police and the local public.

The system of differentiated ethnic status produced social order but with the attendant costs of social inequality, group rivalry, and xenophobia. It reinforced an ideology of Anglo-Saxon Protestant supremacy. Differential ethnic status compromised democracy, because it expressed and ratified group exclusion and hierarchy. By promoting a racially conscious and hegemonic conception of ethnic relations, it was conducive to ethnic conflict and violence.

## The Nexus of Immigrant Citizenship

In the northern ethnic pattern of the early twentieth century, the preparation of new immigrants from southern and eastern Europe for citizenship was the key issue of their incorporation in the polity.[25] Although nativists criticized the potential for dependency and antisocial tendencies of the New Immigrants, a consensus emerged that they could be acculturated to democracy through guided naturalization, progressive education, and by participation in reformed electoral politics.[26] "Good citizenship" would overcome the divisive effects of ethnicity and class in the age of the New Immigration.[27]

The progressives strove to reinvigorate citizenship as a social nexus. They promoted the overriding civic duties to the community, the public interest, and the nation as a means to heal social and economic divisions.[28] Progressive educators introduced behavioristic programs of civic education: student service and government, social studies, patriotic ritual, and an extracurriculum whose main goal was socialization.[29] Progressives also realized that a strong devotion to citizenship hinged upon the capacity of society to provide decent living and working conditions. Thus they coupled the citizenship they offered to immigrants with the establishment of social and labor reforms.[30] Progressivism aimed at ensuring that a polity based on individual rights would function ultimately under higher conceptions of communal and national welfare than afforded by the free market alone.[31]

In the early twentieth century, government took steps that indirectly increased the value and utility of citizenship to immigrants. Citizenship became more desirable because local governments passed laws that specified lesser rights for aliens in access to occupations and property.[32] At the same time, the obtainment of citizenship required more rigorous preparation. Congress modified the nineteenth-century tradition of lax local naturalization into a systematic national test for membership.[33] In 1906, lawmakers raised the qualifications for naturalization by requiring the knowledge of English and civics and stricter verification of a minimum five-year residency, one of the longest probationary periods of any immigrant-receiving nation.[34]

Naturalization, however, was never compelled by law. The transference of allegiance remained based on individual and voluntary initiative.[35] The naturalization law of 1906 reaffirmed that for the New Immigrants naturalized citizenship would not be tied to class and ethnic origin. These features inhibited the development of immigrant labor politics rooted in workplace identity.[36] The New Immigrants acquired the franchise and the civil rights that offered full economic and social participation. T. H. Marshall observed that such rights (which he analyzed by examining the English polity) were "an aid, not a menace to capitalism and the free-market economy, because they conferred the legal capacity to strive for things one wished to possess, without guaranteeing the possession of any one of them."[37]

The New Immigrants were absorbed without sharp discontinuities into republican political traditions. This made possible political alliances with elements of the native middle class and working class to achieve progressive reforms. The acquisition of citizenship rights loosened ethnic identification and allowed American national identity to compete with it.[38] The rights of citizenship offset social-class distance with civic integration.[39] This condition contrasted with the situation of industrializing European nations in which fixed and limited corporate distribution of citizenship reinforced social distances opened up by the proletarianization of the working class.

For the New Immigrants, individual private rights to opportunity were functional in the major social and economic arenas.[40] They concentrated on the full utilization of their rights to opportunity rather than the pursuit of greater rights to equality of condition. These equal-opportunity rights complemented a politics based on the territorial community rather than social class.

The socioeconomic and cultural integration of European immigrant groups was achieved without internecine violence and civil insurrections in territorial communities. This was a major historical achievement and cannot be dismissed as an inevitable or easy result because of a common European heritage. The social historian Oscar Handlin once rhetorically highlighted the importance of this accomplishment by wondering, "Why didn't these peoples so different from each other kill each other?" After all, the Poles and Jews, the Russians and Germans, the Irish and English, who lived side by side in the same northern industrial cities were often locked in a seemingly inexhaustible cycle of intergroup hostilities in homeland regions. Contextual factors of the northern industrial city such as access to a dynamic and expansive modern economy and the geographic space that offered the opportunity to form economic and residential enclaves promoted the social mobility and self-regulated communal life that probably helped to keep competition for resources from reaching hostile and violent levels. Perhaps the most important conditions reducing violence were the disciplines, both formal and informal, of living and working in the modernizing city. The regimentation of the factory, the police enforcement of orderly public behavior, the spread of public education, the legalization of society, and the tight organization of urban schedules encouraged ordered coexistence.[41]

Notwithstanding the array of historic, contextual forces that reduced the potential for violent conflict, a polity based on liberal citizenship probably played an equally important role in producing the relatively harmonious integration of European minorities.[42] The rights of liberal citizenship ensured equal access to the opportunities and resources afforded by urban, industrial communities. It proffered shared participation in government. The eschewal by government of involvement in ethnic maintenance sharply limited the tendency to turn government into a battleground for the promotion of group interests.

In the northern ethnic pattern, universal access to citizenship moved a ranked ethnic order closer to an unranked order. Citizenship rights to equal opportunity organized ethnic relations into a fluid and shifting array of diverse groups structured by the individual exercise of civil and political rights. Widespread social mobility eroded social-class entrenchment of particular groups and produced a cumulative intergenerational rise in the social position of others.[43]

Citizenship functioned as a building block of ethnic-territorial political communities: the neighborhoods that served as the matrix for working-class public culture.[44] The New Immigrants learned American values and ideals in neighborhood institutions, such as churches, schools, clubs, mutual benefit societies, and settlement houses that generated progressive civic culture. Perhaps the apotheosis of progressive civic integration was John Dewey's attempt to turn the public school of the immigrant city into a vehicle for participatory and active citizenship.[45] The neighborhood community produced a consumerism of mass-culture and material commodities that expressed public values and integrated people across ethnic lines.[46] A formularized civic culture took shape, a unifying code of ideals and values for citizenship, in which nationality was divorced from ethnic culture. John Higham has noted, "For integrationists the linchpin of a rightly ordered society is a set of ideals, a body of principles, in our own case what Gunnar Myrdal called an 'American Creed.' A people who aspire to universality and consist largely of detached and mobile individuals will rely heavily on the beliefs they hold in common. Indeed, they may share little else, for all who subscribe to the official creed should be received in to membership."[47] The code was an ideological paradigm of public identity and culture. The adoption of symbols of official Americanism produced American national identity. Progressives did not concentrate on extinguishing ethnic identification or culture. Instead their primary objective was maintaining a unified civic iconography that could be learned and given expression by a variety of groups. Each ethnic group was thus assumed to have the capacity to adopt American nationality and thereby achieved a kind of public equality.

## Toward Equal-Opportunity Antidiscrimination

From the New Deal to the Great Society, liberal reformers sought to make the northern ethnic pattern the national norm for ethnic relations. The New Immigrants from Europe achieved socioeconomic progress and acculturation without group sponsorship by government. Integration by the liberal right to equality of individual opportunity had sufficed in promoting the transition toward an unranked ethnic order.

The pursuit of a national regime of equal-opportunity antidiscrimination intensified during the Depression and war years. Mexican American leadership created new organizations to combat segregation and to achieve full citizenship.[48] The assault on prejudice gained additional impetus from the ideological and political reaction to Nazism. Jewish self-defense organizations launched educational and legal campaigns and sponsored studies that attacked prejudice as a pathology.[49] They supported organized efforts to outlaw lynching and to provide legal justice to blacks. Immigrant leadership and labor joined with blacks to establish state commissions against discrimination, making antidiscrimination an institutionalized function of government.[50] A mutual security alliance developed among the leadership of European immigrant communities and the leadership of racial minorities.[51]

The civil-rights movement from World War II to the Great Society was integrative and its petition drives were based on peaceful demonstration. It drew support from the social justice movements of the immigrant community, because the civil-rights model of integrationist equality coincided with the European immigrants' struggle to realize their citizenship. Southern black leaders united with northern reformers to move toward equal opportunity through executive and judicial administration, as well as through the vote.[52] They pressured the President to desegregate the armed services through executive orders and to establish a Fair Employment Practices Commission. The Warren Supreme Court enlarged the scope of judicial intervention into race relations to promote equality of opportunity for members of minorities. Steps toward full civic inclusion for Asians sprang from the reform of immigration and naturalization policy. In 1952, the McCarran-Walter Immigration Act repealed all exclusions of Asians from admissions and naturalization.[53] Hawaii's attainment of statehood in 1959 marked the overcoming of historic resistance to granting equality to a territorial political community in which the majority were Asians and Pacific Islanders.[54] For Asians it established their collective right to full inclusion in the American nation. The passage of the Hart-Celler immigration act of 1965, spearheaded by advocates from the immigrant constituency, ended discriminatory national quotas which had legally signified that Asians and other ethnic groups from outside northern Europe were less desirable as citizens.

New efforts were made to make ethnic relations conform to the democratic ideology used to authorize America's international leadership role during World War II and the cold war. Intellectuals and statesmen realized that the health of American ethnic relations would be a standard used to judge American leadership against the appeal of fascism and communism.

In this atmosphere, the immigrant experience developed into a national and global touchstone of American freedom. Oscar Handlin, the major American social historian of the early cold war, established the key historical role of immigration in the conception of American nationality and its liberal tradition (1951, 1963a). He sharply criticized discrimination in immigration law and in intergroup relations (1957). Nathan Glazer, the most active commentator on the sociology of American ethnic relations, carved out a view of ethnicity prescribing a free democratic pluralism for all races.[55] Glazer revisited Horace Kallen's theory of pluralism which only accommodated European immigrants and demanded permanent identification with an ancestral group. Both Handlin and Glazer advocated an ethnic pluralism that was fluid, pragmatic, and consistent with the rights of the individual. Their writings developed the thesis that urban blacks were functionally like earlier European immigrants in the process of assimilation, on the path toward social and civic inclusion.[56]

## The Rise of Preferential Policies

In the early 1960s, it appeared that the northern ethnic pattern would become the national paradigm for ethnic relations. The federal government established laws guaranteeing political rights, civil rights, and equal opportunity for individuals of all races. The civil rights movement achieved success through nonviolent and multiracial protest tactics aimed at fulfilling integrationist ideals.

In the 1960s, the nexus between differential status and a ranked ethnic order dissolved at an accelerating pace. The forces of dissolution came from two directions. The first was unprecedented legislation and enforcement activism by the federal government to ensure equal opportunity in jobs and voting to all citizens regardless of race.[57] The second was the rising multigenerational level of social mobility attained by blacks, Hispanics, and Asians that resulted in racial boundaries moving beyond class lines.

In the turning point of the mid-1960s, as a national regime of ethnic relations based on "race-blind" principles gained strength, calls for preferential group treatment by minority leaders initiated a momentous change in antidiscrimination policy. Demands for remedial tactics and equality of outcome began to rise. Minority advocates laid claims to compensation for setbacks due to historic discrimination against groups, not individuals. Policymakers established new rights for minorities to remediation for cumulative historical disadvantage verified by a record of disparate representation in social, political, and economic structures. Underrepresentation of groups was assumed to be due chiefly to historic as well as ongoing discrimination.[58]

Lawmakers and judges saw these preferential policies—labeled "affirmative action"—as the most aggressive way of moving an ethnic order in which racial minorities had a low social rank to a more egalitarian order. They defined equality of condition as numerical representation equal to the proportion of a group in the population, not representation accorded to individual achievements based on a universal standard.[59] Lawmakers promoted group equality through affirmative action and proportional electoral representation.[60] Legally, the term "discrimination" came to signify a historical and structural exclusion of minorities from the key spheres of society that could be measured by statistical correlation with membership in the population.

A by-product of the movement toward positive group discrimination was the growth of protections for the alien class increasingly composed of immigrants from the third world. Through the expansion of the equal-protection and due-process principles, aliens maintained social and economic rights comparable to those of citizens; undocumented aliens received special opportunities for normalizing their residential status.[61] Mexican-American advocacy leaders began to propose returning to the nineteenth-century pattern of alien enfranchisement.[62]

Minority advocates asserted that they were merely reversing the differential status system of the early twentieth century. In doing so, they espoused the continuance of the principle of differential status over universal citizenship, but for putatively benign ends of minority empowerment. They felt that the former rather than the latter would be more effective in moving from a ranked to an unranked order.

Preferential policies entailed that status by group identity eclipsed status by individual identity. These developments introduced an American version of a European-style estate system of functional political representation: the legal recognition and ranking of corporate groups according to their functional relationship to government powers.[63] Samuel Beer distinguished the features of functional representation in an analysis of the historic British polity:

> [Functional representation] refers to any theory that finds the community divided into various strata as having a certain corporate unity, and holds that they ought to

be represented in government. From one historical period to another, such group-ings have been differently named—estates, ranks and orders, interests, classes and vocations—and have differed greatly in their internal structure, relations with the community, and mode of representation. The similarity lies first in the fact that they are regarded as performing an important function in the community as a whole (as the knights in medieval society performed the function of defense, or as the workers in some industry carry on an activity necessary to the economy of modern Britain). Moreover, the unity of such a stratum is not that of mere volun-tary association which stresses common ideas and moral judgments. On the con-trary, its integration is seen as arising especially from objective conditions that give its members a function and are the ground for deeply rooted, continuing—even "fixed"—interests. Recognizing this function and these common interests, the members act as a unit and find in this group a sphere of moral fulfillment and an instrument of political action. This anti-individualist bias is common both to older corporatist attitudes and to modern pluralism.[64]

American minority leaders moved to legitimize the status of mi-norities as separate functional political groups. To support claims for official corporate status these advocates developed an anti-assimilationist ideology that drew on a historical critique of American social development and institutions. Minority advocates criticized the ideology of assimilation and free pluralism as overpredicated on the European immigrant experience. The Vietnam War served them as a negative paradigm for the history of American ethnic relations as im-perialism, racism, and exploitation. The ethical decline of assimilation and the melting pot occurred in academic scholarship, journalistic opin-ion making, and policy making in the late 1960s.[65]

New forms of cultural liberation challenged what was seen as the oppressive cultural reductionism of assimilation. Minority militants discovered Cuban, Maoist, and third-world alternative models of eth-nic liberation. The sympathies of intellectuals grew toward recovery of pre-industrial cultures that were resistant to assimilation and capi-talist modernization.[66]

In the 1960s, the historic Western ethnic pattern of multiracial sta-tus became the basis for a coalition of "third-world" groups that broad-ened the movement for preferential policies. This alliance developed a political ideology based on the deterministic power of sociological factors, particularly race. It requested that groups such as the Chinese and Mexicans be treated in terms of their racial identity rather than their social identity as immigrants. Challenging the liberal assumption that ethnic groups were unified by a common citizenship, the Western-pattern minority activists asserted that minorities were interdependently linked through subjection to an obdurate and pervasive racism: a regime of internal colonialism.[67] Consequently, their new agenda was to form an alliance of racial blocs to petition to move beyond the liberal opportunity system rather than to consummate it.

The ideology of racial oppression and liberation contained theoretical abstractions such as "people of color" and "oppressed minorities" that crafted a sense of multiracial unity and were implicitly adversarial toward what was seen as a monolithic white community. In reality, group rights created competition between minorities over whom was entitled to what rights. Because the ideology was constructed out of utopian and nationalist assumptions, at first it influenced only a radicalized subgroup in the minority populations.

By the 1970s, however, the multiracial coalition pressed to advance the commitment to the functional representation of minorities in the American polity. They turned a threefold rationale to this purpose. A defensive rationale held that minorities required protected group status because of the pervasiveness of racial prejudice and discrimination. This was the objective condition that gave minorities the deeply rooted, "fixed" interest, described by Samuel Beer, that had to be fulfilled in efforts to create a good society. A positive rationale for functional group status was also propounded. Minorities would police the polity to ensure that discrimination and prejudice as general social ills would be systematically counteracted. Because of their historical experience with discrimination and prejudice, minorities had special skills to perform this task. Finally, the minority coalition claimed that if multiracial functional representation occurred in politics, employment, education, residency, and the media, minorities would diversify and enrich American culture. By the 1980s, the minority coalition promoted this idea under the rubrics of "diversity" and "multiculturalism." Functional ethnic representation thus was seen as providing a necessary social good benefitting all constituencies, not just providing remediation to particular minorities for historical group disadvantage.[68] On the logical justification of this policy, the thoughts of Samuel Beer once again are illuminating:

> [In functional representation of interest groups] the design of the good society legitimizes their needs; hence, their wishes, reflecting the needs of this mode of life, ought to have a voice in government. . . . [Moreover] the needs of the class or interest in question should be considered not simply because they are legitimized by the design of the good society, but also because this element (whether stratum or lesser community) carries out a function important to the social whole. This justifies giving it power to protect itself. But what is especially relevant in modern

society, it also means that the knowledge of those performing this function may well be necessary for the good governing of the wider community. They have special skills, experience, *expertise* which government must have at hand if it is to understand control the complex and interdependent social whole.[69]

The minorities who had suffered status inequality in the early twentieth century experienced an elevation of status in a time of federal government intervention in the social structure. Welfare politics connected the issue of rights for minority groups with socioeconomic status. Differential minority rights were bound in with the objective of ending social inequality. Because of the Democratic party's activist conception of federal government, the minority coalition tended to operate within it. For American minorities, the movement for expanded rights resembled the enfranchisement of the working class in Europe. Both originated in an organized petition movement by the disfranchised against the government. The minority coalition learned to pressure and access the national government as interest groups. Moreover, the increasing centralization and bureaucratization of the American federal government provided a limited, well-defined target that was easier to strike. By the 1980s, the civil-rights movement's original adversarial stance toward national government had turned into a clientage system for official corporate minorities operated by the growth of a regulatory bureaucracy.[70]

Under official ethnic corporatism, individuals learned to assert their interests through ethnic groups and ethnic cultures. This tendency heightened the potential for intergroup competition and conflict. Most importantly, ethnic conflict was channelled *pro forma* into political arenas. In general, ethnic competition and conflict became politicized and driven by group ideology. American society was increasingly divided by group identification and group membership. Relationships between whites and non-whites were riven by collective adversarialism.

From the 1960s a revolution in racial consciousness radically intensified the subjective elements of race relations. Ideological symbolism, separatist pride, and self-worth became keys to race relations.[71] The mass riots in inner-city black neighborhoods adumbrated this trend.[72] These riots differed from racial clashes in the early twentieth century in that they aimed at a kind of symbolic and institutional destruction. The rioters destroyed the property of what was perceived as the white power structure.[73] Moreover, they were not a mechanical reaction to overall economic setbacks. The disorders of Harlem (1964),

Watts (1965), Newark (1967), Detroit (1968), and Miami (1980) occurred in a time of improving conditions for blacks.[74] These outbreaks also inflicted great destruction upon black communities.

A psychology of grievance and conspiracy assumed an increasing role in the evolution of interracial riots. The precipitants for the riots in Harlem, Watts, Miami, and Los Angeles were police violence or the acquittal of police brutality that signified racial oppression. In New York City in the 1980s, the perception of racist conspiracies in the Tawana Brawley, Bensonhurst, and Crown Heights affairs triggered violent street protests by black militants.[75] According to surveys, a large percentage of blacks believed that a genocidal plot caused the AIDS and drug epidemics. Radical Afrocentrists and black Muslims asserted that Jews had played historic roles in oppressing blacks.

Subjective race relations were heightened as the representation of ethnic culture and became a cardinal status issue. Culture itself was politicized as groups saw culture as a means to empowerment. Minority advocates demanded that government manage and sponsor ethnic culture to produce multicultural diversity. They also demanded that government and the public should increase sensitivity toward group feelings and interests.[76] Government should engage in symbolic actions that enhanced the status of groups.

The pursuit of esteem and self-esteem became a key aspect of cultural empowerment. J. R. Pole called attention to "this most emotive category"[77] of American egalitarianism, earlier examined by James Bryce in *The American Commonwealth*. The enlistment of government to support therapeutic cultural empowerment of minorities, particularly through public education, became a new kind of preferential policy.[78] The critical reaction to the Moynihan Report calling attention to the widespread breakdown of the black family signified the rising sensitivity to ethnic esteem issues.[79] Government at federal and local levels embarked on an unprecedented course in the history of the American polity. They began to use public resources to promote ethnocultural maintenance involving bilingual and ethnic-heritage programs, particularly in the schools.[80]

Central governmental direction of ethnic empowerment could spill over into conflict and violence. Preferential polices for minorities engendered a white backlash that was sometimes expressed in violent communal resistance. Perhaps the outstanding occurrence of this type was the hostile opposition to court-ordered busing in multiracial cities.[81]

Protest by groups who felt that institutions failed to empower them adequately or fairly led to conflict and violent outbreaks within schools and colleges. The enhancement of minority student rights aggravated preexistent tensions caused by the increasing enrollment of multiracial student populations.[82] In Los Angeles in 1991, rioting broke out between black and Mexican students who felt that they had separate and antagonistic group interests within the life of the public school.[83]

Nativism with a potential for intergroup violence grew out of popular conspiratorial views that new immigrants arriving from Asia and Latin America had special entitlements and advantages. The new nativism had many faces. It arose both in economically declining white and black communities who resented "welfare immigrants" and competition with economically mobile immigrants. Resentment over the mobility of Asian newcomers overlapped with fear of international Asian economic competition to provoke assaults against Asian Americans. Acts of anti-Asian violence increased from the 1980s to the early 1990s. The perception that Cambodians were unfairly entitled refugees produced hostilities in Lowell, Massachusetts. Blacks in New York City and Los Angeles assaulted, picketed, and harassed Korean small shopkeepers whom they regarded as exploitative and alien intruders. Black advocacy leaders saw policies to empower Hispanic immigrants as unfairly depriving programs to empower blacks.[84]

The phenomenon of urban rioting moved in a new direction with the growth of new immigrant populations from Asia and Latin America in transitional neighborhoods once occupied by white ethnic groups.[85] In Miami in 1980, black rioters killed two persons of Cuban ancestry. In Washington, D. C. in 1991, ethnic conflict between black members of the city's police force and Hispanic immigrants precipitated an interracial riot that led to looting of Latino stores.[86] In Los Angeles in 1992, blacks attacked Korean neighborhoods and destroyed much of their property. The new immigrants living and working in areas adjoining central city districts became the constituency for law and order.

The recent developments in intergroup conflict and violence indicate that these pathologies no longer revolve centrally around hegemonic conflict between whites and non-whites. All groups appear to be ensnared in a web of intergroup hostilities. Ironically, the decades from the 1960s have been a time of unprecedented socioeconomic integration and even primary-level assimilation (for instance, the rising rates of intermarriage) for white and non-white groups.[87] Despite the hardening of a black underclass in the 1980s, the black middle class continued to expand to unprecedented size.[88] It is proper to ask whether race relations based on a new politics of status have become so powerful as to obscure the objective trends of structural fusion and to divert energy from social reform not based on group agendas.

## Conclusion

In twentieth-century America, the tactics for expanding rights originated from the minority groups created out of the legal segmentation of the class structure according to race and nativity. In England and European industrial states, class-designated citizenship promoted alliances between the leaderships of working-class organizations in the pursuit of equality, while in the United States ethnically determined status produced historically evolved alliances between the leaderships of different minority groups.

The republican ideal of universal citizenship and nationality retreated in the early twentieth century before nativism and racism. Ethnic conflict in the early twentieth century came from efforts by groups of British Protestant origin to use law and custom to restrict opportunity and power, permitting them to fashion and to dominate a ranked ethnic order. The most subjective element in ethnic relations was an ideology of Anglo-Saxon supremacy and tutorialism of dependent races. Nevertheless, a political system for greater ethnic equity and concord developed in the northern pattern of European immigrant assimilation. The once proletarian New Immigrants from southern and eastern Europe achieved social mobility and acculturation through equal-opportunity citizenship, moving the northern ethnic pattern toward an unranked order, without provoking destructive social movements.

The effort to expand the northern ethnic pattern of assimilation to a national paradigm for ethnic inclusion shaped official policy from the New Deal to the Great Society. To realize this ideal, government abandoned its traditional policy of nonintervention in group relations and institutionalized laws and programs to reduce prejudice and discrimination. Group differences were to be subsumed under an expanded citizenship and nationality that was inclusive of all ethnic and racial minority groups and secured by government regulation of discrimination.

Since the 1970s, a radical "equal rights" revolution among minorities demanded a corporatist polity of functional political communities based on fixed categories of ethnicity. A multi-racial coalition called for the recognition of the historical exceptionalism of minorities to the polity of liberal democracy. At first they demanded preferential policies of remediation to amend historical injuries to groups and to protect them from putatively pervasive discrimination. Subsequently, they moved beyond the rationale of remediation and protection to preferential policies. In the new prescription, preferential policies would promote multicultural diversity as social goods by ensuring proportional ethnic representation in institutional and social arenas.

The rise of preferential and multicultural policies marked the expansion of citizenship to include social rights in addition to political rights. T. H. Marshall and other scholars have shown how European states enlarged citizenship rights to social rights by recognizing the social duties performed by groups. These social rights, however, became constitutive of a decentering subnational citizenship when they were apportioned according to official groups.

Preferential policies replaced the workings of social process with the employment of government power to advance group interest. In this way, the conflictual process of ethnic social mobility was aggravated by the ethnic politicization of social mobility. These policies officialized group identity and culture to make groups amenable to classification and administrative management. Official group identity inescapably led toward tendencies to formularize and essentialize identity, to overlook heterogeneous individuality. The political authorization of ethnic essentialism formed a slippery slope toward dehumanization of outsiders and thus heightened the potential for destructive intergroup conflict. Ultimately, these tendencies threatened the democratic rights to individually chosen identity. It stifled dissent and difference within groups, by encouraging the phenomenon of official spokesmanship for group political orthodoxies. These spokesmen often acted to silence dissenters by political threats and personal intimidation.

By politicizing the sponsorship of multicultural diversity, the new functional ethnicity intensified the subjective forms of race relations. The new polity advanced beyond intergroup tolerance to the realm of intergroup competition for symbolic and hegemonic esteem. The heightened subjectivism of group relations produced an atmosphere of preoccupation with ethnic recognition and pride issues. It cultivated an intense awareness of pervasive, covert racism and its manifestations. This volatile sensitivity in intergroup relations increased the chances for ethnic conflict and its escalation into violence. It also foregrounded a symbolic politics of group status that diverted from a politics of pragmatic cooperation.

In the American polity, citizenship and nationality have been eroded by the ethnic revival of the late twentieth century.[89] The unity of their legal basis has been compromised by preferential policies creating separate spheres of rights for different groups. The political culture of citizenship lost ground to official group identity. The new efforts to protect aliens from the third world reduced the marginal advantage of citizenship. These trends probably have increased the risk for group conflict. The legal scholar Peter Schuck has worried:

> As citizenship's value and significance decline, therefore, we should expect that people's more parochial loyalties may loom correspondingly larger and may be asserted with greater intensity. Such a shift may yield neighborly pride, ethnic solidarity, and other emotional satisfactions. But it may also encourage a retreat from civic commitment toward some darker feelings that are never wholly absent from American life: xenophobia, petty localism, intolerance, and privatistic self-absorption.[90]

Prescriptive solutions to these problems portending heightened group conflict are difficult to formulate, but a historical perspective on twentieth-century America suggests some possibilities. A modernized and resuscitated version of the workings of the northern ethnic pattern and the historic, but abortive, effort to nationalize it is a promising path. If ethnic relations realigned around universal citizenship and the liberal ideal of equal rights to opportunity for individuals, the divisive tendency to pursue self-interest through politicized groups and cultures would be curbed. Concomitantly, equality of citizenship and its rights to opportunity should be protected by vigorous government activism. Multicultural pluralism should be linked to the historic and ongoing reality of America's culture as a constantly changing plural culture that all have shaped and shared. Schools should recognize the diversity of student populations but encourage the continuities and correspondences between different cultures and American culture. Thus a realistic understanding of the fusion or mutual assimilation of cultures and identities would produce a constructive equilibrium between cultural unity and diversity. Ethnic pluralism should remain voluntary in the neighborhood community and expressed through its unifying public culture. If government eschewed sponsorship of therapeutic cultural security, the subjective focus of race relations can be limited.

These measures would inhibit ethnic essentialism and separatism. This outcome would allow people to build individual civic identity and to know one another free of the reductionism of group identity. Under these conditions, it is possible that intergroup tensions could be sufficiently reduced to permit the continuance of mass global immigration and the absorption of multiracial populations, without fear of escalating ethnic conflict.

The United States achieved national coherence out of its multiethnic population by supporting the mutual relationship of inclusive citizenship and weak legal boundaries. Citizenship remained weak in the sense that voluntary ideological allegiance substituted for primordial and statist authoritarianism. Legal and civic boundaries were separated from the place of an individual in the social structure. Legal boundaries between groups were historically weak after World War II for ethnic groups who did not come from Europe. Unitary civic identity and open legal boundaries between groups coincided strongly from World War II to the 1960s, a time in which ethnic equality and intergroup discord decreased in tandem.

The character of American civic identity and group boundaries grew out of social experience. A common social tradition of mass migration, settlement, and the mutual character of nation building anchored inclusive citizenship and weakened boundaries. This was the advantage in developing these official parameters for shaping group relations held by the United States over European states without a modern history of nation building through immigration.

In contrast, nation building in Europe involved the development of homogeneous and exclusive forms of nationality facilitating state empowerment. Citizenship was unitary but it was stronger in its statist and nationalistic ties and nationality itself was limited because of cultural and legal closure of the social nation that grew out of historic territorial identity or a concept of *Volk* identity. Under these conditions, the absorption of immigrants was conflictual, violent, or even impractical.

As different as the American polity has been from that of European nation-states, the historic inclusive principle of American civic identity, if not the exact form of American citizenship and nationality, is not without parallel in the evolution of modern European states. These developments have occurred since World War II, when countries in Western Europe became magnets for immigrants and refugees from

Asia, the West Indies, North Africa, and Eastern Europe. The long-term solution to the problem of absorbing permanently resident new-comers may lie in the evolutionary path taken by nations like England and France, which have recently received large infusions of immigrants from outside Europe. In these countries, nationality and the forms of civic culture, with its essential Anglo-Saxon and Gallic character, expanded to assimilate alien populations and to be shared by all groups in the late twentieth century. Despite local deviations and differences, England and France moved toward the inclusive forms of nationality and citizenship early developed by the United States because it was the first modern state to forge a unified society out of international mass migration.[91]

The alternative to efforts towards inclusion to suppress the potential for group conflict arising out of global population transfers would entail the application or reinforcement of exclusionary measures. Nations with historically closed boundaries of citizenship and nationality, such as Germany, can choose to lower the potential for group conflict by more exclusionary admissions policies or greater commitment to the maintenance of a permanent alien class.

The United States, for the moment, has rejected this path by building on the advantage of its pluralistic social history. The gates for admission have been kept open. But with the rise of official group rights, history's quintessential immigrant nation stands at the crossroads. It remains to be seen if the division of society into official groups and identities will achieve a permanent and expanded place in the polity, a development that would represent nothing less than a historic departure from the vision of society as a melting pot resulting from heterogeneous and voluntary fusion. Already, a populist nativism has been generated by fears that the newest immigrants encased in official group compartments will not assimilate. Political pressures have intensified to restrict immigration portending the end of global immigration on the scale seen in the 1970s and 1980s.

## Notes

1. Horowitz 1985, pp. 21–24.
2  Glazer 1982, p. 133.
3. Hartz 1955; Kramnick 1982; Appleby 1982; Diggins 1984; Pocock 1975; Murrin 1980; Ross 1980.

4. Handlin, p. 47; DeLeon 1983, pp. 8–9; Meier and Rivera 1972, p. xvi; Romo 1983, pp. 94, 127.
5. Adams 1918, p. 409; Bannister 1979, p. 193; Montejano 1987, pp. 220–234.
6. Daniels 1962, p. 49; Frederickson 1981, pp. 189–191, 277.
7. Warner 1936, pp. 234–237; Dollard 1957, ch. 5.
8. McGovney 1911, pp. 231–250, 326–347; McGovney 1923, pp. 129–161; Malcolm 1921, pp. 77–81; Wigmore 1894, p. 827; Gulick 1918, ch. 5; Konvitz, Ithaca 1946; Konvitz 1953, ch. 3; Kansas 1936, pp. 28–33.
9. Moore and Pachon 1976, pp. 33, 49; Romo 1983, pp. 160–161.
10. Lasch 1958.
11. Cabranes 1979.
12. Gettys 146–159.
13. Alexander 1931; Kohler 1909, pp. 275–293; Konvitz 1946; MacKenzie 1937.
14. Garcia 1981, pp. 98–99.
15. Fuchs 1961, pp. 275–277; Wollenberg 1976, pp. 38–47, 72–75; Bell 1973, p. 79; Garcia, pp. 110–111; Montejano, pp.168–169.
16. Kansas 1936, pp. 23–24; Heizer and Almquist 1971; Garcia, pp. 1–9, 127, 231, 234; Grisworld del Castillo 1979, pp. 115–117; tenBroek et al. 1954, ch. 1; Bogardus 1930.
17. Cell 1982, pp. 171–180.
18. Horowitz 1983, p. 189.
19. Woodward 1974; Raper 1933.
20. Horowitz 1983, p. 189.
21. Higham 1956, pp. 169, 209, 264, 295.
22. Rudwick 1964; Spear 1967; Tuttle 1970.
23. Daniels 1962, pp. 33–34; Montejano 1987, pp. 122, 204; Acuna 1981, pp. 326–327.
24. Brown 1975, pp. 29–30; Feldberg 1975; Grimsted 1972; Richards 1970; Coolidge 1909, pp. 254–277.
25. U.S. Immigration Commission 1911; U. S. Commissioner-General of Immigration 1927, pp. 21–22; Shaler 1904, pp. 200–206.
26. Brewer 1902, pp. 25–27; Bryce 1909, pp. 106–107; Park and Miller 1921, pp. 267–273; Davis 1920, pp. 600–606; Drachsler 1920, ch. 8, 9.
27. Merriam 1934, pp. 54ff.
28. McCormick 1981, pp. 264–265; Thelen 1972, pp. 55–56, 82–85; Weeks 1917; Cleveland 1908; Hadow 1923; Newman 1928.
29. Skinner 1900; Clarke 1918; Woellner 1923; Stewart and Hanna 1928.
30. Gompers 1917, pp. 28–31, pp. 35–43.
31. Hofstadter 1955, pp. 257–271; Thelen 1972, pp. 55–56.
32. Wise 1906, p. 7.
33. Williams 1912, pp. 399–427.
34. U.S. Congress 1905, p. 10.
35. Kettner 1974, pp. 208–242; Rundquist 1975; Mann 1979, pp. 55–60; Ueda 1980.
36. Katznelson 1981, pp. 65–72.
37. Marshall 1950, p. 35.
38. Ueda 1992.
39. Carpenter 1927; Gavit 1922.
40. Handlin and Handlin 1961, p. 47.
41. Handlin 1963b; Lane 1968; Monkonnen 1981; Silverman 1981.
42. Handlin 1961, pp. 113–154; Glazer 1975, pp. 3–22.
43. Handlin 1961, pp. 123–154; Thernstrom 1973, ch. 6–7; Barton 1975, ch. 5–6; Kessner 1977, ch. 5; Lieberson 1980, ch. 11; Sowell 1981, ch. 1.

44. Katznelson 1981, ch. 2–3; Bodnar 1985, ch. 7.
45. Cremin 1961.
46. Rosenzweig 1983; Couvares 1984; Peiss 1986; Cohen 1990.
47. Higham 1984, p. 235.
48. Garcia 1989, ch. 2.
49. Higham 1984, p. 221; Adorno et al. 1950.
50. Berger 1952.
51. Rustin 1966; Glazer 1983, pp. 29–43.
52. Glazer and Ueda 1980.
53. Reimers 1985, pp. 20–22.
54. Fuchs 1961.
55. Glazer and Moynihan 1963; Glazer 1975, 1983.
56. Glazer and Moynihan 1963, pp. xxii-xiv; Handlin 1959; Handlin 1964.
57. Glazer 1975, pp. 33–76.
58. Glazer 1975; Sowell 1990.
59. Eastland and Bennett 1979, pp. 116–138.
60. A. Thernstrom 1977.
61. Schuck 1985, 1989.
62. Chavez 1991, p. 133.
63. Bendix 1977, p. 91.
64. Beer 1965, pp. 17, 71, 73.
65. Mann 1979, pp. 1–18.
66. Gutman 1973.
67. Carmichael and Hamilton 1967, pp. 2–32; Blauner 1972.
68. Carter 1991; MacDonald 1992, p. 60.
69. Beer 1965, p. 72.
70. Williams 1982.
71. Bayes 1982, pp. 25–34, 92–94.
72. Brown 1975, p. 31.
73. Janowitz 1969, pp. 412–415; Feagin and Hahn 1973, pp. 268–269, 300–301; Caplan 1971, pp. 343–345, 358–359.
74. Wilson 1978; Horowitz 1983; Farley 1984; Graham 1990.
75. Sleeper 1990.
76. Ravitch 1990.
77. Pole 1978, pp. 335–337.
78. Ravitch 1990; Schlesinger 1991.
79. Moynihan 1965; Rainwater and Yancey 1967.
80. Chavez 1992; Porter 1990.
81. Lukas 1985; Formisano 1991.
82. Palmer 1992.
83. Woo and Kowsky 1991.
84. Miles 1992.
85. Skerry and Hartman 1991.
86. Lane 1991.
87. Petersen 1970; Sowell 1980; Farley 1984; Graham 1990; Bean and Tienda 1987; Portes and Rumbaut 1990; Fugita and O'Brien 1991; Chavez 1991.
88. Wilson 1987; Jones 1992; Hacker 1992; Jencks 1992; Mead 1992; Wolfe 1992.
89. Janowitz 1983, pp. 106–144.
90. Schuck 1989, pp. 62–63.
91. Horowitz 1992, pp. 7–10; Brubaker 1992, pp. 97–98.

# References

Adams, Henry. 1918. *The Education of Henry Adams*. Boston: Little, Brown.

Alexander, Norman. 1931. *Rights of Aliens Under the Federal Constitution*. Montpelier, VT: Capital City Press.

Appleby, Joyce. 1982. "Commercial Farming and the 'Agrarian Myth' in the Early Republic," *Journal of American History* 68, 833–849.

Arieli, Yehoshua. 1964. *Individualism and Nationalism in American Ideology*. Cambridge, MA: Harvard University Press.

Bannister, Robert C. 1979. *Social Darwinisim: Science and Myth in Anglo-American Social Thought*. Philadelphia, PA: Temple University Press.

Bayes, Jane H. 1982. *Minority Politics and Ideologies in the United States*. Novato, CA: Chandler and Sharp.

Bean, Frank and Marta Tienda. 1987. *The Hispanic Population of the United States*. New York: Russell Sage Foundation.

Beer, Samuel. 1965. *British Politics in the Collectivist Age*. New York: Vintage.

Bell, Derrick A., Jr. 1973. *Race, Racism and American Law*. Boston: Little, Brown.

Bendix, Reinhard. 1977. *Nation-Building and Citizenship*. Berkeley, CA: University of California Press.

Berger, Morroe. 1952. *Equality by Statute: Legal Controls Over Group Discrimination*. New York: Columbia University Press.

Blauner, Robert. 1972. *Racial Oppression in America*. New York: Harper and Row.

Bodnar, John. 1985. *The Transplanted: A History of Immigrants in Urban America*. Bloomington, IN: Indiana University Press.

Bogardus, Emory S. 1930. "The Mexican Immigrant and Segregation," *American Journal of Sociology* 36, 74–80.

Brewer, David J. 1902. *American Citizenship*. New York: Charles Scribner's and Sons.

Brown, Richard Maxwell. 1975. *Strain of Violence: Historical Studies of American Violence and Vigilantism*. New York: Oxford University Press.

Brubaker, Rogers. 1992. *Citizenship and Nationhood in France and Germany*. Cambridge, MA: Harvard University Press.

Bryce, James. 1909. *Hindrances to Good Citizenship*. New Haven, CT: Yale University Press.

Cabranes, Jose A. 1979. *Citizenship and the American Empire: Notes on the Legislative History of the United States Citizenship of Puerto Ricans*. New Haven, CT: Yale University Press.

Caplan, Nathan. 1971. "The New Ghetto Man: A Review of Recent Empirical Studies," in David Boesel and Peter H. Rossi (eds.), *Cities under Siege: An Anatomy of the Ghetto Riots, 1964–1968*. New York: Basic Books.

Carmichael, Stokeley and Charles Hamilton. 1967. *Black Power: The Politics of Liberation in America*. New York: Vintage Books.

Carpenter, Niles. 1927. *Immigrants and Their Children*. Washington, D.C.: Government Printing Office.

Carter, Stephen L. 1991. *Reflections of an Affirmative Action Baby*. New York: Basic Books.

Cell, John W. 1982. *The Highest Stage of White Supremacy: The Origins of Segregation in South Africa and the American South*. Cambridge: Cambridge University Press.

Chavez, Linda. 1991. *Out of the Barrio: Toward a New Politics of Hispanic Assimilation*. New York: Basic Books.

Clarke, Kate Upson. 1918. *Teaching the Child Patriotism.* Boston, MA: The Page Company.

Cleveland, Grover. 1908. *Good Citizenship.* Philadelphia, PA: Henry Altemus.

Cohen, Lizabeth. 1990. *Making a New Deal: Industrial Workers in Chicago, 1919–1939.* Cambridge: Cambridge University Press.

Coolidge, Mary Roberts. 1909. *Chinese Immigration.* New York: Henry Holt and Company.

Couvares, Francis G. 1984. *The Remaking of Pittsburgh: Class and Culture in an Industrializing City, 1877–1919.* Albany, NY: State University of New York Press.

Cremin, Lawrence. 1961. *The Transformation of the School: Progressivism in American Education, 1876–1957.* New York: Alfred A. Knopf.

Daniels, Roger. 1962. *The Politics of Prejudice: The Anti-Japanese Movement in California and the Struggle for Japanese Exclusion.* Berkeley, CA: University of California Press.

Davis, Philip, ed. 1920. *Immigration and Americanization: Selected Readings.* Boston: Ginn and Company.

DeLeon, Arnaldo. 1983. *They Called Them Greasers: Anglo Attitudes Toward Mexicans in Texas, 1821–1900.* Austin, TX: University of Texas Press.

Diggins, John Patrick. 1984. *The Lost Soul of American Politics: Virtue, Self-Interest, and the Foundations of Liberalism.* New York: Basic Books.

Dollard, John. 1957. *Caste and Class in a Southern Town.* 3d ed. Garden City: Doubleday.

Drachsler, Julius. 1920. *Democracy and Assimilation: The Blending of Immigrant Heritages in America.* New York: Macmillan.

Eastland, Terry and William J. Bennett. 1979. *Counting by Race: Equality from the Founding Fathers to Bakke and Weber.* New York: Basic Books.

Farley, Reynolds. 1984. *Blacks and Whites: Narrowing the Gap.* Cambridge, MA: Harvard University Press.

Feldberg, Michael. 1975. *The Philadelphia Riots of 1844: A Study of Ethnic Conflict.* Westport, CT: Greenwood Press.

Formisano, Ronald. 1991. *Boston against Busing: Race, Class, and Ethnicity in the 1960s and 1970s.* Chapel Hill, NC: University of North Carolina Press.

Frederickson, George M. 1981. *White Supremacy: A Comparative Study in American and South African History.* New York: Oxford University Press.

Fuchs, Lawrence H. 1961. *Hawaii Pono: A Social History.* New York: Harcourt Brace Jovanich.

Fugita, Stephen S. and Dale O'Brien. 1991. *Japanese American Ethnicity: The Persistence of Community.* Seattle, WA: University of Washington Press.

Garcia, Mario T. 1981. *Desert Immigrants: The Mexicans of El Paso, 1880–1920.* New Haven, CT: Yale University Press.

———. 1989. *Mexican Americans: Leadership, Ideology, and Identity 1930–1960.* New Haven, CT: Yale University Press.

Gavit, John P. 1922. *Americans by Choice.* New York: Harper and Brothers.

Gettys, Luella. 1934. *The Law of Citizenship in the United States.* Chicago: University of Chicago Press.

Glazer, Nathan and Daniel P. Moynihan. [1963] 1970. *Beyond the Melting Pot: The Negroes, Puerto Ricans, Jews, Italians, and Irish of New York City,* 2d. ed. Cambridge, MA: MIT Press.

Glazer, Nathan. 1976. *Affirmative Discrimination: Ethnic Inequality and Public Policy.* New York: Basic Books.

————. 1982. "The Politics of a Multiethnic Society," in Lance LIebman (ed.), *Ethnic Relations in America.* Englewood Cliffs, NJ: Prentice-Hall.

————. 1983. *Ethnic Dilemmas, 1964–1982.* Cambridge, MA: Harvard University Press.

Glazer, Nathan and Reed Ueda. 1980. "Policies Against Prejudice and Discrimination," in Stephan Thernstrom (ed.), *Harvard Encyclopedia of American Ethnic Groups.* Cambridge, MA: Harvard University Press.

Gompers, Samuel. 1917. "Address of Samuel Gompers" and "Address of J. M. Berkey," in *Proceedings of the First Citizenship Convention.* Washington, D.C.: Government Printing Office.

Graham, Hugh Davis. 1990. *The Civil Rights Era: Origins and Development of National Policy, 1960–1972.* New York: Oxford University Press.

Graham, Hugh Davis and Ted Robert Gurr. 1969. *Violence in America: Historical and Comparative Perspectives.* New York: Bantam Books.

Grimsted, David. 1972. "Rioting in its Jacksonian Setting." *American Historical Review* 77, 361–397.

Griswold del Castillo, Richard. 1979. *The Los Angeles Barrio, 1850–1890: A Social History.* Berkeley, CA: University of California Press.

Gulick, Sidney L. 1918. *Asian Democracy and Asiatic Citizenship.* New York: Charles Scribner's Sons.

Gutman, Herbert G. 1973. "Work, Culture, and Society in Industrializing America, 1815–1919," *American Historical Review* 78, 531–588.

Hacker, Andrew. 1992. *Two Nations: Black and White, Separate, Hostile, Unequal.* New York: Scribner's.

Hadow, Will. 1923. *Citizenship.* London: Oxford University Press.

Handlin, Oscar. 1951. *The Uprooted: The Epic Story of the Great Migrations that made the American People.* Boston, MA: Little, Brown.

————. 1954. *The American People in the Twentieth Century.* Cambridge, MA: Harvard University Press.

————. 1957. *Race and Nationality in American Life.* Boston, MA: Little, Brown.

————. 1959. *The Newcomers: Negroes and Puerto Ricans in a Changing Metropolis.* Cambridge, MA: Harvard University Press.

Handlin, Oscar and Mary Handlin. 1961. *The Dimensions of Liberty.* Cambridge, MA: Harvard University Press.

Handlin, Oscar. 1963a. *The Americans: A New History of the People of the United States.* Boston, MA: Little, Brown.

————. 1963b. "The Modern City as a Field of Historical Study," in Oscar Handlin and John Burchard (eds.), *The Historian and the City.* Cambridge, MA: MIT Press.

————. 1964. *Firebell in the Night: The Crisis in Civil Rights.* Boston, MA: Little, Brown.

Handlin, Oscar and Lillian Handlin. 1992. *Liberty in Peril, 1850 to 1920.* New York: HarperCollins.

Hartz, Louis. 1955. *The Liberal Tradition in America: An Interpretation of American Political Thought since the Revolution* New York: Harcourt, Brace.

Heizer, Robert F. and Alan F. Almquist. 1971. *The Other Californians: Prejudice and Discrimination under Spain, Mexico, and the United States to 1920.* Berkeley, CA: University of California Press.

Higham, John. 1956. *Strangers in the Land: Patterns of American Nativism, 1860–1925.* New Brunswick, NJ: Rutgers University Press.

————. 1984. *Send These To Me: Immigrants in Urban America.* Revised Edition. Baltimore, MD: Johns Hopkins University Press.

Hofstadter, Richard. 1955. *The Age of Reform: From Bryan to F.D.R.* New York: Knopf.

Horowitz, Donald L. 1983. "Racial Violence in the United States," in Nathan Glazer and Ken Young (eds.), *Ethnic Pluralism and Public Policy: Achieving Equality in the United States and Britain.* Lexington, MA: D. C. Heath and Company.

Horowitz, Donald L. 1985. *Ethnic Groups in Conflict.* Berkeley, CA: University of California Press.

————. 1992. "Immigrants in Two Democracies: French and American Experience," in Donald L. Horowitz and Gerard Noiriel (eds.), *Immigrants in Two Democracies: French and American Experience.* New York: New York University Press.

Irons, Peter. 1983. *Justice at War.* New York: Oxford University Press.

Janowitz, Morris. 1969. "Patterns of Collective Racial Violence," *Violence in America: Historical and Comparative Perspectives.* New York: Bantam Books.

————. 1983. *The Reconstruction of Patriotism: Education for Civic Consciousness.* Chicago: University of Chicago Press.

Jencks, Christopher. 1992. *Rethinking Social Policy: Race, Poverty, and the Underclass.* Cambridge, MA: Harvard University Press.

Jones, Jacqueline. 1992. *The Dispossessed: America's Underclasses from the Civil War to the Present.* New York: Basic Books.

Kansas, Sidney. 1936. *Citizenship of the United States of America.* New York: Washington Publishing Company.

Katznelson, Ira. 1981. *City Trenches: Urban Politics and the Patterning of Class in the United States.* New York: Pantheon.

Kettner, James H. 1974. "The Development of American Citizenship in the Revolutionary Era: The Idea of Volitional Allegiance," *American Journal of Legal History* 18, 208–242.

Kohler, Max J. 1909. "Un-American Character of Race Legislation," *Annals of the American Academy* 34, 275–293.

Konvitz, Milton R. 1946. *The Alien and the Asiatic in American Law.* Ithaca, NY: Cornell University Press.

————. 1953. *Civil Rights in Immigration.* Ithaca, NY: Cornell University Press.

Kramnick, Isaac. 1982. "Republican Revisionism Revisited," *The American Historical Review* 87, 629–664.

Lane, Charles. 1991. "Over the Rainbow," *The New Republic* 204(23):15–18.

Lane, Roger. 1968. "Urbanization and Criminal Violence," *Journal of Social History* 2, 1956–63.

Lasch, Christopher. 1958. "The Anti-Imperialists, the Philippines, and the Inequality of Man," *Journal of Southern History* 24, 319–331.

Lieberson, Stanley. 1980. *A Piece of the Pie: Blacks and White Immigrants Since 1880.* Berkeley, CA: University of California Press.

Lukas, J. Anthony. 1985. *Common Ground: A Turbulent Decade in the Lives of Three American Families.* New York: Knopf.

MacDonald, Heather. 1992. "Divided Self," *Commentary* 93, 60–62.

MacKenzie, Norman R. 1937. *The Legal Status of Aliens in Pacific Countries.* London: Oxford University Press.

Malcolm, Ray. 1921. "American Citizenship and the Japanese," *Annals of the American Academy* 93, 77–81.

Mann, Arthur. 1979. *The One and the Many: Reflections on the American Identity.* Chicago: University of Chicago Press.

Marshall, T. H. 1950. *Citizenship and Social Class*. Cambridge: Cambridge University Press.

McCormick, Richard L. 1981. "The Discovery that Business Corrupts Politics: A Reappraisal of the Origins of Progressivism," *The American Historical Review* 86, 247–274.

McGovney, D. O. 1911. "American Citizenship," *Columbia Law Review* 11, 231–250; 326–347.

———. 1923. "Race Discrimination in Naturalization," *Iowa Law Bulletin* 8, 129–161; 211–244.

Mead, Lawrence. 1992. *The New Politics of Poverty: The Non-Working Poor in America*. New York: Basic Books.

Meier, Matt S. and Feliciano Rivera. 1972. *The Chicanos: A History of Mexican Americans*. New York: Hill and Wang.

Merriam, Charles E. 1934. *Civic Education in the United States*. New York: Charles Scribner's Sons.

Miles, Jack. 1992. "The Struggle for the Bottom Rung: Blacks versus Browns," *The Atlantic* (October).

Monkonnen, Eric. 1981. *Police in Urban America*. Cambridge: Cambridge University Press.

Moore, Joan W. and Harry Pachon. 1976. *Mexican Americans*. 2d ed. Englewood Cliffs, NJ: Prentice-Hall.

Murrin, John M. 1980. "The Great Inversion, or Court versus Country: A Comparison of the Revolution Settlements in England (1688–1721) and American (1776–1816)," in J.G.A. Pocock (ed.), *Three British Revolutions: 1641, 1688, 1776*. Princeton, NJ: Princeton University Press.

Newman, Sir George. 1928. *Citizenship and the Survival of Civilization*. New Haven, CT: Yale University Press.

Palmer, Thomas C., Jr. 1992. "Minority Demands, Majority Unrest at UMass," *Boston Globe*.

Park, Robert E. Park and Herbert A. Miller. 1921. *Old World Traits Transplanted*. New York: Harper and Brothers.

Peiss, Kathy. 1986. *Cheap Amusements: Working Women and Leisure in Turn-of-the-Century New York*. Philadelphia, PA: Temple University Press.

Petersen, William. 1970. *Japanese Americans: Oppression and Success*. New York: Random House.

Pocock, J. G. A. 1975. *The Machiavellian Moment: Florentine Political Thought and the Atlantic Republican Tradition*. Princeton, NJ: Princeton University Press.

Pole, J. R. 1978. *The Pursuit of Equality in American History*. Berkeley, CA: University of California Press.

Porter, Rosalie Pedalino. 1991. *Forked Tongue: The Politics of Bilingual Education*. New York: Basic Books.

Portes, Alejandro and Ruben G. Rumbaut. 1990. *Immigrant America: A Portrait*. Berkeley, CA: University of California Press.

Rainwater, Lee and William L. Yancey. 1967. *The Moynihan Report and the Politics of Controversy*. Cambridge, MA: MIT Press.

Raper, Arthur F. 1933. *The Tragedy of Lynching*. Chapel Hill, NC: University of North Carolina Press.

Ravitch, Diane. 1990. "Multiculturalism: E Pluribus Plures,"*The American Scholar* 59, 337–354.

Reimers, David M. 1985. *Still the Golden Door: The Third World Comes to America*. New York: Columbia University Press.

Richards, Leonard L. 1970. *"Gentlemen of Property and Standing": Anti-Abolition Mobs in Jacksonian America.* New York: Oxford University Press.

Romo, Ricardo. 1983. *East Los Angeles: History of a Barrio.* Austin, TX: University of Texas Press.

Rosenzweig, Roy. 1983. *Eight Hours for What We Will: Workers and Leisure in an Industrial City, 1870–1920.* Cambridge: Cambridge University Press.

Ross, Dorothy. 1980. "The Liberal Tradition Revisited and the Republican Tradition Addressed," in John Higham and Paul K. Conkin (eds.), *New Directions in American Intellectual History.* Baltimore, MD: Johns Hopkins University Press.

Rudwick, Elliot M. 1964. *Race Riot at East St. Louis, July 2, 1917.* Carbondale, IL: Southern Illionois University Press.

Rundquist, Paul S. 1975. "A Uniform Rule: The Congress and the Courts in American Naturalization, 1865–1952." Ph.D. thesis: University of Chicago.

Rustin, Bayard. 1966. "Black Power and Coalition Politics," *Commentary* 42, 35–40.

Schlesinger, Arthur M., Jr. 1990. *The Disuniting of America: Reflections on a Multicultural Society.* Whittle Direct Books.

Schuck, Peter H. 1989. "Membership in the Liberal Polity: The Devaluation of American Citizenship," in William Rogers Brubaker (ed.), *Immigration and the Politics of Citizenship in Europe and North America.* Lanham, MD: University Press of America.

Schuck, Peter H. and R. Smith. 1985. *Citizenship Without Consent: Illegal Aliens in the American Polity.* New Haven, CT: Yale University Press.

Shaler, Nathaniel S. 1904. *The Citizen: A Study of the Individual and the Government.* New York: A.S. Barnes and Company.

Silverman, Robert. 1981. *Law and Urban Growth: Civil Litigation in the Boston Trial Courts, 1880–1900* Princeton, NJ: Princeton University Press.

Skerry, Peter and Michael Hartman. 1991. "Latin Mass," *The New Republic* 204 (23): 18–20.

Skinner, Charles R., ed. 1900. *Manual of Patriotism: For Use in the Public Schools of the State of New York.* Albany, NY: Brandow.

Sleeper, Jim. 1990. *The Closest of Strangers: Liberalism and the Politics of Race in New York.* New York: W. W. Norton.

Sowell, Thomas. 1981. *Ethnic America: A History.* New York: Basic Books.

———. 1990. *Preferential Policies: An International Perspective.* New York: William Morrow and Company.

Spear, Allan H. 1967. *Black Chicago: The Making of a Negro Ghetto, 1890–1920.* Chicago: University of Chicago Press.

Stewart, Grace Hull and C. C. Hanna. 1928. *Adventures in Citizenship: Literature For Character.* Boston: Ginn and Company.

tenBroek, Jacobus et al. 1954. *Prejudice, War and the Constitution: Causes and Consequences of the Evacuation of the Japanese Americans in World War II.* Berkeley, CA: University of California Press.

Thelen, David P. 1972. *The New Citizenship: Origins of Progressivism in Wisconsin, 1885–1900.* Columbia, MS: University of Missouri Press.

Thernstrom, Stephan. 1973. *The Other Bostonians: Social Mobility in the American Metropolis, 1880–1970.* Cambridge, MA: Harvard University Press.

Thernstrom, Abigail. 1987. *Whose Votes Count?: Affirmative Action and Minority Voting Rights.* Cambridge, MA: Harvard University Press.

Tuttle, William M., Jr. 1970. *Race Riot: Chicago in the Red Summer of 1919.* New York: Atheneum.

U. S. Immigration Commission. 1911. *Reports*. Washington, D.C.: Government Printing Office.

U. S. Commissional General of Immigration. 1927. *Annual Report*. Washington, D.C.: Government Printing Office.

U. S. Congress, House of Representatives. 1905. *Report of the Naturalization Commission*. Washington, D.C.: Government Printing Office.

Ueda, Reed. 1980. "Naturalization and Citizenship," in Stephan Thernstrom (ed.), *The Harvard Encyclopedia of American Ethnic Groups*. Cambridge, MA: Harvard University Press.

———. 1992. "American National Identity and Race in Immigrant Generations," *Journal of Interdisciplinary History* 22, 483–491.

Warner, W. Lloyd. 1936. "American Caste and Class," *American Journal of Sociology* 42, 234–237.

Warren Commission. 1968. *Report of the National Advisory Commission on Civil Disorders*. New York.

Weeks, Arland D. 1917. *The Psychology of Citizenship*. Chicago: A. C. McClurg and Company.

Wigmore, John H. 1894. "American Naturalization and the Japanese," *American Law Review* 28, 818–827.

Williams, Hattie Plum. 1912. "The Road to Citizenship: A Study of Naturalization in a Nebraska County," *Political Science Quarterly* 27, 399–427.

Williams, Walter E. 1982. *The State Against Blacks*. New York: New Press.

Wilson, William Julius. 1978. *The Declining Significance of Race: Blacks and Changing American Institutions*. Chicago: University of Chicago Press.

———. 1987. *The Truly Disadvantaged: The Inner City, the Underclass, and Public Policy*. Chicago: University of Chicago Press.

Wise, John S. 1906. *A Treatise on Citizenship*. Northport, NY: E. Thompson.

Woellner, Fredric P. 1923. *Education for Citizenship in a Democracy*. New York: Charles Scribner's Sons.

Wolfe, Alan. 1992. "The New American Dilemma," *The New Republic* 206, 30–37.

Wollenberg, Charles M. 1976. *All Deliberate Speed: Segregation and Exclusion in California Schools, 1855–1975*. Berkeley, CA: University of California Press.

Woo, Elaine and Kim Kowsky. 1991. "Schools' Racial Mix Boils Over," *Los Angeles Times*.

Woodward, C. Vann. 1974. *The Strange Career of Jim Crow*. 3d. rev. ed. New York: Oxford University Press.

# 5

# Nations, States, and Sovereignty: Meanings and Challenges in Post-Cold War International Security

*James Gow*

Nationalism is a cardinal force in international politics. Its place in questions of international order depends on the relationship of the designated nation in question to the international system as a whole and, in particular, to four crucial "S-words": sovereignty, statehood, self-determination, and security. These represent a viciously hissing snake which was stirred anew by the end of the cold war and which presents the major challenge to international society.[1]

Nationalism linked to sovereignty and statehood has generated three waves of nation-state formation in the twentieth century. The first of these followed the break-up of the continental European empires—the German, the Russian, the Austro-Hungarian and the Ottoman—at the end of World War I. This led to the formation of independent states in Central and Eastern Europe, such as Poland, Lithuania, Czechoslovakia, Romania, and Yugoslavia. The post-World War I condition of Europe, of course, gave rise to a different wave, one of revisionist nationalism. That culminated in Nazism and the horrors of World War II. The second wave of nation-state formation in the century came after World War II and saw membership of the United Nations, formed in the wake of that war, grow from its original fifty in 1946 to 163 in the 1980s. The reason for this was decolonization—the process through which territories, mostly in Africa and Asia, formerly under imperial rule became independent states. In each of these cases "nationalist" pressures for "self-determination" resulted in the formation of new states.

The end of the cold war provided a new set of nationalist challenges to international order, resulting in the third wave of state formation in the twentieth century and increasing UN membership to 180 in 1993. Three communist federations—Yugoslavia, the Soviet Union and Czechoslovakia—gave way to new states formed by the erstwhile federal elements. In turn, many of those new states were themselves subject to disintegrationist pressures. This process of challenge and formation was accompanied by violent unrest and war—most prominently in the former Yugoslavia. The events in Yugoslavia and elsewhere have pushed the concepts of sovereignty, statehood, self-determination, and security onto the international agenda, both for students of international society and for policymakers and practitioners in national governments and international bodies such as the CSCE or the UN.

These are all words which can have different uses or meanings, depending on the user and the context. What they are taken to mean will depend on the interpretation, either explicit, or implicit, of another word replete with ambiguity: nation. All four S-words can be conjoined with "nation" to articulate a cardinal precept in the international canon: national sovereignty, national self-determination, nation-state, national security. A better understanding of what these concepts entail is crucial to the resolution of Europe's post-communist conflicts and has ramifications around the world. Until it has been established who is entitled to do what and in what circumstances, the representatives of the international community will find life confusing, painful, and crippling—whether dealing with the break-up of states, or making judgments on the question of external, particularly, humanitarian intervention in internal crises and conflicts . For, one of the major problems manifest in the international handling of the disintegration of Yugoslavia has been the absence of established international standards for dealing with the challenges involved and, even, a general lack of understanding of concepts at the heart of debates.

In the post-cold war world there can be no doubt that something has changed. This is attested not only in the content of academic and political discussion, but in practice in cases such as the Kurds of northern Iraq, Bosnia and Herzegovina, Somalia, and, in a different context, Libya.[2] Understanding of the key concept of sovereignty has clearly moved: as yet it is not clear where to. Often the content of contemporary thought on sovereignty and these other key concepts is not entirely new—interpretations may recall theoretical work from earlier periods. What is new, however, is the relevance of these ideas to security crises at the end of the twentieth century and, concomitantly, their bearing on policy and practice in international relations.

The aim of this paper is twofold. First, through use of the particularly virulent Yugoslav example, it will explore the nature of the challenge to international security issued by nationalism at the end of the twentieth century. Secondly, it will indicate the ways in which the ethnonationalist challenge has induced reassessment of the key concept in international relations—sovereignty. Following the end of the cold war, the protection from outside interference in matters of domestic jurisdiction offered to states by traditional interpretations of sovereignty has changed: it is now clear that the internal affairs of a state may be a matter of concern to international bodies. This has two consequences. First, on a more or less consensual basis, bodies such as the CSCE or the UN will have a role in the internal affairs of certain states. Secondly, in certain cases, however, as a consequence of changing interpretations in relation to the principle of noninterference, states may be subject to unwanted external intervention—which may, in extreme circumstances, involve the use of armed force.

### The Sovereign State System

States are the necessary components of an international system and the principle by which they are ordered is that of sovereignty. The key to sovereignty's position as the cornerstone of international relations is the precept of nonintervention. In what is traditionally described as an "anarchical society,"[3] each state is regarded as having absolute jurisdiction within its territorial bounds, but has no right to interfere in the internal sphere of other states. Thus, in spite of the absence of an overall sovereign in the international system—that is, the equivalent of a ruling authority within a state—some order can be found among states. The international system is anarchical because there is no overarching sovereign to provide rule, but social because there is a principle which regulates and orders life between the individual entities.

Sovereign states are the necessary components because all discourse in international relations is shaped by and around the existence of the nation-state. Environments of the international system (these may be, for example, economic, environmental, religious, or ideological) may place pressures on sovereign states, or create opportunities for them. But, critically, it is always in the purview of the sovereign state to decide for itself how to respond. The state can resist external pressure, or it can choose to accommodate it, which in some cases, may mean reapportioning some aspect of its sovereignty. This has been the case, for example, in the EU, where, by the end of the 1980s (in the then European Community) twelve states had "reached the limit of their possibilities," so if they did not act through the Community, they would "not do it through any other."[4] But, even in examples such as the EU where some aspects have been "pooled," the pooling of those aspects was a sovereign act in which each state made decided "to limit its freedom by making commitments," as Waltz would characterize it,[5] to the Union. A corollary of this is that a sovereign decision to reapportion some aspect of sovereignty may, presumably, be revoked by a subsequent exercise of sovereignty—as, it may be argued was the case in the dissolution of Yugoslavia (see below).

The origin of the sovereignty system lies in the Treaty of Westphalia of 1648. The important aspect of the Treaty was its legal codification of sovereign statehood, for the first time providing a general and formal principle of law to govern relations between states and taking sovereignty into the international sphere, giving it an external character—that of mutual recognition by other sovereigns—in addition to its previous internal qualities. The Treaty did not mean a rejection of the use of force, however. It merely meant that doctrinal difference between branches of the Christian faith and religious intolerance would not constitute a *casus belli*. Instead of them, it substituted reasons of state.

Whilst the principle of the Westphalian regime became the key to international relations, it did not fix the political-territorial dispensation in Europe indefinitely. Indeed, geopolitical boundaries in Europe shifted during the eighteenth and nineteenth centuries, largely in response to the growth of modern nationalism—that is, the phenomenon of political movements formed around the popular principle and ethnicity seeking to form nation-states (rather than more ancient manifestations of nationalism, as identified, for example, by Conor Cruise

O'Brien[6]). Crucially, however, in each phase of transition, new entities confirmed the sovereignty system by seeking membership of it and agreeing to be governed by its key principle. In this way, they conformed with Giddens's view that the principle of sovereignty is impelled through the international system: the nation-state is born into an already established global structure.[7]

Sovereignty is one of the concepts which falls into a category of ideas where a great part of their value is to be "essentially contested."[8] In practical use, it has a number of purposes, as Alan James has pointed out,[9] all of which may entail different definitions of its content. It is because sovereignty carries with it a particular status that it is much played on and much sought after—it is the qualification, in conventional thought on international relations, for membership of the society of states. In practice, as Robert Jackson has argued with reference to the developing world, as others have argued generally and as will be discussed below with reference to post-communist states in Europe,[10] the quality of sovereignty associated with any particular state may vary—which means that the content of sovereignty will change from one state to another.

Certainly, the meaning and content of sovereignty will often change according to the need of a particular government at a particular time—it is a plastic term which means that a government can justify almost any action, whether assertive or contrite, in terms of exercising its sovereign rights. Essentially, this means it has decided for itself what to do. It is the "power of action without being bounded unto others."[11] Whilst often taken to be a fundamentally legal concept in international relations,[12] sovereignty is, in reality, both legal and political. Indeed, it is ultimately a political concept because, as I shall emphasize below, the basic meaning of sovereignty is the political supremacy to make law (even though, in modern practice, the makers of law, themselves, are likely to be subject to legal restraint).

Whilst sovereignty may be susceptible to different interpretations, its general importance and formal content have remained constant: the key to the Westphalian system was mutual recognition between sovereigns. The content of sovereignty changed in one essential way as the system of which it was the guiding principle was extended. Whereas the Westphalian agreement had been made between sovereigns who were individuals (monarchs), this prescriptive mode of sovereignty had been generally supplanted by a popular one in Europe by the twentieth century—meaning that the exercise of sovereign rights was no longer the prerogative of a single personality, but that of the representatives of the state's governing institutions. Increasingly, if somewhat hypocritically, the degree to which power holders are seen to embody the interest of the people of a particular state through an "act of national self-determination based on the will of the majority" has become a factor in their being accepted and granted recognition as representatives of the sovereign by others in international society.[13]

## Nationalism, Sovereignty, and Self-Determination

The rise of the importance of the principle of self-determination alongside the shift from prescriptive to popular sovereignty went hand in hand with the rise of modern nationalism.[14] Associated especially with the shift from monarchical to republican rule in France, the idea of the "nation-state" developed. The idea of the nation was based on an ethnic community, sharing a collective name, a myth of common ancestry, social solidarity and certain elements of culture—often language and religion,[15] which should have the right to decide on its own government. By analogy with the freedom of individuals, nations were taken, paraphrasing Mill, to be free to pursue their own good, in their own way so long as they did not deprive others of theirs, or impede their efforts to obtain it.[16]

Following the French Enlightenment, the nation became politically supreme. Essentially, sovereignty was transferred to the nation, being assumed to be the source of all authority and, therefore, of law making: "The nation exists before all, it is the origin of everything. Its will is always legal, it is the law itself."[17] The nation and the people were taken to be synonymous, which created little problem in a country more or less ethnically and linguistically homogeneous, such as France.

The critical difference between an ethnic group, defined by a separate culture, of which over 8,000 have been identified,[18] and an ethnic community which may be regarded as a nation is the degree in which it is politically dynamic. More precisely, the distinction between an ethnic community *qua* ethnic community and a nation is its relationship to statehood and, by implication, sovereignty: nations either form a sovereign state, have or seek a constitutional stake in one, or are politically engaged in trying to form one, or define themselves vis-à-vis one. Thus, historically, Gypsies have never formed a national, or nationalist homeland; rather, they have been a (usually despised) ethnic community in whichever of the countries they were to be found. In contrast, another historically dispersed group, the Jews, had a politically dynamic character, at least in the Middle East, where they sought the formation of an independent state. Nationalism, therefore, is simply that phenomenon where the sentiment of common, usually ethnic, identity is used to mobilize political sentiment—at which point, the quintessential nature of nationalism means that political community— who constitutes "we" and who are "they"—is brought into question. Any ethnic group can form a nationalist movement, once it seeks to assert, or defend, itself politically as a community. The political action of one nationalist program forces others to address their own identity.[19] One group's claim for political status challenges that of other groups in a quest for political supremacy.

In the multiethnic, or multinationality, empires in Central and Eastern Europe the notion of a single nation concomitant with the state made no sense. Even after the collapse of those empires, few of the states formed in Central and Eastern Europe after World War I were ethnically homogeneous.[20] This left the majority of them vulnerable to nationalist challenges. Yet, a major component of the drive for national self-determination, led by U.S. President Woodrow Wilson, was the idea that each nation should be self-governing.

Those states which were formed as a result of the self-determination tide in 1919, whether ethnically homogeneous or heterogeneous and, therefore, challenged, all embraced the sovereign state system eagerly. Between the two World Wars, the League of Nations made attempts to preserve the sovereign state system and, at the same time, to assure the position of ethnic minorities in Central and Eastern Europe.[21] Whilst the League system was generally seen to have failed, it did further imbed the idea of the sovereign nation state.

In the UN era, whilst a global international society has been empirically established for the first time through the very existence of the organization and its comprehensive membership, the UN system, principally through the Charter and through practice, confirmed the preeminence of the sovereign state as the primary unit of international relations. This was taken to be established by article 2 of the UN Charter, in paragraphs 4 and 7. It is these paragraphs which determine legally and, often, politically and practically, international relations. Conventionally, it is these paragraphs which confirm the sanctity of the state and its right to be free from interference in its internal affairs. Paragraph 4 proscribes "the threat or use of force against the territorial integrity or political independence of any state," whilst paragraph 7 establishes the concept of "domestic jurisdiction":

> Nothing contained in the present Charter shall authorise the United Nations to intervene in matters which are essentially within the domestic jurisdiction of any state.

In addition, among its key principles, stated in article 1, the Charter established the role of the Security Council in dealing with matters of international peace and security and "on respect for the principle of equal rights and self-determination of peoples."

At the same time, the UN Charter established, as formulae, at least, two significant developments in international relations. Both concern the right to use armed force. The initial effect of the Westphalian system had been to remove religion as a *casus belli*. But, this had left all other issues as potential reasons rightfully to launch a war. The UN Charter left the right to use armed force with the state in only one case—that of self-defense (article 51 of the Charter) and even this could be restricted by resolutions issued by the UN Security Council under chapter VII of the Charter. The second development also related to chapter VII and the Security Council. This involved the centralization of the right to use armed force in the UN Security Council. Thus, in principle, the UN era was one in which any use of armed force that was not in self-defense or initiated by the Security Council was in breach of international law and a matter for the Security Council to deal with. The point of all of this, however, was to underline the primacy of the inviolability of the sovereign state in international society.

Whilst these aspects of the UN Charter reflect the degree to which it was a product of World War II, to a large extent, it was also drafted in response to the second wave of nationalist pressure for the formation of new states in the twentieth century. As with the first wave, however, the second created a new set of states a good number of which were vulnerable to internal ethnic and nationalist challenges. Indeed, the UN Charter perhaps also fostered this phenomenon, as the second wave came in response to what has been termed "anti-colonialist nationalism."[22] In this phase, "nationalist leaders more often than not mobilised diverse groups who shared a hostility to colonial rule rather than a pre-colonial group sentiment or identity of interest."[23] The physical product of this process was a large number of new states, many of which were in crucial respects weak.[24]

This process of state-formation came, as with its predecessor at the end of World War I, as a result of the notion of self-determination. An idea historically associated with liberal thought,[25] paradoxically, self-determination for groups required individuals to be subject to the demands of a collective, at least in a limited historical phase, effectively making them prisoners of a political community. However, the reality of post-World War II anti-colonial self-determination was to limit the exercise of the right to self-determination. Implicitly, self-determination, sovereignty, and statehood were inseparably linked: self-determination meant the right to form a sovereign state. The right, however, was applied to predefined territorial units. Formal sovereignty in the international system was restricted to states (this will receive further discussion below).

Statehood was determined by territorial parameters: the territory of former colonial units was inherited by the new state. As a consequence, in all those cases where "diverse groups" with only a common opposition to colonial governance meant ethnically divided societies, the right of other groups which might seek to continue the process of self-determination was, in effect, curtailed—in an attempt to "freeze the political map."[26] In short, the concept of national self-determination was confined to "anti-colonial self-determination." In Africa, despite the almost complete absence of congruence between ethnic communities and state borders, in 1963, the leaders of the members of the Organization of African Unity, in spite of nationalist challenges to the border regime established under colonialism, opted to preserve the state sovereignty system, reasoning that to attempt to redraw boundaries would create more problems than it would solve.[27] With the single exception of the secession of Bangladesh from Pakistan, until the collapse of the communist federations at the beginning of the 1990s led to a wave of new state formation, no group or territory claiming to exercise a right to self-determination beyond the anti-colonial context achieved international recognition of its claim to sovereignty and statehood.

This is because the state is the primary unit of international relations. Moreover, the single principle which provides for minimal order, or society, in international relations is mutual recognition of sovereignty between states. This is generally understood as the principle

of noninterference. The reason for this is that it is international society, based on the principle of noninterference in sovereign affairs,
which provided states with the minimal security available in the absence of an international sovereign which would make and enforce
rules. However, in the post-cold war world this arrangement has been
put under pressure not by demands for self-determination in the framework of anti-colonial nationalism, but of substate groups motivated by
nationalism—that is, political instrumentalisation of group identity and
sentiment. As will be seen below, the double usage of nation to refer
both to the population of a territorially defined state and to a politically mobilized ethnic community within a state, in this context, needs
reevaluation.

### The Serbian Snake

The critical case in which resurgent nationalism has decisively challenged order and security in post-communist Europe is the former
Yugoslavia. Analysis of this case provides a useful reference point for
discussion of the issues at stake in such situations. It also provides an
example of a specific "hissing snake" which has spit its venom bitterly
in the early 1990s and which is a model of the general challenge
presented in many places where there are mixed ethnic communities.
The unique lens through which to explore the concepts of nation,
sovereignty, statehood, self-determination, and security is the hissing
snake peculiar to the Yugoslav context: that of Serbian nationalism.
   Although a model of the four *S*s which make the snake, Serbian
nationalism has four *S*s of its own which illustrate clearly the kernel of
all nationalisms, no matter how the nation is construed, or how positive a particular swell of nationalist fire may be at a certain time. The
Serbian-cum-Yugoslav example allows a peculiar opportunity to look
at the lexical ambiguity of some of the key concepts at the heart of this
paper. It also points to the bearings being taken in the international
community towards more useful definition of the four S-words.
   The Serbian version of the snake derives from the four Ss which
appear on the traditional Serbian emblem, now regarded by some as a
companion to the Nazi swastika: a cross with four cyrillic *S*s (which
look like *C*s to those used to Latin script) placed in the four corners.
(See p. 181) These stand for "Samo sloga srbina spasava"—often
translated as "Only unity saves the Serbs."[28] The four *S*s around the

cross emblem is a reference to the medieval Serbian kingdom and the professed part the Serbs played in the defence of Christendom against the Muslim Turks in the fourteenth century. Symbolically, it is only gathering around the cross in solidarity that enables Serbian survival. The ultimate responsibility for the 1990s war of dissolution in Yugoslavia lies with the military-political elite in Belgrade,[29] although the break-up of the old federation and the reality of the war result from a number of factors. However, the primary condition for war was Serbian nationalism. This was focused on Serbian solidarity: all the Serbs should live in one state, in which they would only be secure if they were able to live in solidarity alone, or with others who accepted Serbian supremacy. This was the backdrop for the practice called "ethnic cleansing."[30]

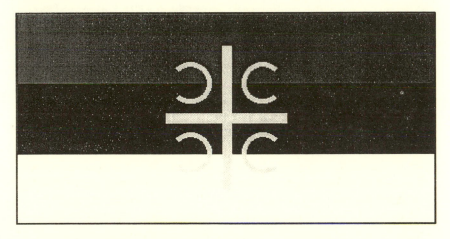

The Serbian national question was decisive in the violent break-up of Yugoslavia. It was also critical in the formation of the state, 1 December 1918, as the Kingdom of Serbs, Croats, and Slovĕnes (it was renamed Yugoslavia in 1929). The creation of a common South Slav state—Yugoslav means "South Slav"—was the culmination of two ideas.[31] The first of these, "the Yugoslav idea," emerged from mixed groups of South Slav intellectuals, mainly Croats and Slovĕnes, in the Austro-Hungarian Empire. The basis of this idea was that all the South Slavs speaking the same, or related languages, should be able to live together in a common state which would allow them expression of their right to "national self-determination."

The second idea was found among Serbian intellectuals: the unification of all Serbs in one state. In the course of the nineteenth century, an independent Serbian state had attained independence from the Otto-man Empire. However, many Serbs were left beyond the borders of this "narrow Serbia," either in Bosnia and Herzegovina, or in Croatia-Slavonia and Dalmatia within the Habsburg Empire. The ideal of unit-ing all the Serbs in one state was, therefore, obvious in a nineteenth century in which the same aspiration was embraced by other groups such as the Germans and the Italians.[32]

The formation of Yugoslavia represented the coming together of these two ideas. In principle, it was a state for all the South Slavs: Croats, Slověnes, and others would achieve self-determination and fulfil their Slavic potential, whilst all the Serbs would be united. How-ever, in practice, the 1918–41 Yugoslav state was a unitary Serb King-dom, where the other South Slavs felt second class and were treated with suspicion by the Serbs as potential (or actual) traitors to the state. When the Axis powers invaded in April 1941, Yugoslavia disinte-grated. It was reconstituted by Josip Broz Tito's communist-led Parti-sans, the victors in a multifaceted war combining elements of civil war, revolution, and liberation. The communist success in creating a second Yugoslav state was, in good part, due to the promise to correct the failures of the first Yugoslavia by creating nation-state formations, which would fulfil the aspirations to self-determination non-Serbs had sought, but not found, in the first Yugoslavia. This was especially important in providing Croatian communists with means to win the support in Croatia for the new state.[33]

A copy of the Stalinist Soviet constitution provided the legal frame-work for this. A "voluntary" federation of peoples in their nation-state formations was created. These were sovereign entities, called Socialist republics, which gave expression to the various peoples' rights to self-determination. However, these republics retained the right to secede from the federation under the Constitution. Together, they formed the Federal People's Republic of Yugoslavia. However, it is important to note that the Yugoslav communists did not intend the provisions of the 1946 constitution to have any meaning.[34]

Meaning accrued to the Constitution after Stalin expelled Tito from the Soviet bloc; to survive, the Yugoslav communists had to prove that, in the dispute with the Soviets, they were in the right. This meant going back to Marx and Lenin in order to prove that they were differ-ent from and better than the Soviets—that is, that they were better communists. The Yugoslavs came up with their own communist variant, socialist self-management, in which control of economic units was to be devolved from the center. This implied concomitant political decentralization. Like the 1946 constitution, this new program was not intended to have much meaning. However, pressures grew in the republican political elites to give formal provisions real content.

The history of the Yugoslav state, especially Tito's version, was one of tension between center and periphery, with power and authority passing incrementally throughout the second Yugoslavia from the federation to the republics. This situation was codified in the 1974 Constitution of the newly renamed Socialist Federative Republic of Yugoslavia. That was, *de facto*, a confederal arrangement. While Tito was alive, most problems could be solved by the assertion of his authority. In the decade following his death in 1980, economic, social, and political reforms were all stymied because authority lay, ever more, with the republics. Reform required inter-republican consensus. The chasm between the republican leaderships, however, proved unbridgeable.

As the future of Yugoslavia was debated at the end of the 1980s and communist rule waned, the republican leaderships and populations fell back on ethnonational identity as a source of strength and security, and on sovereignty as the means of self-protection.[35] The Slovenian leadership invoked sovereignty as it responded to a popularly perceived threat from Belgrade. This happened in 1988, against the background of a martial clampdown by Belgrade in the Autonomous Province of Kosovo in southern Serbia, where an 80 or 90 percent ethnic Albanian population had been living under repression since riots in the Province in 1981. Slovenia sought self-protection through recitation of the magic word, whilst Serbia asserted its claim to sovereignty over Kosovo. In different ways, both effectively challenged the sovereignty and integrity of the Yugoslav federation—the internationally perceived object of sovereignty.

When dissolution of Yugoslavia became inevitable with the declarations of independence by Slovenia and Croatia in June 1991, the key concepts were the right to self-determination and the property of sovereignty. However, the question of "national self-determination" was raised in another context: Serbs began to invoke the notion—if others were to be allowed to exercise the right to self-determination, then why not the Serbs, came the cry?[36] It was a cry compounded by different interpretations of the Yugoslav Constitution.

## Sovereignty and Self-Determination:
## Yugoslavia and the Meaning of Nation

In the two years leading up to the declarations of independence by Slovenia and Croatia, and in the wake of those declarations, different understandings on the question of right-holders were in conflict with reference to the rights to sovereignty and self-determination. These conflicting conceptions were addressed in the European Community's Conference on Yugoslavia, held first in The Hague and later in Brussels. In particular, they were considered by a legal advisory and arbitration commission established by the Conference under President of the French Constitutional Council, Robert Badinter. It was their interpretation of constitutional and international legal matters which provided the framework for the Council of the European Community to act politically to settle these questions, at least partially.

At the heart of the constitutional-political dispute, although not a part of it, as such, was the meaning given to "nation." This was linked to different interpretations of the principles of sovereignty and self-determination.[37] Divergent interpretations of "nation" rendered radically different outcomes in terms of the compound concepts "national self-determination" and "national sovereignty." Nation refers to people who are, with small exceptions, born together into a particular community. Nation may, therefore, refer to all the people born within the territorial boundaries of a political community in which they have citizenship rights - it is in this sense that U.S. presidents often address "the Nation." Nation may also, however, allude to all the people born within a particular ethnonational group (which might be defined by genetic, linguistic, cultural, religious—and so forth—characteristics) irrespective of the territorially defined political communities in which they find themselves.[38]

Nation, defined as all the people living within the territorial boundaries of a given political community, and nation, defined as all the members of a particular ethnonational group, lead to terminological trouble where the two senses of nation do not coincide. (There are perhaps as few as twenty cases in which the two actually coincide to the extent that less than five percent of the population is not from the titular nationality.) Where the same ethnonational group is found within more than one state, problems of sovereignty and self-determination may arise.

These were sharply focused in the break-up of Yugoslavia. Declarations of independence by Slovenia and Croatia were based in claims to sovereignty and the inalienable right to national self-determination for the republics and their populations. These were directly opposed by a Serbian claim to the sovereignty of the Serbs as an ethnonational people, wherever they were to be found, with the fundamental and inalienable right to national self-determination. Both claims were made on the basis of the Yugoslav Constitution.

The right to national self-determination, up to and including the right to secession, was granted in the preamble to the Yugoslav Constitution.[39] Each republic was a "nation-state" formation which was endowed with sovereignty.[40] The general problem of defining the right-holder—that is, which "nation" is repository of these inalienable rights—is compounded in the Yugoslav case. "Narodna samoupravlenje"—"national self-determination" in Serbo-Croat intensifies the terminological tension.

In Serbo-Croat, "narod" means both "people" and "nation." In both senses, it can refer to the ethnonational group or to the inhabitants of a state. The difficulty here is amplified with reference to the "United Nations" (that is, the global organization of states) which can be rendered as "Ujedina Naroda," or "Ujedina Nacija"—that is, in some cases, a separate word was used to refer to nation-as-state.[41] This implies that, in Serbian minds, the term "narodna samoupravlenje" was taken (both really and, where appropriate, disingenuously) to refer to the Serbian people wherever they were.

The ambiguity over national self-determination in the Yugoslav context has peculiar features. These, however, are particulars which only add emphasis—they do not render the Yugoslav example itself unique. Outside that context, the issue has generally been more clearly defined. Indeed, the general understanding, received from previous periods, particularly decolonization, in which self-determination and sovereignty were key questions informed the Badinter Commission as it considered the Yugoslav case.

The Commission effectively rejected the Serbian claim to sovereignty for the ethnonation, in its official opinions. It deemed sovereignty to rest with territorial units, that is, the republics. It was less categoric, when the Serbian camp sought clarification about the right of the Serbs in Croatia and in Bosnia and Herzegovina to self-determination. It did not express the opinion that a right to self-determination was not available to the Serbs in Croatia and in Bosnia and Herzegovina.[42] Rather, it implied that there might possibly be a second level at which self-determination operated. In this case, self-determination could be regarded as a principle which extended from the protection of individual human rights and involved the possibility of individuals claiming membership of an ethnic, religious, linguistic, or other group. Groups of this kind, would be entitled to respectful treatment by states under the imperative norms of international law (*jus cogens*).[43]

The Commission's opinions were based largely on traditional international law and convention, although, to some extent, there was innovation appropriate to the Yugoslav problem. Whereas, in theory, self-determination might be interpreted as applying, at the lowest level, to individuals, it is, essentially, a collective right. In practice, application of the right has been restricted to specific circumstances—and only with regard to predetermined territorial units, mostly in the course of decolonization.[44] Badinter made clear that the principle of *uti posseditis*, originally established in the context of decolonisation, pertained to Yugoslavia. This meant that, in the absence of peaceful agreement to alter frontiers which were changing status, "the former boundaries acquire the character of boundaries protected by international law."[45]

According to this opinion, the protection in international law of their boundaries was extended to the emerging states. A number of nonbinding international documents, including the Helsinki Final Act were referred to in support of this finding. Most importantly, however, it was backed by reference to the UN Charter. In effect, the Commission judged that the republics were entitled to the protection and provisions of article 2 of the UN Charter concerning the territorial integrity and political independence of states.[46]

The following is a synthetic summary, derived from the Arbitration Commission's opinions, of what is implied by the terms sovereignty and self-determination: the former applies to territorial units, as does self-determination, up to and including statehood; however, self-determination may also apply to other "national" (that is, self-defining ethnic, religious, genetic, cultural, linguistic, and so forth) groups, as an expression of its members' individual human rights; this does not, though, include the right to form a state, although it entails the right to status, including levels of autonomy—that is, political and cultural prerogatives and powers, perhaps of self-governance, operable within the boundaries of a state.

The blending of elements of international law (*uti posseditis juris*) with the provisions of the Yugoslav Constitution offered clarification of the issues at stake. Sovereignty and statehood were both linked to territory; national self-determination was linked to them in cases where "nation" referred to the people living within the boundaries of a defined territorial unit; sovereignty, statehood and national self-determination were not necessarily linked and were not juridically to be combined where "nation" alluded to the members of an ethnonational community which formed part of one or more states, or territorial units with the potential to become states.

Whilst none of this ruled out completely the possibility of statehood for an ethnonational group seeking to exercise a right to self-determination, it meant that there would be a bias against this happening. The emphasis would remain on preserving existing states. In the Yugoslav context, this meant that once the Vance-Owen plan (which would have preserved a single Bosnian state on the basis of ten provinces), had been abandoned in May 1993, it was replaced by discussions on the basis for an internal division of the country which would create a Union of Republics with sovereignty granted to each of the three ethnically defined republics which would form the Union.[47] This, of course, sowed the seeds for possible dissolution of the Union at some stage in the future, if required conditions were met.

When a general framework for peace was achieved towards the end of 1995, the arrangement fell somewhere between these earlier options.[48] In the talks at Dayton, Ohio (signed as an agreement in Paris on 14 December 1995), there was agreement to shape Bosnia as a single state on the basis of two entities and three peoples. The entities, unlike the Union of Republics concept, were not endowed with sovereignty or a formal entitlement to independence. But, there was understood to be a degree of ambiguity on this issue as this was the only way of reconciling wholly opposed positions. It was not wholly excluded that there could be a parting of the ways, but the provisions would not make this straightforward. Rather there was a division of sovereignty on what was effectively a mixture of territorial and nonterritorial bases: the entities—Federation of Bosnia-Herzegovina (primarily comprising Croats and Muslims) and the Republika Srpska (essentially comprising Serbs) were important elements in the constitution of the country, but the network of projected political institutions effectively created a gridlock: each ethnic group could operate a veto on matters which were of vital interest, thus making consensus a pre-requisite for any decisive steps. The agreement, ableit with a provi-sional aspect, was based on an assumption: Bosnia's sovereignty had to be divisible. From this it followed that any peaceful and viable future for the country rested on a redistribution of that divisible sover-eignty.

This process of redistribution has not yet been fully recognized—and never may be. However, as I shall suggest, reinventing one of the wheels of sovereignty in this way is essential to the promotion of security and settlement of conflicts. Accompanying this, there is a gradual shift towards acceptance, that, through (at least, temporary) division of sovereignty with international bodies, the sovereignty in-herent in a state throughout its territory may be partitioned and par-celled into new territorial packages. Each of these may form part of a compound sovereignty, throughout the state's territory, shared both within the state and with an external agent. An extension of this, is that, ultimately, the new distribution of sovereignty could provide the mechanism for a change in the external borders of the state where the sovereign components of the whole are territorially based and where the other elements of the compound do not exercise the veto provided by their own portion of sovereignty to prevent this happening.

In cases such as Bosnia and Herzegovina where the international community made enormous military (the NATO-led IFOR, then SFOR) and civilian commitments following the Dayton accords, there is un-likely to be an environment where positive intercommunal relations can emerge, or reemerge, without help from the outside world. The possibilities for states further to share sovereignty with international bodies are still under investigation, although the UN role in the peace settlement in Cambodia and the holding of elections there offers one framework. Other examples where this is already the case, albeit in extremely limited senses, were mentioned above.

The UN involvement in Cambodia was significant. The UN estab-lished a Transitional Authority in Cambodia (UNTAC). This was to administer the country until the first post-settlement elections had taken place. Although there were a number of other tasks to be undertaken, such as mine clearance and repatriation, ensuring that the elections took place and were reasonably fair was the primary mission for UNTAC.[49] In order to do this, in excess of 20,000 UN peacekeepers were deployed. Whereas the UN had taken responsibility for transitional votes—partially in Namibia (jointly with South Africa) and wholly in the Western Sahara and in Angola, Cambodia was distinct in that the UN took responsibility for major government ministries, thus redistributing, for the transitional phase, aspects of sovereignty to the UN, whilst formally, a twelve member Supreme National Council governed the country, purportedly a coalition of all the warring parties.

In spite of problems, UNTAC was a relative success. The open hostility of one of the former belligerents, the Khmer Rouge, which withdrew its consent to the UN presence and delayed and complicated the deployment of large parts of the UNTAC peacekeeping force, was a particular problem.[50] So was a campaign sponsored by the former Hun Sen government to undermine UNTAC through low-level intimidation of its opponents.[51] The elections were able to be conducted in a relatively free and fair way—including the participation of more than half the 370,000 refugees returned by UNTAC from Thailand, with 4.7 million Cambodians being registered to vote. However, whilst the elections were a relative success, UNTAC was unable to accomplish its mission to demilitarize the country. In part this was due to the difficulty and cost of mine clearance where millions of land mines had been laid. More significantly, less than 5 percent of the estimated 200,000 troops due to be cantoned and disarmed by July 1992 had been. The reason for this was the Khmer Rouge renunciation of the agreement which, whilst it did not lead to complete breakdown and a return to war, meant that the other parties would not be prepared to put down their weapons. Thus, the UN involvement in Cambodia was initially successful, but it would take at least a decade before the initial outcome could be regarded as fully secure. But, it was significant that the UN's sharing of sovereignty in the transitional period had made sure that the majority of parties could not question the impartiality of the administration and that no party could ruin, or manipulate, the elections through control of, for example, the interior ministry. A temporary UN stake in Cambodia had increased confidence among the Cambodian factions. The long-term problem, however, could prove to be that, without the UN, but still not demilitarized, Cambodia could fall back on fighting in the future.

A similar external role was discussed often with reference to the future of Bosnia and Herzegovina. The much discussed, much criticized and much misunderstood Vance-Owen Plan would have been underpinned not only by a significant UN and EC involvement in the

Plan's implementation, but would also have seen a UN administration for the capital city, Sarajevo, and EC administration for the regional capital of Herzegovina, Mostar. In addition, each of the ten provinces foreseen in the plan, would have had a complicated governmental structure, including a governor nominated by representatives of the largest ethnic group, a deputy from the second largest group, and proportional representation in the provincial government of all the ethnic groups. There would also have been a mechanism for protection of minority ethnic groups within the provinces.[52] All of this would have been underpinned by a UN implementation force, both military and civilian.

Although the Vance-Owen Plan was replaced by the idea of a Union of Republics, comprising three ethnically based mini-states, the international perspective remained one in which it was thought unrealistic that there could be any settlement in Bosnia without an element of external administration. When international efforts secured an end to the bombardment of Sarajevo in February 1994, the next moves were to begin to work towards a UN administration of the city. However, it was not reasonable to expect this to work effectively without a more comprehensive settlement having been established in the rest of the country and supported by UN peacekeepers. Even with a UN presence, there would be the prospect of one party, or more, reneging on the settlement as happened in Cambodia. Without one, a return to hostilities would be almost certain.

This would be the case whether or not the outcome of the Bosnian war was a unitary state, internal partition, or complete international partition. Whatever the details, the key to any outcome, remained the willingness of the Bosnian government to agree to the redistribution of some of its formal sovereignty—both within Bosnian territory and beyond it (and, of course, the preparedness of others, to be part of any sovereignty rearrangement). As indicated above, when a peace agreement was achieved at Dayton at the end of 1995, the basis for provisional settlement was division of Bosnia's sovereignty.

The need for "collapsed" states, riven by internal animosities, to have an external prop for a transitional period if they are in any way to be restored seems to have become a feature of international relations. However, these remain specific and exceptional cases dealt with on their own merit. There were significant moves in the early 1990s towards the creation of new international norms which not only indicated the importance in terms of international security of regulating the scope of states with regard to their populations. Although initial fumbles in the darkness, these stirrings were an indication that those concerned with international relations might be beginning to follow the lead made by constitutional theorists (from the sixteenth century onwards) in recognizing that sovereignty, whilst absolute in its quality, is divisible—and that states may share some parts of their sovereignty with international bodies.

In addition, there is one more small, but paramount, instance of states conceding part of their sovereignty to the international community—one which is unparalleled and beyond question, but which is usually forgotten. That is the abdication of sovereignty made in the sphere of international peace and security by all states signing the UN Charter, where in the last clause of article 2(7), and in Chapter VII, the limit of state sovereignty is imposed at the point where the UN Security Council determines a threat to international peace and security under Chapter VII.

## Chapter VII Measures: Intervention and Enforcement after the Cold War

Although article 2 of the UN Charter generally sets down the independence, integrity, and freedom from external meddling in internal affairs due to states and, in Chapter VII, Article 51 grants the inherent right to self-defense, both these cease to apply in specific circumstances. These are when the UN Security Council has determined a "threat to international peace and security". In 2(7), the last clause sets out the limit of the principle of noninterference: " . . . this principle shall not prejudice the application of enforcement measures under Chapter VII." Similarly, article 51, which establishes the "inherent right to individual and collective self-defense," also has the caveat that this is so only until the Security Council has "determined a threat to international peace and security" in order to take enforcement measures, whether military (Article 42), or non-military (Article 41).

What this means is that sovereignty in the sphere of matters of international peace and security lies with the UN Security Council: it decides what constitutes the kind of threat to international peace and security that warrants suspension of a state's otherwise inherent rights. Conventionally, this has been taken to be applicable only in cases of an act of aggression by one state against another, although in the cases of Rhodesia (1966), especially, and South Africa (1977) this was not strictly the case, as internal policies were in question (*a propos* of South Africa, there was also an external dimension). What happened following the end of the cold war, beginning with the Kurdish situation in northern Iraq, was that interpretation of what could be regarded as constituting a threat to international peace and security was significantly altered.

It became clear that there was no longer a single, more or less fixed definition, understood by all. Instead, the concept of a threat to international peace and security had become elastic and became applicable in a variety of circumstances, all of which challenged traditional views of sovereignty. In January 1992, the Heads of Government and State of the members of the UN Security Council issued a declaration making this clear:

> The absence of war and military conflict amongst States does not in itself ensure international peace and security. The non-military sources of instability in the economic, social, humanitarian and ecological fields have become threats to peace and security.[53]

In line with this, Chapter VII resolutions were passed by the Security Council with regard to the extradition of suspected terrorists from Libya (Resolution 748, 1992), the restoration of peace and security within a country, Somalia, Resolution 733, 1992) and with regard to arms supplies and involvement in war with reference to the former Yugoslavia (Resolutions 713, 1991; 757, 770 781, all 1992; 816, 820, 836, all 1993). The Security Council resolutions on Bosnia and Herzegovina, Libya, and Somalia are radical departures in terms of sovereignty in international relations. In particular, with reference to Somalia and Libya, previously unthinkable definitions of a threat to international peace and security were given.

The growth in the use of Chapter VII measures, as well as the broadening of the situations in which they would be used, was a product of the international handling of the Iraqi invasion of Kuwait in 1990. The post-cold war cooperation between the Soviet Union and the West gave rise to a situation in which to an unprecedented degree, the UN functioned as a collective security organization, as had been intended at its inception.[54] Although it is possible to question the UN response to the Gulf conflict philosophically as an act of collective security (because of the degree to which events were driven by particular interests, rather than by an absolute commitment to international peace and security), there is little doubt that, in form and effect, it became the first occasion on which the UN acted fully in terms of collective security.

On one previous occasion, the UN had acted partially in the manner intended: Korea. Although Chapter VII had been implied in UN Security Council Resolution 82 (1950) on Korea in which it was determined that "this action constitutes a breach of the peace," there was no explicit reference to it. Nor was there any reference to the Chapter in the two subsequent resolutions which led to the expedition of an international force to repel the North Korean advance across the thirty-eighth parallel, the line which had been agreed between the Soviet Union and the United States as demarcating their sectors of occupation in 1945. That force was authorized to have a unified command under the UN flag; the United States was asked to provide a commanding officer and be responsible for organizing the combined forces.

The role of the UN in Korea was essentially to provide "international legitimacy for the United States efforts to aid South Korea."[55] The use of the UN in Korea was only made possible by a Soviet boycott of the Security Council at the time. Had the Soviet Union not been seeking to promote membership by the newly established People's Republic of China, it would have been in a position to veto the resolutions—in most other instances in the first forty years of the UN the veto in the hands of the five permanent members of the Security Council (the United States, the United Kingdom, the Soviet Union—inherited by the Russian Federation, France, and China) meant that the work of the Security Council was stalled as the cold war adversaries had different perspectives on most issues.

In the case of Korea, there was not so much an act of collective security by all states, as a use of the UN mechanism by one side in a divided world against the other—a use only made possible by the Soviet absence. In reality, Korea was an act of collective defence by non-communist countries against communist ones. After U.S.-led forces had gone far towards not only restoring the *status quo ante*, but also towards the reunification of the two Koreas, intervention from the People's Republic of China led to a situation in which the division along the thirty-eighth parallel was restored. Although both sides supported the reunification of the country, they did so on incompatible terms and the division of Korea became imbedded and remained a question for the UN in the 1990s.

The Gulf conflict was different from Korea because there was general unanimity, notably among the great powers. Iraq had invaded Kuwait in what constituted a textbook case of interstate aggression. With the cold war in abeyance and China seeking to reestablish international links following the outrage following the Tiananmen Square massacre in 1988, almost unique global conditions allied with a peculiarly straightforward act of aggression created a situation in which it was possible for the UN security mechanism to work. Between the Iraqi invasion of Kuwait on 2 August 1990 and 17 June 1991, the Security Council issued nineteen resolutions, only two of which were not clearly Chapter VII resolutions dealing with an act of aggression. The outcome was the restoration of the territorial integrity of Kuwait, under the aegis of the UN, by a coalition of forces, as with Korea, led by the United States.

However, in the course of the handling of the Gulf conflict, there was a significant departure from traditional practice. This was the improvisation of "safe havens" for the Kurds in northern Iraq. These were established by the coalition partners following media-led pressure once it became clear that having been apparently led on by the coalition partners to rise up and overthrow repression from the Iraqi authorities, the Kurds were being subject to genocidal reprisals. Although the coalition partners began to establish the "safe havens" *de facto*, they also sought the cover of Security Council Resolution (SCR) 688 (1991). However, this was one of the two resolutions which did not clearly rely on Chapter VII. When the coalition partners transferred responsibility for the "safe havens" to the UN, the Secretary General insisted on the signing of a memorandum of understanding with the Iraqi government before accepting responsibility. This was because of the implications for the interpretation of sovereignty in the international system inherent in the creation of "safe havens." These were breaches of territorial integrity and infringements of state sovereignty, in traditional terms. This had implications for ideas of humanitarian intervention and for the understanding of sovereignty in the state system (see below).

The Security Council cooperation over the Gulf conflict was the first in a series of actions where the traditional understanding of that which constituted a threat to international peace and security became broader. Following the precedent of the Kurds in Iraq, humanitarian questions became matters of international intervention. In the former Yugoslavia and in Somalia, the Security Council authorized a variety of interventionist measures, military and nonmilitary, which relied on explicit or implicit references to chapter vii.

The first time the Security Council addressed the conflict in former Yugoslavia was on 25 September 1991, exactly three months after declarations of independence by Slovenia and Croatia, when it imposed an embargo on the transfer of armaments to the then Yugoslav state and any of its territories. This was a mandatory measure, but, following the Kurdish model, it dealt with what had been traditionally within the purview of domestic jurisdiction. Whilst it was evidently the case that the Yugoslav federation had entered a phase of transition and was becoming a number of separate states claiming a right to self-determination and was a proto-interstate conflict, in terms of the UN it remained an internal conflict, outside the established understanding of what could trigger a Chapter VII resolution, that is, an interstate act of aggression. Instead, the only reference to an external dimension was reference to the movement of refugees into Europe which the war in Croatia was producing. Indeed, the decision to take enforcement measures was "hidden" in the fifth operative paragraph, rather than being emphasized in the resolution. Many countries, indeed, were deeply sensitive to the implications of taking Chapter VII action where the only international threat was the prospect of more refugees. For China, the Soviet Union, India and Zimbabwe on the Security Council at that time the critical factor which had swayed them to authorize the resolution was the speech to the Security Council by the Yugoslav foreign minister in which he had requested the embargo.[56]

Once that initial step had been taken, it was some time before further Chapter VII action was taken with regard to Yugoslavia. By the time sanctions were imposed under SCR 757 (1992), three former Yugoslav republics had become independent and the context of that action was more consistent with traditional interpretations of international conflict—the Federal Republic of Yugoslavia (Serbia and Montenegro) was being held responsible for the conflict in Bosnia and Herzegovina. However, a variety of subsequent resolutions mostly making express reference to Chapter VII were issued with regard to the creation of an air-exclusion zone, the delivery of humanitarian assistance, and the declaration of safe areas. It is significant that there was interplay between the different sets of resolutions which were taking international society into uncharted—some would argue un-Chartered—waters. Resolutions in one area with reference to a particular problem made it easier to issue similar resolutions with regard to another—although there was also the reality of a resolution issued on one conflict creating pressure for a similar one on another crisis.

A clear example of this was the Security Council's arms ban with reference to Somalia. Whereas the Yugoslav case had been processed with caution and reservation, Resolution 733 (1992) on Somalia could be adopted because the Yugoslav resolution had already established a precedent—the form of the resolution was very similar. In Somalia, however, there was to be a critical further extension of the new scope for defining threats to the peace and for authorizing mandatory interventionist action. Going beyond the Security Council resolutions on Iraq and Bosnia, as well as failing to make even a passing reference to the subject of refugees (which had been the case with Resolution 733 (1992)), the situation in Somalia was declared a threat to international peace and security and, for the first time, a full military enforcement mission *within* the borders of a member state had been authorized.[57]

The UN had first begun its involvement in Somalia in mid-1992 when UNOSOM I was established with a force of 500 troops (later increased to 3,500), although the first 500 of these, a Pakistani battalion, did not arrive until the following October. This force was deployed into a complex situation in which, effectively, there was no Somalia—there had been no government of central authority since January 1991 when the government of dictator Siad Barre fell. UNOSOM I could not operate—the Pakistani battalion was kept in barracks in the Somali capital Mogadishu and other units were unable to deploy. In the light of a report on UNOSOM I, facing embarrassing questions on inaction in Bosnia (and possibly wishing either to leave office in glory, or bequeath trouble), outgoing U.S. President George Bush offered to commit 24,000 troops to Somalia, at an estimated cost of $450 million.

This deployment was groundbreaking. First, it was the first UN operation to have U.S. troops wearing UN blue helmets and taking part in a UN operation (rather than one authorized by the UN, such as Korea and the Gulf conflict). More significantly, SCR 794 which established the Unified Task Force (UNITAF) in which the United States took the lead role, was mandated to use all measures necessary to

establish a secure environment for humanitarian relief operations—
that meant stopping the local warlords and their militias, as well as
bandits, from looting humanitarian supply convoys. This resolution
required the Security Council to determine that the situation in Somalia constituted a threat to international peace and security in order to
authorize enforcement measures under Chapter VII.

This force involved military personnel from twenty countries, total-
ling 37,000. However, its mandate was restricted to 40 percent of
Somalia and did not include disarmament of militias. A further resolution,[58] extended the mission, creating UNOSOM II. This mandated the
UN force to "assume responsibility for the consolidation, expansion
and maintenance of a secure environment throughout Somalia." This
created a situation in which UN forces were effectively mandated to
restore law and order in the country. This mandate was further expanded in June 1993, following the death of 46 UN soldiers in
UNOSOM II and 300 Somalis in clashes between the UN forces and
the Somali National Alliance led by General Mohammed Farah Aideed.
Security Council Resolution 837 reaffirmed UNOSOM II's mandate
and added to its authority to seek out, detain, and punish those ob-
structing the force from carrying out its mandate. In effect, this meant
UNOSOM II going to war with at least one of the Somali factions.[59]

The intervention, unthinkable in 1990, took the UN into new territory, well beyond the conventional notion of sovereignty and the associated principle of noninterference. The UN Security Council had not
only authorized activity inside the boundaries of a Member State, but
had extensively taken responsibility for the maintenance of law and
order in the state and rehabilitation of the country. Although the Security Council was at pains to point out the exceptional circumstances in
Somalia, including the complete collapse of the state and to declare
that the Somali case was not necessarily a precedent, it was difficult to
disguise the radical nature of the UN intervention in Somalia.

Indeed, it was only the operational problems which cast real doubt
on future excursions into Chapter VII territory for situations in which
humanitarian, or other concerns, constituted a threat to international
peace and security. The first is the dilemma, faced in Bosnia and
elsewhere, of needing both to use force to secure compliance with
agreements, but also of needing to develop a relationship with the
population based on confidence: in the Somali example, the use of
force worked against the need to generate "a maximum measure of

local support,"[60] in order to operate successfully. The operational balance between use of force and the building of trust was delicate.

In addition, UN interventions in relatively complicated situations, such as those in Cambodia, Somalia, and the former Yugoslavia are associated with practical difficulties. Many of these concern command, control, and communications problems. The major difficulty the UN faces is finding sufficient troops to carry out mandates—calls by the force commander and the secretary general for further troops in the former Yugoslavia twice failed to produce an adequate response between September 1993 and February 1994 (in the latter case, potentially jeopardizing ceasefire agreements in Bosnia). Behind the inability to attract adequate troop contributions, there is the financial crisis at the UN, which means that the UN is unable to pay for the operations already under way—indeed, it was already $463 million in debt on the peacekeeping budget before the three large operations in Cambodia, the former Yugoslavia, and Somalia were initiated in 1992.[61] Thus, whilst there had been a major conceptual shift with regard to UN intervention and the content of sovereignty, there were strong practical constraints which seemed likely to limit such interventions for some time to come.

In the rubric of changed attitudes to sovereignty and the place of the state in the international system, even the case of Somalia is not so radical as that of Libya. In SCR 731 (1992) (not under Chapter VII), Libya was called on to respond to requests from the United Kingdom and others to cooperate in investigations into the case in which Pan Am flight 103 had exploded over Lockerbie in Scotland as a result of a terrorist bomb planted on board, as well a terrorist attack on UTA flight 772. In particular, the United Kingdom and the Security Council were seeking the extradition for trial of two suspects in the Lockerbie case, alleged to have been sponsored by Libya. The Libyan authorities did not cooperate. This led the Security Council to act under Chapter VII to impose sanctions against the country on the grounds that the "failure of the Libyan Government to demonstrate by concrete actions its renunciation of terrorism and in particular its continued failure to respond fully and effectively to the requests in resolution 731 (1992) constituted a threat to international peace and security."[62] Libya contested the authority of the Security Council at the International Court of Justice (ICJ), arguing in its defense that, under the terms of the Montreal Convention governing extradition, it could not be obliged to extradite its individuals to a country with which it did not have an extradition treaty already. The ICJ, however, ruled that the Security Council, acting under Chapter VII, was supreme in a matter which concerned international peace and security. Whilst it seemed unlikely to happen immediately, this ruling left open the possibility that if the nonmilitary sanctions against Libya did not yield the suspected terrorists, nor further measures of the same kind, then it would be conceivable that the Security Council could authorize military enforcement measures against Tripoli. Similarly, the same situation might arise elsewhere, or there could be different situations in which the Security Council would determine a threat to peace and security and authorize an intervention—for example, in cases such as North Korea or Ukraine where nuclear capabilities could be held to menace international society.

Thus, the changes in the understanding of the place of state sovereignty in the international system and the interpretation of that which may be deemed to present a threat to international peace and security developing through the early 1990s were confirmed. The protection once thought to be the immovable and inalienable right of states under Article 2 (7) of the UN Charter had slipped through the window of the last clause in the article which removed protection when the Security Council determined a threat to international peace and security. In retrospect, it is clear that this protection was only afforded by the cold war and self-imposed limits of the meaning of the key phrase "threat to international peace and security." Sovereignty was not the state's alone, but was part of an international division of sovereignty and security with the UN. In the space of three years, between 1990 and 1993, the definition of a threat to international peace and security had stretched from cases which concerned external aggression, to humanitarian intervention, to cases involving cases of self-determination, to involvement in intrastate wars, or transitional wars, neither purely internal, nor purely external aggression, to state involvement in, or support of, terrorism. However, although it became clear that the delineation of Chapter VII situations could be far broader than had conventionally been the case, there was no indication of what the limits were to the expanding understanding of what could entail a threat to international peace and security.

In sum, both in terms of peace building, discussed above, and peace enforcement, under Chapter VII, of the UN Charter, there have been notable shifts in the sovereignty paradigm. It is necessary that for a (not too long) period, there will be further reflection and reassessment of the nature of sovereignty in the international system and its relationship to security questions. This will mean, *inter alia*, recognition that in specific areas certain states—and in one particular domain, all signatory states to the UN Charter—have found it vital and in their interest to transcend the narrow (and somewhat erroneous) interpretation of state sovereignty as being absolute and indivisible in terms of the international system. Within the scope of Chapter VII of the UN Charter, each state's sovereignty is already split with the UN Security Council. It is likely that the future will bring broader definitions of what constitutes a threat to international peace and security. However, this represents the more negative side of the problem—measures taken once a problem has emerged. There is, perhaps, a greater requirement to evolve positive measures which can contribute to the avoidance of critical situations and the building of security.

In this regard, the emphasis is on identifying ways in which sovereignty can be shared both between different communities within states, yet not create greater insecurity and, crucially, not bring the territorial *status quo* in the international system into question, as far as possible. It is increasingly clear that, "states should be encouraged, under specific circumstances, to surrender a certain amount of sovereignty to ethnonational minorities within the state's borders in the name of security."[63] It is also fairly evident that minority communities within states are unlikely to have confidence in any arrangement unless there is some international dimension providing a minimum guarantee of any particular arrangement—which will mean the concomitant surrender of portions of sovereignty to international bodies, not only of a particular state, but of states in general. This implies much for the understanding of sovereignty and security in the international security system.

## Sovereignty and Security: New Bearings

The security implications of situations in which one group within a state rejects that state are clear in the Yugoslav case: if weapons are available, there will be violence. In these cases, the two versions of the nations come into conflict: the sovereignty of the nation-state is challenged by the effective exercise of political sovereignty by an ethnonational group within it. The result of this is tension between the "national security" of the nation-as-state and the "national security" of the ethno-nation. The two are, however, intimately linked. Security of the state depends on ensuring that all those embraced by its borders are happy to accept the embrace. Nation-state security and ethnonational security are interdependent. Whereas "national security" could previously be taken to refer to the military and diplomatic efforts of a state to preserve both its physical integrity and its core values, in the post-cold war world, it is increasingly evident that security is gaining a wider meaning. One part of that broadened meaning involves the reinterpretation of and reallocation of sovereignty.

The notion of the "security dilemma" may also have changed. The security dilemma was the problem of security dependent on armed force. In a threatening situation, if you have a gun, you feel safe because you feel that you can defend yourself. However, your having a gun can appear to threaten somebody else. Likewise, their having a gun threatens you. So, the sense of security is compromised. A new version of the security dilemma can be identified which addresses the question of ethnic security.[64] By asserting collective identity, one group feels safer because those within it feel they belong and are protected by each other. But, their identity can only be asserted at the expense of someone else's, which makes another community feel threatened. The second community asserts its own identity, thereby appearing to threaten the first. Both engage on an escalator of tension which will come to manifest itself in the form of the original security dilemma. The difference is that the dilemma operates between peoples within the boundaries of one state, rather than between the peoples of two separate states with their own governments and armed forces.

Security is no longer something which only concerns the defense forces of states, as such.[65] Instead the focus must be on security as a feeling. Security is a *cathectic* notion.[66] It is something people, as individuals or groups, feel, not something which can be rationally described. In the unsteady societies of post-communist Europe, and by implication for the rest of Europe, it is clear that this feeling or its absence will be a major determinant of international stability. Security is something which people have to work out for themselves. It is something which they can only come to through negotiation, cooperation, and the building of confidence. This has implications for sovereignty.

The kind of security practice offered by the Ukraine and suggested in the Yugoslav context by the EC, means a new dispensation in state sovereignty with a view to enhancing security. Sovereignty is being reapportioned both at the expense of the collective rights of groups within states and of the rights of the international community to intervene in some way on behalf of those groups. This process of development has begun, but it is not yet clear where it will finish. However, several indications have already been given in international arenas of the ways in which this kind of change is developing.

In June 1992, the changing nature of international security problems was reflected in the UN Secretary General's report *An Agenda for Peace*. In it, Boutros Boutros Ghali emphasized the need to improve activities such as preventative diplomacy, peacemaking, peacekeeping, the reconstruction of peace after wars (civil or international), the alleviation of economic despair, social injustice, and political oppression. He continued:

> The foundation-stone of this work is and must remain the State. Respect for its fundamental sovereignty and integrity are crucial to any common international progress. The time of absolute sovereignty, however, has passed; its theory was never matched by reality. It is the task of the leaders of states today to understand this and to find a balance between the needs of good internal governance and the requirements of an ever more interdependent world. Commerce, communications and environmental matters transcend administrative borders; but inside these borders is where individuals carry out the first order of their economic, political and social lives.[67]

This reveals increasing appreciation that international security depends on the internal political development of states. This is especially the case in the post-communist countries of Europe where the position of national minorities is commonly (and increasingly perceived to be) a security concern both within and between states.

This comes, to some extent, from the increased attention accorded to humanitarian values since the end of the cold war. It underlines the significance of the human dimension of the CSCE in undermining the former communist regimes, as well as the realities of instability in Eastern Europe. Finally, it owes something to the initial optimism raised by the prospect of a "new world order" resulting from the international cooperation shown in the handling of the Iraq-Kuwait war. The articulation of a "new world order" had a particularly emotional appeal because it included "justice" as one of its core qualities[68]: this implied that the "new world" would be a better one.

Popular pressure on Western governments, evoked by that optimism, produced "Operation Provide Comfort" to protect Kurds in northern Iraq who were being pursued and persecuted by Iraqi forces. This humanitarian intervention, although limited, clearly signalled that it was no longer impossible for there to be external interference, including, even, the insertion of armed forces, in the internal affairs of an individual state. Even though, the Kurdish question and the international response to it was a function of specific circumstances, it fuelled debate. This concerned the character of external intervention in a state's internal affairs, definition of the conditions which would make this possible or justified and the degree in which a state's internal problems could constitute a threat to international peace and security.

International intervention in the realm of humanitarian issues would inevitably disturb political life inside a state. International engagement in favor of individuals or groups could only come at the expense of the rights of states and governments. For this reason they could be slow to allow too great an accent on humanitarian affairs. Where situations emerge in which their could be common interest between states, progress should be possible. However, before a suitable international regime is established, there are likely to be circumstances in which the international community may find an overriding interest in collectively interfering in a particular state, without that state's consent.[69]

Ideally, states would subject themselves to measures of external involvement in internal affairs. A relatively small, though psychologically vast, first step in this direction was taken in a 1987 treaty between the member states of the Council of Europe. This established a body, with a view to preventing abuses, which would have a right of intrusive inspection of all locations in signatory states where people were deprived of their liberty. Where fault was found, either private recommendation, in the first instance, or failing that, public disclosure could be used to obtain suitable adjustments. A more general shift towards human values, especially with regard to minorities, would radically alter both the internal and external politics of many countries were it to be achieved, as well as having consequences for international peace and security.

Explicit recognition of this came in the Moscow Document of the CSCE which abolished the possibility of referring to the "Principle of nonintervention in 'human dimension' cases":

The commitments undertaken in the field of the human dimension of CSCE are matters of direct and legitimate concern to all participating states and do not belong exclusively to the internal affairs of the state concerned.[70]

This was conceived as a moral premise. It reflects, however, the reality that the "moral" and "political" health of societies is a determinant of stability and international security. It forms part of a series of initiatives within the CSCE to make progress in collective regulation of human-rights matters, particularly, with regard to minorities. The Moscow Human Dimension Mechanism and the preceding Vienna Human Dimension Mechanism provided a number of limited ways in which human-rights doubts about a particular state could be addressed. The most extensive of these, agreed in Moscow, was the possibility that any state, with the support of at least nine others from the fifty-two-strong membership, could activate a mechanism whereby a commission of experts could be formed to investigate cases where a particular state was suspected of failing to meet its commitments under the human dimension of the CSCE.

Finally, and perhaps most critically, at its July 1992 Helsinki Summit, the CSCE decided to create a High Commissioner on National Minorities.[71] This happened in response to events in parts of both the former Yugoslavia and the former Soviet Union, where conflicts which might have been ameliorated by preventative prior engagement had reached armed hostility before external bodies could formally address them. It was, therefore, in direct response to the wave of nationalism creating security crises in post-communist Europe. The role of the High Commissioner was essentially restricted to being part of an "early warning mechanism." Cases where violence had already erupted not generally part of the remit—although the only specific exclusion was for "national minority issues in situations involving organised acts of terrorism."[72]

The real task of the High Commissioner is to identify potentially violent national, or ethnic, questions, to seek to remedy them, and in the final analysis issue a statement of early warning to the Council of the CSCE where the prospect of open armed hostility is close. In its short period of activity in this area, the CSCE has been associated (along with the EU [previously the EC], the Council of Europe and the International Court of Justice in seeking to deal with a number of problems.[73] One relatively successful example is the problem of Hungary, Slovakia, the Hungarians in Slovakia, and a dam close to the border between the two countries which, if built would damage the livelihood of ethnic Hungarian farmers. However, there remain questions to be solved with regard to the status of the Hungarians in Slovakia.

The foregoing emphasizes that, at the end of the twentieth century, security problems seem less likely to be concerned with a rapid invasion from a neighboring country than with the quest of groups for identity, self-determination, and freedom from the fear and uncertainty. This is especially the case in Eastern Europe and the former Soviet Union, where the gap emerging between political and economic expectations and their fulfillment—the no-man's land between communism and liberal-democracy—breeds frustration. International attention is necessarily and increasingly focused on security below the level of the state as a means of ensuring security at the level of the state. This is particularly so with regard to problems of national minorities.

The steps already taken in addressing the questions of national minorities, nations, sovereignty, statehood, self-determination, and security are only the first. The aim is the formation of an overall strategy for creating what might be called "ethnic security" and for dealing with manipulation of fears by old authoritarians, or nationalist newcomers, as well as working towards an international political norm with regard to the position of minorities within the borders of states.

It is critical that such norms should be backed with the possibility of intervention by the international community to ensure security. It is also vital that part of the norm should be that concern and intervention are better expressed through the international community than by individual neighboring countries with an interest in a particular minority. Security in post-communist Europe and many other regions has to be built at the domestic level. However, this will only be achievable through the involvement of the international community and the establishment of generally accepted values. The burden is, therefore, incumbent on Western policymakers, policy-actors, and policy-shapers. For them, the biggest part of the burden is to overcome the hang-ups of "skeletonism."[74] Only then will Western governments be able properly to reconsider the meaning and position of sovereignty.

## Conclusion

The acceptance internationally of absolute sovereignty in the internal sphere can no longer be taken for granted. Discussion on sovereignty within states and on the sovereignty of states in the international system is the linchpin for a reevaluation of the meaning of all the other concepts which compose the hissing snake. Self-determination, statehood, security and, ultimately, national, or ethnic status, are all determined in relation to sovereignty. Sovereignty, like all the other concepts, is in question in certain ways.

The outcome of that review cannot be known. But, the direction of the changes which have taken place is towards the recognition that, just as within states, at the international level, sovereignty cannot be allowed to be indivisible if abuses of it are not to be tolerated. Something equivalent to the constitutional separation of powers within states in order to validate and control power-holders may be in the process of evolving, although it is, as yet, clearly not codified. Developments could include the formal incorporation of particular communities within a state (on either a territorial, or nonterritorial basis) in the constitutional order, or, the presence of an external actor in an internal constitutional order. It certainly means states subscribing to international norms on the accommodation of various communities within their territorial limits and, eventually, becoming signatories to an international convention, or treaty, in which the concentration of sovereignty in certain parts of the state is dissipated and, instead, shared, both within its boundaries and beyond its boundaries—something which is likely to emerge under the banner of the Council of Europe, in Europe, in the mid-1990s.

Nothing of this kind will be easy to attain and whatever materializes will surely take time. If achieved, however, it would both place a limit on the potential for the presently evident potential for a state to abuse its sovereignty and promote greater international security. It would also go some way towards accommodating the change being forced on the international system by nationalist pressures after the cold war by creating new conceptual, normative, and legal frameworks in which to deal with nationalist conflicts over sovereignty, self-determination, ethnic and state security, and statehood. A better understanding of the implications of these words-with-two-meanings, including an awareness of their existence, is required before the trouble which arises from their ambiguity can be addressed. The repercussions of differing understandings are clear in the former Yugoslavia.

Some elucidation of the issues emerge from that war, though. The principal one is that, where nation and state do not coincide, sovereignty and self-determination conflicts are possible. These may pitch the international legal sovereignty of the state against the violent ethnonational political sovereignty of a particular ethnic group. In such cases, the only solutions can be those in which the divisibility of sovereignty is recognized and a mechanism for sharing it through possession of parts of a compound whole are found—creating a division of sovereignty not only within the state, but between the state and international bodies. The result may be that divisibility, or sharing, of sovereignty paradoxically strengthens the state and its security. The sooner the gradual process of making sovereignty in the international system, *de facto*, divisible is recognized and established openly as a norm of international relations, the sooner the nationalist snakes will have less to hiss about.

## Notes

1. I first adopted the "hissing snake" characterization in "Whose Sovereignty? Which Nation? Interpreting the International Lexicon after the Cold War and Taming the Hissssing Sssssnake," a paper for the SSRC-MacArthur International Workshop on Sovereignty and Security in Contemporary International Affairs at the Center for International Affairs, Harvard University, 2–4 April 1993. Sections of this chapter draw on and make developments from that paper.
2. See for example the following discussions: Paul Fifoot, "Functions and Powers, and Inventions: UN Action in Respect of Human Rights and Humanitarian Intervention," in Nigel Rodley (ed.), *To Loose the Bands of Wickedness: International Intervention in Defence of Human Rights*, Brassey's, London, 1992; Jarrat Chopra and T.C. Weiss, "Sovereignty is No Longer Sacrosanct: Codifying Humanitarian Intervention," *Ethics and International Affairs*, vol. 6, pp.95–117; Christopher Greenwood, "Is There a Right to Humanitarian Intervention?' *The World Today*, vol. 49, no. 5, May 1993 and "Human Rights and External Intervention," Ditchley Conference Report no. D93/8; Gregory H. Fox, "New Approaches to International Human Rights: the Sovereign State Revisited," paper for the SSRC-MacArthur International Workshop on Sovereignty and Security in Contemporary International Affairs, Department of War Studies, King's College London, 3–4 December 1993.
3. Hedley Bull, The Anarchical Society: A Study of Order in World Politics, Macmillan, London, 1977.
4. Peter Ludlow, director, Centre for European Policy Studies, Brussels, giving expert evidence to the House of Commons Foreign Affairs Committee, 15 January 1992, Foreign Affairs Committee, op. cit., pp. 213–4.

5. Kenneth Waltz, *The Theory of International Politics*, Addison-Wesley, Reading, MA, 1979, p.96.
6. Conor Cruise O'Brien, "The Wrath of Ages: Nationalism's Primordial Roots," *Foreign Affairs*, vol.72, no.5, November-December 1993.
7. Anthony Giddens, *The Nation State and Violence Polity* 1985.
8. Similar notions are liberty and justice—see W.B. Gallie, *Philosophy and the Historical Understanding*, Chatto and Windus, London, 1964, ch.8.
9. Alan James, "Sovereignty in Eastern Europe," *Millennium: Journal of International Studies*, vol.20, no.1, 1991.
10. See Jackson, *Quasi-States*, and Barry Buzan, *People, States and Fear: An Agenda for International Security Studies in the Post-Cold War Era*, Harvester-Wheatsheaf, Hemel Hempstead, 1991, pp.67–9.
11. Gordon Pocock, "Nation, Community, Devolution and Sovereignty," *Political Quarterly*, vol. 61, no.3, 1990, p. 323.
12. For this reason, many international lawyers, in particular, Americans, assume sovereignty to be not only a legal concept, but to refer to a "constitution," because, in the United States, "the Constitution" is held to be invested with sovereignty—although in reality, domestic sovereignty is shared between the executive and legislative branches of government and the judiciary and, of course, the people. The case for purely legal conceptions of sovereignty is made, for example, by Gregory H. Fox, loc. cit.; Fox draws on Ian Brownlie, *Principles of Public International Law*, 4th ed., Clarendon Press, Oxford, 1990.
13. See James Mayall, *Nationalism and International Society*, Cambridge Studies in International Relations 10, C.U.P., Cambridge, 1990, p. 28.
14. See Alfred Cobban, *The Nation State and National Self-Determination*, Collins, London, 1969.
15. Benedict Anderson, *Imagined Communities*, rev. ed., Verso, London, 1991, p.6, argues that these are imagined communities because, among other reasons, because the members "will never know most of their fellow members, meet them, or even hear of them, yet in the minds of each lives the image of their communion."
16. J.S. Mill, *On Liberty*, Penguin, Harmondsworth, 1974, p. 60.
17. Abbé Sieyès, *What is the Third Estate?*, quoted by Conor Cruise O'Brien, "The Wrath of Ages: Nationalism's Primordial Roots," *Foreign Affairs*, vol. 72, no.5, November-December 1993, p. 143.
18. Ernest Gellner, *Nations and Nationalism*, Blackwell, London, 1983, p.43ff.
19. Slavenka Drakulic, "Overcome by Nationhood," *Time*, 20 January 1992.
20. David Welsh, 'Domestic Politics and Ethnic Conflict', *Survival*, vol. 35, no.1, Spring 1993, p. 65, suggests that as a few as twenty states are homogeneous to the extent that no more than five percent of the population does not belong to the titular nation.
21. See Jonathan Eyal, "A Framework for Handling Ethnic Minority Isues in Eastern Europe," in Foreign Affairs Committee, *Central and Eastern Europe: Problems of the Post-Communist Era (First Report)*, vol. 2, HMSO, London, February 1992, p.115.
22. See Mayall, *Nationalism and International Society*, p.47.
23. Ibid., p.49.
24. See Robert H. Jackson, *Quasi-States: Sovereignty, International Relations, and the Third World*, Cambridge Studies in International Relations 12, C.U.P., Cambridge, 1990.
25. See, for example, John Stuart Mill, *Considerations on Representative Govern-*

*ment*, in Mill *Utilitarianism, Liberty, Representative Government*, introduction by A.D. Lindsay, Everyman, London, 1957,

26. See Mayall, *Nationalism and International Society*, p.56.
27. Ibid., p.56.
28. For example, Serbian groups operating in the United Kingdom and the United States use this translation in their English language publicity. A more precise definition of "sloga" might be "concord," or "harmony"—the meaning, however, would remain the absence of discord among the Serbs, rather than harmony with others, even though the latter would benefit the Serbs more.
29. See James Gow, "One Year of War in Bosnia and Herzegovina," *RFE/RL Research Report*, vol.2, no. 23, 4 June 1993.
30. "Ethnic cleansing" describes the practice of killing, terrorizing, and forcibly expelling the members of other ethnic communities from areas of mixed population, or where there are strategic assets. It is important to be aware of this last point: the Serbian ethnonational project combined with Belgrade's desire to have control over strategic assets, but with potentially hostile populations removed.
31. See Ivo Banac, *The National Question in Yugoslavia: Origins, History, Politics*, Cornell University Press, Ithaca, NY, 1984, pp.79–80.
32. In addition, there was a strong strand in Serbian linguistic-ideological thought which regarded most of the other South Slavs, who spoke almost the same language to be Serbs who confessed a different faith and simply did not yet realize that they were Serbs. See Banac, *The National Question*.
33. See Aleksa Djilas, *The Contested Country: Yugoslav Unity and Communist Revolution 1919–1953*, Harvard University Press, Cambridge, MA, 1991.
34. When looking at these aspects of the formation of the Yugoslav state, it is crucial to be aware that the communists believed that the state would wither away and that the nation upon which the nation state was based would wither with it. See ibid.
35. See James Gow, *Legitimacy and the Military: The Yugoslav Crisis*, Pinter, London, 1992, pp. 89–94.
36. This was a cry taken up by John Zametica in his partisan Adelphi Paper, *The Yugoslav Conflict*, Brassey's for the IISS, London, 1992. Zametica, despite a Slav Muslim father, was firmly in the Serbian camp, being part of the Bosnian Serb team attending the London Conference, afterwards moved to Geneva as the International Conference on the Former Yugoslavia, where he began to appear as an official representative of the self-styled Serbian Republic in Bosnia and Herzegovina. The Adelphi Paper included a number of questionable assertions, among which the assertion that Albanians were engaged in "ethnic cleansing" of Serbs in Kosovo in the 1970s stands out for its pernicious misrepresentation.
37. As discussed above, despite the consideration that has been devoted to establishing what it means and who possesses it, in the final analysis, the concept means only one thing: the sovereign, whoever or whatever it might be in particular circumstances, is the inalienable ultimate authority—that is, has the right not to be overruled. (See Michael Akehurst, *An Introduction to International Law*, George Allen and Unwin, London, 1970.) Self-determination is the right accorded to "all peoples" in, among other places, the UN charter and the International Covenant on Civil and Political Rights (1966), in which "the people" were given the right "freely" to "determine their political status and freely pursue their economic, social and cultural development." Although it is a general right which is usually assumed to include the right to statehood for all communities which seek to rule

themselves, in practice, its application has been more limited. However, it has remained an evocative and affective symbol.

38. Tomaž Mastnak, "Is the Nation-State Really Obsolete?" *The Times Literary Supplement*, 7 August 1992, p.11, points out the interchangeable use of "nation" and "state," in some instances.

39. *Ustav Socijalističke Federativne Republike Jugoslavije*, Službeni List, Belgrade, 1991 (with amendments), p.9.

40. "The Socialist Republic is a state, founded on the sovereignty of the nation . . . " Ibid., art.3, p. 23.

41. Both *narod* and *nacija* could be used in both senses, all Serbo-Croat variants. However, this example is offered to highlight the confusions and ambiguities involved.

42. See Marc Weller, "The International Response to the Dissolution of the Socialist Federal (sic.) Republic of Yugoslavia," *The American Journal of International Law*, vol.86, no.3, July 1992, p.591.

43. I am grateful to Ben Kingsbury for this point and others which benefitted from his international lawyer's perspective.

44. The entities which have had claims to statehood granted have fallen into the following cases: mandated, trust, and other territories treated as non-self-governing under Chapter IX of the UN Charter; distinct political-geographical entities subject to *carence de souveraineté* (the only successful case here is Bangladesh; on the basis of a plebiscite held with the agreement of the parties involved in a particular territory; formerly independent entities reasserting their independence; and, following the demise of communist federation in Yugoslavia, the Soviet Union and Czechoslovakia, federating republics from a dissolved state.

45. Avis no.3, 11 January 1992, cited by Weller, "The International Response," *The American Journal of Law*, p.590.

46. See Nigel Rodley, 'Collective intervention to protect human rights and civilian populations: the legal framework', in Rodley (ed.), *To Loose*, p.14 ff.

47. See Graham Messervey-Whiting, *Peace Conference: the Politico-Military Interface*, London Defence Studies no.23, Brassey's for the Centre for Defence Studies, London, 1994.

48. On the General Framework Agreement for Peace in Bosnia, see James Gow *Triumph of the Lack of Will: International Diplomacy and the Yugoslav War*, Columbia University Press, New York, 1997, ch. 10.

49. David Roberts, "Cambodia: Problems of a UN-Brokered Peace," *The World Today*, vol.4, no.7, July 1992, p.130.

50. Gerald Segal and Mats Berdal, "The Cambodian Dilemma," *Jane's Intelligence Review*, vol.5, no.3, March 1993, p.131.

51. Mats R. Berdal, *Whither UN Peacekeeping?*, Adelphi Paper no. 281, IISS/Brassey's, London, 1993, p.29.

52. On the Vance-Owen Plan, see Messervey-Whiting, op.cit.

53. UN Doc. S/23500, 1992.

54. The essence of collective security is that all states have a common and necessary interest in the maintenance of international peace and security and will therefore all act collectively to ensure that any of their number which breaches the peace is dealt with through the pressure of all for the one offended against, against the transgressor.

55. A. Le Roy Bennett, *International Organisations: Principles and Issues*, 5th ed., Prentice-Hall, Englewood Cliffs, NJ, 1991.

# Contributors

*Assaad Azzi* received his Ph.D. in psychology from the University of Pennsylvania. After serving as an assistant professor at Yale University, he took up a social psychology chair at the Université Libre de Bruxelles.

*Christopher Dandeker*, B.Sc.(Soc.) Ph.D., is Professor of Military Sociology and Head of the Department of War Studies at King's College London. He is joint founder and Secretariat member of the British Military Studies Group which is affiliated with the Inner-University Seminar on Armed Forces and Society (IUS). Professor Dandeker's other publications include *The Structure of Social Theory* (Macmillan, 1984) and *Surveillance, Power, and Modernity* (Polity, 1990).

*James Gow* is Reader in War Studies, King's College London and Research Associate of the Centre for Defence Studies, University of London. He is author of *Triumph of the Lack of Will. International Diplomacy and the Yugoslav War* (1997) and *Legitimacy and the Military: the Yugoslav Crisis* (1992), as well as co-editor of *Bosnia by Television* (1996). From 1994 until 1996 he was an expert military advisor to the Office of the Prosecutor at the UN International Criminal Tribunal for the former Yugoslavia, and he continues to work with the Tribunal as an expert witness. He was recently appointed as a member of the UK Secretary of State for Defense's Expert Panel for Strategic Defence Review.

*Harold James* is Professor of History at Princeton University, and author of many articles on economic and political history. His books include: *The German Slump: Politics and Economics 1924–1936* (Oxford University Press, 1986), *A German Identity* (Weidenfeld and Nicolson, 1989), and *International Monetary Cooperation Since Bretton Woods* (Oxford University Press, 1996).

*Reed Ueda* received his Ph.D. from Harvard University and is a member of the Department of History of Tufts University. He is also a member of the Inter-University Committee on International Migration, at the Center for International Studies of MIT, and the author of *Postwar Immigrant America: A Social History* (St. Martin's Press, 1994).

# Index